Critical Reflection for Nursing
and the Helping Professions

Critical Reflection for Nursing and the Helping Professions

A User's Guide

Gary Rolfe
Dawn Freshwater
and
Melanie Jasper

First published 2001 by
PALGRAVE MACMILLAN

Palgrave Macmillan in the UK is an imprint of Macmillan Publishers Limited, registered in England, company number 785998, of Houndmills, Basingstoke, Hampshire RG21 6XS.

Palgrave Macmillan in the US is a division of St Martin's Press LLC, 175 Fifth Avenue, New York, NY 10010.

Palgrave Macmillan is the global academic imprint of the above companies and has companies and representatives throughout the world.

Palgrave® and Macmillan® are registered trademarks in the United States, the United Kingdom, Europe and other countries.

ISBN-13: 978-0-333-77795-4

This book is printed on paper suitable for recycling and made from fully managed and sustained forest sources. Logging, pulping and manufacturing processes are expected to conform to the environmental regulations of the country of origin.

A catalogue record for this book is available from the British Library.

Printed and bound in Great Britain by
CPI Antony Rowe, Chippenham and Eastbourne

Contents

List of tables and figures

■ Tables

■ Figures

Acknowledgements

The authors and publishers wish to thank the following for permission to use copyright material: Blackwell Science for a figure from H.S. Kim (1999) 'Critical Reflective Inquiry for Knowledge Development in Nursing Practice', *Journal of Advanced Nursing*, 29, 5, p. 1208 and a figure from Heath and Freshwater (2000) 'Clinical Supervision as an Emancipatory Process', *Journal of Advanced Nursing*, 30, 5, pp. 1298–1306; Routledge for a table from Sharples (1999) *How We Write*, pp. 116–17 and a figure from Page and Wosket (1994) *Supervising the Counsellor*, p. 34. Every effort has been made to trace all the original copyright-holders but, if any have been inadvertently overlooked, the publishers will be pleased to make the necessary arrangement at the first opportunity.

To our students, for helping us to learn.

The teacher is ahead of his students in this alone,
that he still has far more to learn than they —
he has to learn to let them learn.

(Martin Heidegger, 1951)

Preface: How to Read this Book

■ Critical reflection

As reflection continues to grow in popularity, more and more books are beginning to appear which claim to offer help and guidance to the reflective practitioner. This book, *Critical Reflection for Nursing and the Helping Professions: A User's Guide*, aims to offer something a little different. Firstly, as the title suggests, it is concerned with *critical* reflection, that is, with using the reflective process to look systematically and rigorously at our own practice. We all reflect on our practice to some extent, but how often do we employ those reflections to learn from our actions, to challenge established theory and, most importantly, to make a real difference to our practice? In the course of the eight chapters that make up this book, we will help you to think about your practical and theoretical knowledge, to consider where it comes from, and to explore how you might gain access to it and employ it more effectively to improve your practice.

There are, however, already more than enough books that claim to tell you what you need to know in order to practice more effectively or more efficiently, and we have no wish to add yet another to the pile. Our belief, in contrast, is that the most important practical knowledge comes not from books but from within yourself. In the words of the psychologist and educationalist Carl Rogers (1969), 'It seems to me that anything that can be taught to another is relatively inconsequential and has little or no significance on behaviour'. Rather, as the philosopher John Dewey (1916) pointed out nearly a century ago, 'We learn by doing and seeing what becomes of our actions'. The aim of this book, then, is to offer some frameworks and structures by which you might better see and evaluate what becomes of your actions, and thereby improve their consequences. If it teaches anything, it teaches how you might best learn for yourself.

■ A user's guide

A clue to the second way in which this book tries to be different lies in its subtitle. It is a user's guide to reflection, aimed at providing a structured learning experience for a wide range of practitioners. As such, you might find that the style and structure of the book is rather different from many traditional texts, and we have therefore included some suggestions on how to go about reading it.

☐ Readership

We have attempted to write this book for a wide readership. It is intended primarily for qualified practitioners from all the helping professions including nursing, midwifery, health visiting, occupational therapy, physiotherapy, social work and so on, either as part of a formal course of study or else on their own or with one or more colleagues. However, you will see from the first two chapters in particular, where we explore the models and theories that underpin critical reflection, that we believe it to be appropriate for practitioners at all stages of professional development, including those still studying for their professional qualifications. Furthermore, although many of the examples that we use refer specifically to one or other of the above professional groups, we maintain that the *processes* of critical reflection are the same, even when the *content* of what is being reflected on is not. When reading the book, then, you might wish to substitute examples from your own discipline where appropriate.

☐ Style

We are very mindful that many academic books adopt a rather aloof style that seems to be aimed at no-one in particular. Indeed, in some texts it is very difficult to find any signs of human life whatsoever, and as Billig (1994) observed, 'Much critical writing . . . is *depopulated*. It is filled with abstract concepts, broad judgements and descriptions of general processes, but it is devoid of people.' Our aim with this book has been to repopulate the text, to reinstate the people. For this reason, it is written almost entirely in the first and second person: *we* attempt to speak as directly as possible (given the rather impersonal medium of the book) to *you*. Where we do lapse into the third person, such as in some of the case studies and examples, we have employed the feminine gender in the absence of any elegant non-gender-specific pronouns. This does not, of course, imply that all members of the helping professions are, or should be, female, but is an attempt to redress the balance in most books of writing from a predominantly male perspective. In texts that *are* populated, it is usually almost entirely with men.

☐ Reading this book

Over four hundred years ago, the philosopher and scientist Francis Bacon wrote 'Some books are to be tasted, others to be swallowed, and some few to be chewed and digested' (Bacon, 1994). We would suggest that the first and third of those methods are particularly appropriate for this book, and would discourage you from swallowing any of the ideas or suggestions whole without giving them a good chew first. Thus, you might wish to get a taste of it by dipping in to specific chapters. If, for example, you are about to set up a supervision group, you will find Chapter 5 particularly relevant, and although you will come across references to ideas from elsewhere in the book, each chapter has been written so that it might be tasted on its own. On the other hand, you might wish to digest the entire book (although not necessarily in one sitting). If you take this approach, you will hopefully find that the chapters are presented in a logical and developmental sequence, and that there is plenty of theoretical justification for the ideas, models and theories that we present. After all, this is a book about *critical* reflection, and we want to encourage you to chew over the contents and spit out anything that doesn't agree with you (or that you don't agree with).

☐ Using this book

But this is not just a book for reading; it is also intended to spur you into action. Two hundred years after Francis Bacon speculated on how books might be read, the philosopher Georg Christophe Lichtenberg wrote 'To read means to borrow; to create out of one's reading is to pay off one's debts' (Lichtenberg, 1969). You are invited to borrow whatever takes your fancy from this book, but we hope also that you will pay back the loan (preferably with interest) by creating something practical from your reading. If you are reading this book by yourself, you might wish to use it to construct your own course of learning on reflective practice (if so, it is better to start with the final chapter on education and the reflective practitioner), and it can also be used by tutors and lecturers to the same end.

☐ *Further reading boxes*

The 'further reading' boxes are intended for the inquisitive or more advanced student, either working independently or as part of a course, who wishes to explore some of the topics in greater depth. The texts recommended in these boxes are intended to build substantially on the issues discussed in this book, and are often quite difficult for the beginning student. In addition to offering support, they are also intended to take the reader off in new directions well beyond the scope and remit of this book.

☐ *Reflective writing boxes*

Reflective writing is one of the cornerstones of critical reflection, and we have devoted an entire chapter to this subject early in the book. We have already asserted our belief that the most important knowledge for practice is not found in the pages of this or any other book, but comes from within yourself, and particularly from the experience that you have accumulated over the years. We therefore see the reflective writing exercises as an integral part of this book, and although you might wish to skip some or all of them, it is these exercises that help to make it a practical workbook. Reflection is a skill that has to be learnt, and like all skills, there comes a point where it is necessary to stop reading about it and start practising it.

As you work through the book, you will notice that the first and last reflective writing boxes are the same in each chapter. These boxes contain the learning plan exercises for the chapter, which help you to identify your own learning needs, the extent to which they have been met through your reading, and the ways in which you might continue to pursue them. If you are using this book by yourself rather than as part of a course, we would suggest that these boxes are particularly important in helping you to keep track of your learning.

☐   *Discussion point boxes*

The third type of box you will come across contains the 'discussion points'. With the exception of reflective writing, most of the methods and techniques for critical reflection presented in this book require interaction with other people. The 'discussion point' exercises are therefore intended to structure and facilitate a reflective discourse with one or more colleagues, and can be employed either by the independent reader or as learning exercises within a formal course.

You will probably have gathered by now that we believe that the most important purpose of this book (and, indeed, the reason that we wrote it) is to help you to learn from and develop your practice. The 'further reading', 'reflective writing' and 'discussion point' boxes are therefore an integral part of helping you not only to read, but to pay off your reading debts by thinking and doing.

Chapter 1

Knowledge and practice

■ Introduction

Our aim in writing this book has been to produce a practical user's guide to critical reflection, and we are therefore concerned mainly with 'what' and 'how' questions such as 'what are the most effective models of critical reflection?' and 'how can I incorporate them into my practice?' But we hope to have written more than just a cookbook of recipes for reflective practice: as well a guide to reflection, we also intend to offer justification in the form of the accompanying theory; and as well as addressing the 'what' and 'how' of reflection, we are also concerned with the 'why'. Our aim, then, is not merely to consider *what* might be the best methods and *how* they might be achieved, but also to explore *why* they are best; to help you not only to develop your skills, but also to add to your knowledge and understanding.

Although these 'why' questions will be addressed throughout the book, this first chapter is concerned almost entirely with a single question: 'why reflect?' In attempting to answer this question, we will try to avoid the obvious and superficial answers such as 'to improve your practice' or 'because it is a good thing to do', and focus instead on the deeper philosophical issues. The short answer to the question 'why reflect?' is that critical reflection produces knowledge about our practice. The long answer is this entire chapter.

Of course, you might wish to skip this chapter altogether and get straight down to the 'what' and 'how' of critical reflection, but we believe that the defining attribute of the reflective practitioner is precisely the inquisitive attitude of taking nothing as given; of following up the answer to every 'what' and 'how' question with a 'why' question. There is nothing wrong with cookbooks, which tell you what to do and how to do it, but if you ever wish to deviate even slightly from the recipes you also need to know why you are doing it.

In attempting to explore the question 'why reflect?' we have a number of aims for this chapter:

1 to examine some of the different philosophical concepts and ideas about knowledge;
2 to explore the relationship between knowledge and practice;
3 to develop a model of practitioner knowledge; and
4 to introduce reflection-on-action as a way of exploring and developing practitioner knowledge.

We have written this book to meet the needs of a wide range of practitioners, and so our aims are necessarily broad and general. We also recognise that you as a reader will bring with you a set of aims specific to your own individual needs, but that these needs are often unstated, and even unacknowledged. In order to get the most benefit from this book, we would therefore encourage you to reflect on your specific aims for each chapter.

REFLECTIVE WRITING

Think carefully about our aims for Chapter 1. Now think about your own practice and how these aims might contribute towards developing it. For example, how might a discussion about different concepts of knowledge benefit you as a practitioner? What kinds of knowledge do you employ in your practice? Are there other kinds of knowledge apart from that generated by research?

Based on our aims above, write down some of your own, both in terms of what you hope to know and what you hope to be able to do after reading Chapter 1. We will return to your aims at the end of the chapter.

■ The nature of knowledge

Acquiring knowledge through reflection is certainly not a recent idea. Well over two thousand years ago, Plato suggested that abstract concepts such as justice, mathematics and goodness are objective and timeless 'Forms' with which we were once all acquainted in a previous existence, but which we have since forgotten. To know something, he argued, requires *anamnesis* or recollection, and is therefore an introspective and reflective process. Similarly, Socrates' method of teaching (the so-called Socratic dialogue), in which the teacher offers no information but asks a sequence of questions through which the pupil eventually discovers the answers within himself, is a form of introspective reflection.

In its modern form, reflection as a way of learning from practice can be traced back at least to the 1930s and the work of John Dewey. Dewey was an American philosopher and educator who was one of the founders of what might be called 'discovery learning' or learning from experience, claiming that 'we learn by doing and realising what came of what we did' (Dewey, 1938). Clearly, Dewey's 'realising what came of what we did' is a form of knowledge, and in order to explore the process of developing such knowledge, we must first attempt to understand a little more about its nature. The focus of this chapter is therefore on the study of epistemology, the 'philosophical theory of knowledge, which seeks to define it, distinguish its principal varieties, identify its sources, and establish its limits' (Bullock *et al.* 1988).

The first thing we must attempt to do, then, is to define what we mean by knowledge, and also to distinguish between knowledge and theory, since as Slevin and Basford (1995) have observed, the two are often used interchangeably. For the purpose of this book, a theory is a way of ordering knowledge in a descriptive, explanatory or predictive framework; it enables us to employ knowledge in order to describe some aspect of the world, to explain it, and to make predictions about it. So, for example, my theory that the world is round allows me to *describe* its shape, to *explain* why ships appear to slowly sink over the horizon, and to *predict* that if I set off in a straight line I will eventually return to my starting point.

The concept of knowledge is rather more complex, so it is essential that we give some thought to exactly what we mean when we say that we know something. We will start with a fairly general philosophical definition of knowledge as *justified true belief*. Thus, for something to count as knowledge, it must firstly be believed by the person making the knowledge claim. It makes no sense to say, for example, that 'I know the world is round but I don't believe it'; to know something is, first and foremost, to believe it to be true. This criterion of belief has some interesting implications, since a belief is personal to whoever holds it. You and I might have completely different beliefs and, hence, different knowledge bases: I might 'know' that the world is round, whereas you 'know' that it is flat. So does that mean that it is possible for two people to know contradictory things about the same object? Surely at least one of us must be wrong.

This, of course, brings us to the second criterion for knowledge, which is the thorny issue of truth. Knowledge is not just any belief; it is *true* belief. The difficulty here is that there are many ways of defining what is to count as truth. On the one hand, there is the 'realist' view that truth implies a correspondence with some sort of external reality: that the statement 'the world is round' is true if, and only if, the world *really is round*. This might seem to be no more than common sense, but the problem is how such judgements about reality are to be made. Let us take a different example to illustrate this point. According to the realists, the statement 'democracy is a good thing' is true if and only if democracy really is a good thing. But how can we judge whether it really is? If, as Plato supposed, there is a world in which the pure objective 'Forms' of democracy and goodness exist, then how do we gain access to it? Few people nowadays would agree with Plato that we simply have to remember back to a previous existence when we were fully acquainted with these ideal Forms, so how are we to 'know' the true nature of democracy (or of anything, for that matter)?

But surely, it could be argued, reality is all around us, and we only need to look and listen in order to see and hear the truth. This, however, supposes that our senses never lie to us, that we perceive the world directly and without distortion. Unfortunately, psychologists tell us otherwise: they are easily able to demonstrate, through a variety of optical, auditory and tactile illusions, ways in which our senses constantly fool us. We can never be certain that what we perceive through our senses is how the world really is, and many philosophers, psychologists and sociologists, as well as some physicists, believe that all of our perceptions are 'theory-laden', that we see the world according to how we expect to see it. The difficulty for the realist view of truth, then, is that if we have no objective and direct access to reality; then we have nothing against which to judge our truth claims.

This has led some thinkers to suggest an alternative view of truth, which we might loosely term anti-realist or 'constructivist', which argues that truth is created in the minds of people rather than discovered in the outside world. So, for example, the statement 'democracy is a good thing' is true because we have decided that it is true. The constructivists do not believe that 'the truth is out there', but rather that it is 'in here' in individual minds. That is not to say that each of us has a totally different conception of truth, but that we collectively decide as a society what is to count as true for us. It also means that truths are not eternal, they are not true for all time, but can shift along with our perceptions of the world. Seen in this way, truth takes on a political dimension, and the question we should ask ourselves is not 'is this true?' but rather 'who decides whether this is true.

 FURTHER READING

Both realism and constructivism embrace a broad range of different positions, to which this book can hardly do justice. One of the most prolific and easy-to-read advocates of realism is Roy Bhaskar, whose book *Reclaiming Reality*, distinguishes between subjectively-held belief and objective knowledge. The constructivist position is outlined equally clearly by Richard Rorty in his book *Contingency, Irony and Solidarity*, which, whilst not denying the existence of a real and objective world, makes a convincing case that we can never have any objective knowledge about it. This constructivist view should not be confused with the far more radical 'idealist' view, which argues that the physical world itself is a construct; that, in effect, the world only exists so long as there is someone present to perceive it. The constructivists are not denying the existence of an objective, physical world 'out there', merely the existence out there of objective knowledge about the world.

Bhaskar, R. (1989) *Reclaiming Reality*, London: Verso.
Rorty, R. (1989) *Contingency, Irony and Solidarity*, Cambridge: Cambridge University Press.

This brings us to our third criterion of knowledge, which is that our true belief must be supported by some form of evidence: to count as knowledge it must be a *justified* true belief. It is not enough to say 'I know the world is round, but I can't (or won't) tell you how I know it'; I must offer proof. For the realists, the justification of the truth of a statement takes the form of some kind of demonstration that the statement corresponds to objective reality. So, for example, I can demonstrate that the world is round by setting sail in a westerly direction and continuing in a straight line until I eventually return to the point that I started from. I can demonstrate that democracy is a good thing by conducting surveys of life in democratic and undemocratic countries and comparing the two. This approach to justification supposes that there is a method by which we can gain access to reality which can somehow overcome all the difficulties mentioned above; that there is an *objective* method which can avoid all the subjective pitfalls such as optical and auditory illusions and other distortions introduced by imperfect individual observers. Most realists accept that the best and most objective method for perceiving reality is the method of science. Some, who often call themselves positivists, argue that the method of science can be applied not only to the physical world, but also to the social world, and even to the study of individual people.

The constructivists, however, would argue that such an approach does not set the search for truth (and, hence, for knowledge) on an objective footing; all that it does is to shift the political decision as to what counts as truth back a stage. Rather than ask the question 'who decides what is to count as truth?', we must now ask 'who decides what is to count as the best method for determining what counts as truth?' The constructivists would therefore call into question the decision to accept science as the best or only way of gaining access to the truth, and would see it as a politically loaded decision taken and maintained by a small group of people who have a great deal to lose if the criteria for truth and knowledge were to change. It might well be the case that knowledge is power, but the constructivists argue that power is also knowledge; if knowledge is constructed by people, then certain people have the power to define what counts as knowledge, who is qualified to undertake the task of generating knowledge, what count as acceptable ways of doing so, who is qualified to disseminate that knowledge, and in which ways.

The power to define knowledge usually rests with governments and their appointed representatives. In some countries, this power is exercised quite overtly by imposing a centralised national educational curriculum whose content is determined by the state, by controlling (and often by owning) the media, and by punishing as dissidents those who challenge the established view of knowledge. Indeed, in some states, such as the former Soviet Union, the 'official' version of what counts as knowledge and reality is so powerful that anyone challenging it is, by definition, out of touch with reality and therefore certifiable as insane. However, many countries, including most western democracies, operate a far more covert policy, which often goes unrecognised and therefore unchallenged.

For example, the British government (DoH, 1993) has defined nursing and healthcare knowledge predominantly in terms of the findings of large-scale generalisable scientific research studies, and in particular, of the randomised controlled trial (RCT). The government also controls, through its funding mechanisms, who may and may not conduct such studies, and, the methods by which they should be disseminated to a wider audience. Small-scale qualitative studies, for example, should be curbed (DoH, 1993), and will not be supported with funding, nor will their findings be disseminated through government-funded units. Many constructivists would argue that this political decision to favour scientific research-based knowledge over other forms such as experiential knowledge was not taken because the former provides a more accurate picture of reality, but firstly because those people who make such decisions (politicians, researchers, civil servants and academics) do not themselves posses very much up-to-date *experiential* knowledge of healthcare; and secondly because they would not have control over its generation or dissemination. For the constructivists, then, scientific research has been chosen as the dominant method for generating knowledge not for any objective reason, but for reasons of power.

 FURTHER READING

The relationship between power and knowledge has been a dominant theme in the work of a number of postmodernist writers. Michel Foucault claimed that knowledge and power are the two sides of the same political coin and cannot be separated, whereas Lyotard, in his book *The Postmodern Condition* argued strongly that science is open to political and financial distortion, such that 'scientists, technicians, and instruments are purchased not to find truth, but to augment power'. In a later book, he recognized that definitions of what counts as knowledge could be imposed on individuals and social groups from a position of power, and claimed that it was the role of the philosopher to act as a go-between or power broker to help resolve disputes between conflicting parties. An exploration of the relationship between power and knowledge with a healthcare focus can be found in Rolfe's book *Research, Truth and Authority*.

Foucault, M. (1980) *Power/Knowledge; Selected Interviews and Other Writings 1972–77*, Brighton: Harvester Press.
Lyotard, J.-F. (1984) *The Postmodern Condition: A Report on Knowledge*, Manchester: Manchester University Press.
Lyotard, J.-F. (1988) *The Differend: Phrases in Dispute*, Minneapolis: University of Minnesota Press.
Rolfe, G. (2000) *Research, Truth and Authority: Postmodern Perspectives on Nursing*, London: Macmillan – now Palgrave.

■ Knowledge and practice

One of the problems for any practice-based discipline with accepting scientific knowledge as the dominant form is that it implies a particular model of the relationship between knowledge and practice. This model, which Schön has termed 'technical rationality', supposes a simple hierarchy with knowledge and theory at the top, and practice at the bottom. In the terminology of the philosopher Gilbert Ryle (1963), it suggests that 'knowing that' precedes and informs 'knowing how'; that we must first learn the theory before applying it to practice (Figure 1.1).

DISCUSSION POINT

Whilst most of us are fairly clear about what we know, we probably never think about the more philosophical question of what knowledge is. Having read the above two accounts, discuss with a friend the pros and cons of both the realist and the constructivist positions and try to arrive at your own theory of knowledge. You might wish to consider some of the following questions:

- Is knowledge objective or subjective?
- Does it exist in the world, waiting to be discovered, or do we construct it as we go along?
- Can you and I both 'know' contradictory things, or is there one right answer to every question?
- If there is a single right answer, how do we know when we have found it?
- Is science the best way of arriving at knowledge, or does it merely serve the interests of those in power?

Attempt to relate your discussion to nursing and/or healthcare.

In the technical rationality model, then, there is a one-way flow from theory to practice, with researchers and academics providing the knowledge and theory for practitioners to apply in their practice settings. This model suggests not only a hierarchical relationship between knowledge and practice, but also between academics and practitioners, or what Elliott and Ebbutt (1985) referred to as 'knowledge generators' and 'knowledge appliers'. We can see that, if followed rigidly, the technical rationality model reduces practitioners to the level of technicians whose only role is to implement the research findings and theoretical models of the scientists, researchers and theoreticians.

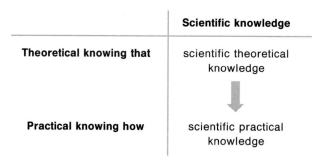

Figure 1.1   A technical rationality model

This model also has implications for professional education, and results in what Hazel Bines has referred to as the technocratic model, which she describes as:

> characterised by the division of professional education into three main elements. The first comprises the development and transmission of a systematic knowledge base, largely, though not exclusively, based on contributing academic disciplines, such as the natural and social sciences, including both 'pure' and 'applied' dimensions. The second involves the interpretation and application of the knowledge base to practice ... and may be based on theoretical models of practice, for example, 'the nursing process' in nurse education. The third element is the supervised practice in selected placements. (Bines, 1992: 12–13)

We can see this technocratic model of education very clearly in the philosophy underpinning the original *Project 2000* nursing syllabus in the UK, and it is reflected in many of the curricula which arose from that syllabus.

Technocratic education, like technical rationality practice, involves a one-way flow of information from teacher to student and, by implication, from theory to practice. This is a top-down 'mug and jug' model of education, in which the students are the mugs who are filled from the teacher's jug of knowledge. The significance of this top-down approach for our discussion of the epistemology of practice is that it supposes that there is only one type of knowledge on which practice is to be based, that is, knowledge derived from research or other scholarly activity. Philosophers usually refer to this type of knowledge as theoretical or propositional knowledge, what Ryle called 'knowing that'. Of course, practitioners also possess practical knowing how, but it is entirely dependent on their propositional knowing that. They know how to do something because they know the theory or research findings underpinning it. The application of the model of technical rationality to practice produces what is essentially research-based practice. So, for example, the research-based nurse knows *how* to respond to a bereaved relative because she knows *that* bereavement follows a well-defined series of stages.

 REFLECTIVE WRITING

Divide your page into two columns. In the first column, make a list of 10 pieces of scientific theoretical knowledge that you have gained from books, journals or lectures. Then in the second column, add 10 associated pieces of scientific practical knowledge, things you know how to do based on each piece of theoretical knowledge.

Put your list to one side. We will return to it later.

This technical rationality model received its first serious challenge in the 1970s and 1980s, not from the healthcare disciplines, but from the teaching profession. This challenge was mounted on two fronts, one practical and the other theoretical. On the practical front, Lawrence Stenhouse led what he referred to as the 'teacher-as-researcher' movement, which encouraged schoolteachers to engage in their own classroom-based research rather than relying solely on the research findings of academics. Thus, he urged:

> If, after comparing the measurement results [from a research study] with your own experience you find yourself uncertain of judgement, then basically there's no alternative to doing your own research. (Stenhouse, 1985: 41)

This was clearly a call to action research and practitioner-based enquiry, and was supported by a number of educational theorists including Wilfred Carr, Stephen Kemmis, David Ebbutt and John Elliott, who constructed a new epistemology of practice in which practical knowledge (Ryle's knowing how) was implicit in every action taken by the experienced practitioner. As Usher and Bryant (1989) noted, 'practical knowledge cannot therefore be derived purely from theoretical knowledge and practice is not something which can be merely "read off" from theory'. Thus, in addition to the scientific knowledge and theory generated by researchers and academics which is applied *to* practice, many educationalists were arguing for another kind of knowledge which is implicit *in*, and which emerges from, practice. As Carr and Kemmis pointed out:

> A 'practice', then, is not some kind of thoughtless behaviour which exists separately from 'theory' and to which theory can be 'applied'. Furthermore, all practices, like all observations, have 'theory' embedded in them. (Carr and Kemmis, 1986: 113)

Schön (1987) referred to these practice-based theories as 'theories-in-use', which are 'implicit in our patterns of spontaneous behaviour', while Usher and Bryant, coined the term 'informal theory', and added:

> Since without such a 'theory' practice would be random and purposeless, we can say that it 'forms' practice. It enables practitioners to make sense of what they are doing and thus appears to have an enabling function. (Usher and Bryant, 1989: 80)

In addition to the technical rationality top-down model of the relationship between theory and practice in which theoretical knowledge was the most important type, these writers were suggesting a bottom-up approach in which the knowledge gained from experience took precedence over theoretical knowledge, such that experiential knowledge was employed in order to construct theory rather than vice versa (Figure 1.2). But in challenging the established hierarchy of knowledge, these writers were also challenging the hierarchy of knowledge generators and knowledge appliers. The search for a new epistemology of practice opened up the potential for practitioners to be their own theoreticians and their own researchers; indeed, experiential knowledge could only come from practitioners themselves. It therefore called into question the entire edifice of technical rationality and created, in effect, a post-technical model of practice in which practical 'knowing how' informed propositional 'knowing that', and academic researchers and theoreticians no longer had a monopoly on the creation of knowledge.

	Experiential knowledge
Theoretical knowing that	experiential theoretical knowledge
	↑
Practical knowing how	experiential practical knowledge

Figure 1.2   A post-technical model

This post-technical model of practice initiated a revival in action research and a revolution in the discipline of education, the reverberations from which are still being felt to this day.

 FURTHER READING

If you are interested in some of the ways that educationalists have employed action research as a means of developing practice, see the books by Altrichter *et al.* and McNiff, both of which offer very practical guides to exploring and developing your practice through action research. Rolfe, in his book *Expanding Nursing Knowledge*, has attempted to apply many of these ideas to healthcare practice. In addition, we shall be examining action research in more depth in Chapter 7.

Altrichter, H., Posch, P. and Somekh, B. (1993) *Teachers Investigate their Work: An Introduction to the Methods of Action Research*, London: Routledge.

McNiff, J. (1993) *Teaching as Learning: An Action Research Approach*, London: Routledge.

Rolfe, G. (1988) *Expanding Nursing Knowledge: Understanding and Researching your own Practice*, Oxford: Butterworth Heinemann.

REFLECTIVE WRITING

Divide your page into two columns again. This time, in the first column, make a list of 10 pieces of experiential practical knowledge, things that you know how to do which you have gained from your own experience. Then in the second column, add 10 associated pieces of experiential theoretical knowledge, explanations of how you are able to do each of the pieces of practical knowledge.

Once again, put your list to one side. We will return to it later.

Nursing and the other healthcare professions have generally taken a far more cautious view of this post technical approach, and have been reluctant to ditch technical rationality for a practitioner-led epistemology. As Dreyfus and Dreyfus pointed out:

> When one sees the importance of practice and intuition, so long neglected in the West, one is tempted to invert the traditional hierarchies in which theory is superior to practice and rationality is superior to intuition, but to invert these terms is to stay within the traditional system of thought . . . Nursing, like all medical practice and the practice of scientific disciplines in general, is a special combination of theory and practice in which it is clear that theory guides practice and practice grounds theory in a way which undercuts any philosophical attempt to say which is superior to the other. (Dreyfus and Dreyfus, 1996: 43)

Both models of practice are important and have their place: the technical rationality model in which scientific theory determines research-based practice *and* the post-technical model in which the knowledge gained directly from practice informs and builds experiential theoretical knowledge. We can therefore place the two models side by side (Figure 1.3) to form a composite model. This simple typology divides knowledge into four categories. Firstly there is scientific theoretical knowledge, which includes findings from scientific research along with more

	Scientific knowledge	Experiental knowledge
Theoretical knowing that	scientific theoretical knowledge	experiental theoretical knowledge
Practical knowing how	scientific practical knowledge	experiental practical knowledge

Figure 1.3 A model of practitioner knowledge

abstract models and theories. For example, a nurse's knowledge that bereaved people experience a number of stages of grieving is scientific theoretical knowledge, since it is something she knows based on a published theory. Secondly (moving in an anticlockwise direction around Figure 1.3), there is scientific practical knowledge, which is the knowing how derived from scientific knowing that, and which results in what is usually referred to as research-based practice. For example, our nurse can follow a model of counselling based on her knowledge of the stages of bereavement; she knows *how* because she knows *that*. Similarly, most nursing procedures are a form of scientific practical knowledge, since they are based on the findings of research. Thirdly, there is experiential practical knowledge, which is a different form of know-how derived not from theoretical knowing that, but directly from experience. Our nurse knows how to counsel bereaved relatives not only from her theoretical knowledge, but also directly from her experience of other bereaved people she has worked with. And finally, there is experiential theoretical knowledge, which is the theoretical knowledge derived not from books or research, but from thinking about experiential practical knowledge. It is this experiential theoretical knowledge which comprises Schön's 'theories-in-use', the knowledge which enables our nurse to make sense of her practice.

 FURTHER READING

This model is a simplified version of Rolfe's typology of knowledge which can be found in full in chapter 13 of his book *Advanced Nursing Practice*. There are, of course, other ways of formulating and understanding practice-based knowledge, and you might wish to explore Barbara Carper's model of nursing knowledge, which is reproduced in an easily digestible form in Kikuchi and Simmons's edited collection *Philosophic Inquiry in Nursing*.

Carper, B. (1992) 'Philosophical Inquiry in Nursing: An Application', in J.F. Kikuchi and H. Simmons (eds), *Philosophic Inquiry in Nursing*, Newbury Park: Sage.

Rolfe, G. (1998) 'Advanced Practice and the Reflective Nurse: Developing Knowledge out of Practice', in G. Rolfe and P. Fulbrook (eds), *Advanced Nursing Practice*, Oxford: Butterworth Heinemann.

The problem which most practitioners quickly discover is that much of this experiential knowledge and theory-in-use is extremely difficult to articulate. Michael Polanyi (1962) referred to it as 'tacit knowledge', knowledge which is impossible to put into words, claiming that we literally 'know more than we can say', and the philosopher Karl Popper (1979) called it 'organismic knowledge', knowledge which is present in our muscles and reflexes rather than stored in our brains. Consider, for example, riding a bicycle. Nobody learns to ride a bicycle by reading an instruction manual. We learn by doing it, and the knowledge required to do it is experiential, organismic knowledge which is stored in our muscles and reflexes. Such knowledge is not easily imparted to others. Part of the reason why no-one has learnt to ride a bicycle by reading a book is that no-one is able to write such a book; the best that any of us can do is to impart a few 'rules of thumb' or heuristics. We can instruct a learner, for example, to lean into a bend, or to turn to the left if she is wobbling to the right, but beyond this all we can do is give her a push and help her up when she falls off.

■ Skills acquisition and expertise

Patricia Benner, in her important and influential study into nursing expertise, argued that this tacit experiential knowledge is the hallmark of expert practice, but that 'capturing the descriptions of expert performance is difficult, because the expert operates from a deep understanding of the total situation' (Benner, 1984). She illustrated her argument with a quotation from an expert psychiatric nurse who was attempting to describe how she recognised psychosis:

> When I say to a doctor, 'the patient is psychotic', I don't always know how to legitimize that statement. But I am never wrong. Because I know psychosis

 DISCUSSION POINT

Now turn back to your four lists of different kinds of knowledge, and discuss the following questions with a partner:

- Which list(s) did you find the most difficult to complete?
- Why was that?
- Which kind(s) of knowledge do you think the healthcare professions value most?
- Why?
- Which kind(s) of knowledge do you find most useful for your own practice?
- Why?
- Which kind(s) of knowledge do you find the least useful?
- Why?

What do your answers to these questions tell you about the different kinds of practitioner knowledge?

from inside out. And I feel that, and I know it, and I trust it. I don't care if nothing else is happening, I still really know that. (Benner, 1984: 32)

The expert nurse cannot say how she knows that the patient is psychotic, and yet she is rarely (if ever) wrong. Benner suggested that the reason that the expert cannot put into words the process of expertise is because there *is* no rational and explicable process. Rather, 'the expert performer no longer relies on an analytic principle (rule, guideline, maxim) to connect her or his understanding of the situation to an appropriate action' (Benner, 1984).

According to Dreyfus and Dreyfus (1986), from whom Benner borrowed much of the theoretical underpinning for her work, the expert arrives at her decision through 'pattern matching', in which the current situation is compared with a mental store of thousands (and possibly millions) of past cases. But as they point out, when called upon to make a decision in the midst of practice, there simply is not enough time to sift through all of these cases in a conscious, rational way; rather, the expert develops an 'intuitive grasp' of the situation which enables her to 'zero in' on the problem without conscious thought. In his later work, Dreyfus (1992) described this intuitive pattern recognition as 'a *bodily skill* basic to all intelligent behaviour' (our italics), thereby linking it to Popper's notion of organismic knowledge which cannot be expressed in words. As Benner (1984) pointed out, when asked to justify her decisions the expert will merely say something like 'Because it felt right', 'It looked good' or 'Well, it all depends'. Expert practice, for Benner, is intuitive and, in a sense, mindless practice based on tacit, organismic 'knowing how' rather than scientific propositional 'knowing that'.

Benner's intuitive expert nurse was at the final stage of a process of skill acquisition which started with novice practice. As Benner pointed out, the novice has no experience on which to base her practice, no exemplars against which to match her current situation. She therefore relies almost entirely on formal propositional knowledge from books and lectures, and as a result her practice is rule-governed, inflexible and extremely limited. In the terminology of our typology, the novice firstly acquires scientific theoretical knowledge such as research findings and theoretical models, which she then employs to construct scientific practical knowledge in the form of rules and procedures (Figure 1.4).

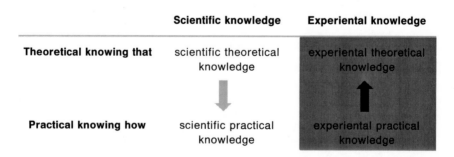

Figure 1.4 Novice practice

	Scientific knowledge	**Experiental knowledge**
Theoretical knowing that	scientific theoretical knowledge	experiental theoretical knowledge
Practical knowing how	scientific practical knowledge	experiental practical knowledge

Figure 1.5   Expert practice

As she acquires more experience she gradually builds a body of experiential practical knowledge, what Benner referred to as intuitive grasp, so that she is able to respond to clinical situations in a fluid and effortless fashion, although she is rarely able to explain or justify her actions to others (Figure 1.5). As we can see, however, what is still missing from the expert's repertoire is experiential theoretical knowledge, the ability to articulate the tacit, organismic experiential knowledge, which is gained directly from practice.

When Benner first published her work on expertise in the early 1980s, it was of no great consequence that the expert practitioner was unable to articulate her *modus operandi*; in fact, it has certain advantages in raising the status of experiential 'knowing how' above scientific 'knowing that'. As Schön observed:

> When people use such terms as 'art' and 'intuition', they usually intend to terminate discussion rather than to open up inquiry. It is as though the practitioner says to his academic colleague, 'While I do not accept *your* view of knowledge, I cannot describe my own'. Sometimes, indeed, the practitioner appears to say, 'My kind of knowledge is indescribable', or even, 'I will not attempt to describe it lest I paralyse myself'. (Schön, 1983: vii–viii)

But whilst this attitude might offer some protection, or even status, to the practitioner, Schön continued by noting that it has also 'contributed to a widening rift between the universities and the professions, research and practice, thought and action'. In addition, expert practitioners are nowadays expected not only to be able to justify their clinical decisions according to some form of evidence, but to pass on their expertise to their colleagues; the attitude expressed by Benner's psychiatric nurse that 'I feel that, and I know it, and I trust it. I don't care if nothing else is happening, I still really know that' simply will not do.

Benner partially recognised this problem and attempted to resolve it by suggesting that the knowledge underpinning expert practice might, in some circumstances, be articulated. She claimed, for example, that:

> When experts can describe clinical situations where their interventions made a difference, some of the knowledge embedded in their practice becomes visible.

And with visibility, enhancement and recognition of expertise become possible. (Benner, 1984: 36)

However, she offered no evidence to back up this statement, which in any case flatly contradicted the observation of her mentors, who wrote that:

> In reality, a patient is viewed by the experienced doctor [and, we might add, nurse] as a unique case and treated on the basis of intuitively perceived similarity with situations previously encountered. That kind of wisdom, unfortunately, *cannot be shared and thereby made the basis of a doctor's rational decision.* (Dreyfus and Dreyfus, 1986: 200, our italics)

If the knowledge-base of expert practitioners is largely tacit, if they truly do know more than they can say, then how is expertise passed on? Or is it the case that more experienced practitioners are of little use in teaching their expertise to junior colleagues, resulting in each generation of practitioners having to start from scratch?

 FURTHER READING

A more recent account of Benner's position on expert practice can be found in chapter 6 of her jointly authored book *Expertise in Nursing Practice*. Dreyfus and Dreyfus' own account of their five-stage model of skill acquisition can be found in chapter 2 of the same book.

Benner, P., Tanner, C. and Chesla, C. (1996) *Expertise in Nursing Practice: Caring, Clinical Judgment, and Ethics*, New York: Springer.

■ Reflection-on-action and the acquisition of knowledge

This problem of how practitioners conceptualise and articulate their knowledge was the focus of Schön's groundbreaking book *The Reflective Practitioner: How Professionals Think in Action*. As he pointed out:

> Professionals have been disturbed to find that they cannot account for processes they have come to see as central to professional competence. It is difficult for them to imagine how to describe and teach what might be meant by making sense of uncertainty, performing artistically, setting problems, and choosing among competing professional paradigms, when these processes seem mysterious in the light of the prevailing model of professional knowledge. (Schön, 1983: 20)

He continued by encapsulating the overriding problem for post-technical practitioners and educators in a single sentence: 'We are bound to an epistemology of practice which leaves us at a loss to explain, or even to describe, the competences to which we now give overriding importance'. Schön's major achievement, as we shall see, was not merely to describe an epistemology of practice, but to outline a method for generating and articulating practice-based knowledge: the method of reflection-on-action.

In fact, Schön advocated two distinct types of reflection, which he referred to as reflection-*on*-action and reflection-*in*-action. Schön considered reflection-in-action, thinking and theorising about practice whilst actually doing it, to be by far the most important form of reflection for experienced practitioners. However, the widespread adoption of Benner's model of expertise has led to a neglect of this form of reflection in nursing, since she claimed that thinking about expert practice while we are doing it leads to a severe degradation in performance. In claiming that 'if experts are made to attend to the particulars or to a formal model or rule, their performance actually deteriorates' (Benner, 1984), she effectively denied the possibility of reflection-in-action as a way of improving practice.

Benner's later work to some extent addresses this issue of thinking about practice whilst doing it, by introducing the concept of 'thinking-in-action' (Benner *et al.*, 1999). However, although this sounds very similar to Schön's notion of reflection-in-action, it is in fact quite different. Thus, 'the thinking we refer to may not be reflective' (Benner *et al.*, 1999), and is based on 'narrative understanding' rather than on any kind of intellectual understanding. All that the expert practitioner can do, then, is to tell her 'story' in the form of a narrative. She cannot offer any sort of rationale for her clinical judgements, since thinking in action is not a rational process which can be brought into consciousness, but is rather an unconscious set of 'patterns and habits of thought and actions' (*ibid.*) which are implicit in her narrative account.

One possible reason why Benner believed that this form of unconscious and mindless expertise was the highest form of practice is that, as we have seen, she based her work on Dreyfus and Dreyfus's model of skill acquisition. Most of the examples used by Dreyfus and Dreyfus involved the acquisition of motor skills such as driving a car and piloting an aircraft, and, as they rightly pointed out, if we concentrate on motor skills as we are performing them our performance inevitably deteriorates. Now of course healthcare professionals are often called upon to perform motor skills, and even simple tasks such as making a bed or changing a dressing are performed less expertly when we consciously think about what we are doing while we are doing it. However, many activities that the expert practitioner carries out are predominantly cognitive rather than motor, and although they *can* be performed mindlessly, there is no evidence to suggest that mindful rational thought will lead to a deterioration in cognitive performance. Even Dreyfus and Dreyfus appeared to recognise the distinction between motor and cognitive performance: having provided several examples of the way in which the performance of motor skills deteriorates when the expert thinks about what she is doing, they then gave the example of the expert chess player, who *can* improve her performance by thinking about it as she does it through a process of 'deliberative rationality' (Dreyfus and Dreyfus, 1986).

Benner, however, failed to make the distinction between motor skills, in which any thought about the process will lead to a deterioration in performance, and cognitive ability, in which deliberative rationality can actually improve performance. In considering nursing solely in terms of motor skills, she not only took the view that thinking about the rules underpinning practice leads to a deterioration in performance, but, as we have seen, took the argument to its (il)logical conclusion by also claiming that 'this does not mean, however, that the rules and formulas just move to the unconscious level or go underground' (Benner, 1984), but rather that there *are* no rules and formulas. As Dreyfus and Dreyfus (1986) put it, 'the expert is simply not following any rules! He is recognising thousands of special cases'. And if there are no rational processes involved, if intuitive grasp really is 'understanding without a rationale' (Benner and Tanner, 1987), then there is no theoretical component to the expert's experiential practical knowledge.

If, along with Dreyfus and Dreyfus, we see practice development in terms of the acquisition of *skills*, then reflection-in-action, in which the practitioner consciously thinks about her practice whilst doing it, leads to a degradation in performance, whereas reflection-on-action is fine for novices and beginners but is of little benefit to expert practitioners who have nothing meaningful to reflect on. Nursing and the healthcare professions have therefore largely ignored reflection-in-action, and have only partially accepted reflection-on-action despite a concerted effort by a number of writers to promote reflective practice and clinical supervision.

If, on the other hand, we adopt a *knowledge* acquisition model of practice, then reflection-in-action becomes a vital part of the repertoire of the advanced practitioner, and reflection-on-action is an essential developmental tool for *all* practitioners. It is therefore on reflection-*on*-action (or what we will refer to as critical reflection) that this book will mainly focus.

Fitzgerald has defined reflection-on-action as:

the retrospective contemplation of practice undertaken in order to uncover the knowledge used in a particular situation, by analysing and interpreting the information recalled. (Fitzgerald, 1994: 67)

This definition makes three points about reflection-on-action. Firstly, it is retrospective; that is, it occurs after and usually away from the scene of the practice. This is in contrast to Schön's notion of reflection-in-action, which occurs during and as an integral part of practice. Secondly, it assumes that practice is underpinned by knowledge, that healthcare practice, unlike riding a bicycle, involves some form of *cognitive* knowing as well as doing. And thirdly, it claims that this knowledge can be uncovered by a process of analysis and interpretation; the reflective process. Reflection-on-action is therefore an active process of transforming experience into knowledge, and as Andrews (1996) pointed out, 'reflection is, therefore, not to be confused with thinking about practice, which may only involve recalling what has occurred rather than learning from it'.

It will be recalled from Figure 1.5 that Benner's expert nurse has acquired a body of experiential *practical* knowledge, what she referred to as tacit intuitive grasp, but cannot articulate the experiential *theoretical* knowledge which underpins it. We have also argued that Benner holds this position largely because she has employed a model of *skills* acquisition rather than *knowledge* acquisition in her attempt to explain and describe expert practice. If we view nursing and healthcare practice in terms of knowledge rather than skills, then we open up the possibility of further levels of practice beyond Benner's expertise. Thus, through reflecting on her practice after and away from the event, the expert practitioner has the potential to develop, explore and (most importantly) articulate her experiential knowledge, and so progress beyond Benner's final stage of expert. The simple model shown in Figure 1.6 illustrates the knowledge acquisition of the practitioner from beginner to advanced, and is intended to demonstrate the importance of reflection-on-action or critical reflection.

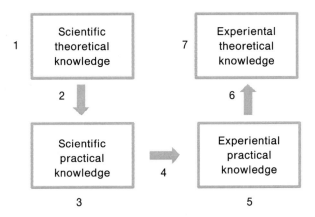

Figure 1.6 A model of knowledge acquisition

As we shall see, the stages in Figure 1.6 roughly follow Benner's stages of skill acquisition:

1 The new student practitioner firstly acquires a body of scientific theoretical knowledge from books and lectures. This is similar to Benner's novice stage.
2 Through supervised practice, she learns to apply this theoretical knowledge to practice.
3 She eventually develops a body of scientific practical knowledge in the form of rules, guidelines and other research- and theory-based procedures. This scientific practical knowledge is largely cognitive (it is stored in the brain) and is easily articulated in words. The practitioner is now at the equivalent of Benner's second stage of advanced beginner.

4   At the same time, she is beginning to internalise some of this practical knowl-
    edge. She begins to act without consciously thinking about what she is doing,
    and she also modifies some of her scientific practical knowledge to meet the
    requirements of real-life situations. She is progressing through Benner's
    stages of competent and proficient.

5   Eventually, after a great deal of experience, she almost totally rejects her
    scientific practical knowledge in favour of experiential practical knowledge.
    This body of knowledge is largely organismic (it is stored in the muscles and
    reflexes) and is very difficult to articulate in words. She usually does the right
    thing, but cannot say how or why it is the right thing. Although she no longer
    uses her scientific knowledge, she has not lost it, and will draw on it when
    faced with a novel situation. This is similar to Benner's stage of expert, and
    was, for Benner, the final and most advanced stage of practice.

6   Through reflecting on her practice, the expert nurse eventually begins to
    recognise, understand and articulate the processes underpinning her exper-
    tise. She realises that there is a rational process underpinning intuitive grasp.

7   She eventually begins to build a body of experiential theoretical knowledge
    out of her experiential practical knowledge. This knowledge is not the
    abstract content-based knowledge of the novice and beginner, nor is it the
    concrete content-based knowledge of the expert. Rather, it is process-based
    knowledge, and is concerned with *how* she practices rather than with *what* she
    practices. Furthermore, it can be shared between practitioners and, as Schön
    noted, transcends professional boundaries and is common to *all* practice-
    based disciplines. We have used the term 'advanced practitioner' to describe
    this level of practice.

   If we conceptualise practice development in terms of knowledge rather than
skill acquisition, then critical reflection takes on a new significance. It allows us
not only to advance our practice beyond Benner's expert stage, but to develop a
body of knowledge about that practice which can be employed to improve our
own performance, to justify it to others as a source of evidence, and to pass it on
to junior colleagues. The remainder of this book is taken up with a variety of ways
in which practitioners can acquire the knowledge and skills of critical reflection
and so develop themselves as advanced practitioners.

REFLECTIVE WRITING

Now turn back to the aims which you identified at the start of the chapter. To what extent have they been met? Write a paragraph outlining the scientific and experiential knowledge you have acquired through reading this chapter and doing the exercises. Write a second paragraph identifying any aims which you feel were only partially met or not met at all. Now divide your page into three columns. Head the first column 'What I need to learn', and make a list of any outstanding issues which you would like to learn more about. For example, you might wish to find out more about improving your practice through action research. Head the second column 'How I will learn it', and write down the ways in which your learning needs could be addressed, for example, through further reading, through attending study days, or through talking to other people. Head the third column 'How I will know that I have learnt it', and try to identify how you will know when you have met your needs. You might, for example, set yourself the task of successfully conducting a small action research project into your own practice.

You have just written your first learning plan for this book. We will be asking you to write one at the end of each chapter.

Chapter 2

Models of critical reflection

■ Introduction

We saw in the previous chapter that not all knowledge for practice comes from textbooks, research journals and lectures, and that in addition to this scientific knowledge, practitioners also informally 'pick up' practical knowledge from their everyday experience. For example, a nurse might acquire the 'know-how' (or what Benner called 'intuitive grasp') about how to recognise when a patient is psychotic from her many past experiences of working with psychotic people. For Benner, this experiential practical knowledge, where the nurse 'just knew' what to do, was the hallmark of expertise and the highest level of practice.

We have argued, however, that there is a level of practice beyond Benner's expertise which can only be attained by the practitioner reflecting on her experiential practical knowledge, thereby creating a body of experiential *theoretical* knowledge about the rational processes which underpin her intuitive grasp. As we noted in the previous chapter, this knowledge is concerned with *how* she practices rather than with *what* she practices, and is common to all practice-based disciplines. Furthermore, because it provides the practitioner with access to the processes by which she makes clinical judgements, she is able to use it to improve her own performance, to justify her actions to others as a source of evidence, and to pass on her expertise to junior colleagues. We have used the term 'advanced practitioner' to describe the person who regularly works at this level.

Having established the need for the kind of experiential knowledge that arises out of reflection (or to be more precise, out of what Schön called 'reflection-on-action'), this chapter is concerned with exploring some of the models, structures and frameworks that can facilitate this reflective process. We have therefore moved from the question '*Why* should I reflect?' posed in Chapter 1, to that of '*How* can I reflect?'

There are two ways of considering the issue of models and frameworks for reflection. Firstly, we can explore the several ways in which reflection-on-action can be facilitated, such as through one-to-one or group supervision, through critical incident analysis in the classroom, or through reflective writing, and these techniques (what we have elsewhere referred to as 'modes' of reflective practice) are the subject of much of the remainder of this book. However, whatever approach is employed to facilitate the reflective process, there is still the need for a framework through which the process is structured, and that is the subject of this chapter. The aims of this chapter are therefore:

1   to examine the practical and philosophical basis of reflection-on-action;
2   to explore and experiment with some simple frameworks and guidelines as structures for reflective practice;
3   to suggest a reflexive framework as a tool for practice development; and
4   to enable you to begin to think reflectively and reflexively in a structured way.

As in the previous chapter, we recognise that you as a reader and practitioner will bring with you a set of aims specific to your own individual needs, which you might now wish to think about.

REFLECTIVE WRITING

Think carefully about our aims for Chapter 2. Now think about your own practice and how these aims might contribute towards developing it. For example, how might a reflective framework help you to explore your own practice?

Based on our aims above, write down some of your own, both in terms of what you hope to know and what you hope to be able to do after reading Chapter 2. We will return to your aims at the end of the chapter.

■ The macro-structure of reflection-on-action

You might recall our brief discussion of reflection-on-action in the previous chapter, where we offered Fitzgerald's definition of:

> The retrospective contemplation of practice undertaken in order to uncover the knowledge used in a particular situation, by analysing and interpreting the information recalled. (Fitzgerald, 1994: 67)

For Fitzgerald, then, reflection-on-action is a process of turning information into knowledge. Boyd and Fales also emphasised the role of reflection in developing the experiential knowledge of the practitioner, and defined it as:

> The process of creating and clarifying the meaning of experience in terms of self in relation to both self and the world. The outcome of this process is changed conceptual perspectives. (Boyd and Fales, 1983: 101)

We can see, however, that whereas Fitzgerald was concerned mainly with knowledge about the situation, Boyd and Fales focused more on the self. They saw the outcome of reflection-on-action as not just new knowledge, but as a *changed conceptual perspective*. Reflection does not merely add to our knowledge, it also challenges the concepts and theories by which we try to make sense of that knowledge. When we reflect on a situation, we do not merely see more; we see differently.

Some writers wish to go even further. Atkins and Murphy, for example, pointed out that:

> For reflection to make a real difference to practice, it is important that the out-come includes a commitment to action. This may not necessarily involve acts which can be observed by others, but it is important that the individual makes a commitment of some kind on the basis of that learning. Action is the final stage of the reflective cycle. (Atkins and Murphy, 1994: 51)

Kim (1999) referred to this emphasis on action in reflection as 'critical reflective inquiry', and located it in the tradition of action science (Argyris and Schön, 1974) and critical philosophy (Habermas, 1984). For Kim, Fitzgerald's notion of reflection as the generation of knowledge about the situation, and Boyd and Fales' notion of reflection as the generation of theory through the transformation of the self, were both part of a broader model which led ultimately to a critical/emancipatory phase of reflection-on-action (Figure 2.1) which 'is a method of changing and correcting professional practice in an on-going fashion' (Kim, 1999). Although Kim's model was designed to be employed by the reflective researcher as a method of data collection, she pointed out that it is equally applicable to reflection-on-action by the practitioner herself.

This model offers a useful 'macro structure' for the process of reflection-on-action, which starts with a descriptive phase in which:

	Descriptive phase	**Reflective phase**	**Critical/emancipatory phase**
Processes	• Descriptions of practice events (actions, thoughts & feelings)	• Reflective analysis against espoused theories (scientific, ethical & aesthetic)	• Critique of practice regarding conflicts, distortions & inconsistencies
	• Examination of descriptions for genuineness & comprehensiveness	• Reflective analysis of situations	• Engagement in emancipatory & change process
		• Reflective analysis of intentions	
Products	• Descriptive narratives	• Knowledge about practice processes and applications	• Learning & change in practice
		• Self-awareness	• Self-critique & emancipation

Figure 2.1 Phases in the critical reflective inquiry (after Kim, 1999)

Descriptive narratives of specific instances of practice in specific clinical situations are written or constructed by nurses, including the descriptions of nurses' actions, thoughts and feelings, as well as the circumstances and features of the situations. (Kim, 1999: 1207)

The aim of these narratives is 'to open a door that has been closed behind, and to look back into the past' (Kim, 1999), and it is the job of the facilitator (or, in Kim's model, the researcher) firstly to keep the narratives at the descriptive level, and secondly to help the practitioner to 'identify what is missing in the descriptions to make them comprehensive and complete' (*ibid.*).

In the second (reflective) phase, these descriptive narratives are 'examined in a reflective mode against practitioners' personal beliefs, assumptions and knowledge' (*ibid.*). The aim here is for the practitioner to uncover her 'espoused theories' relating to the specific situation, what we referred to in Chapter 1 as her experiential theoretical knowledge, so that she 'can discover not only how [she is] able to handle complex situations but also in what ways [she] become[s] entrenched in routinized practice' (*ibid.*). In other words, the reflective phase of the process enables the practitioner to begin to build her own personal and situational knowledge and theory base so that she is able to respond not only from her scientific knowledge, but also from her experiential knowledge.

However, Kim argued that it is not enough merely to construct knowledge from practice settings, and that the practitioner must also reflect on how that knowledge can lead to intentions to act; in other words, how experiential knowledge translates into clinical actions. She pointed out that this is extremely difficult for the practitioner to do alone, and usually requires facilitation, since 'it is not easy for people to free themselves from 'rationalizations' they make of their actions and partition out which actions were intended from which actions were not intended' (*ibid.*).

Kim's third and final 'critical/emancipatory' phase builds on the insights into practice acquired in the reflective phase and 'is oriented to correcting and changing less-than-good or ineffective practice, or moving forward to future assimilation of new innovations emerging from practice' (*ibid.*). In this phase, the facilitator and the practitioner 'engage in the process of critique in order to point out problems that require change in practice' (*ibid.*). The required changes can be either personal or communal, but ultimately require both self-knowledge and self-emancipation, since:

Through the [facilitator's] questioning and probing, practitioners can engage in self-dialogue and argumentation with themselves in order to clarify validity claims embedded in their actions, bringing forth the hidden meanings and disguises that systematically result in self-oriented and unilateral actions or ineffective habitual forms of practice. Self-emancipation is the key desired outcome of this examination as through this process nurses may become open to new models of practice. (Kim, 1999: 1209)

We can see, then, that Kim's three phases of reflection form a developmental continuum along which the practitioner can travel as she gradually develops her reflective abilities. In the 'descriptive phase', she is concerned primarily with building narratives of her practice through which she is able to 'open a door into the past'. The role of the facilitator at this stage is to stop the narrative from becoming too analytic and to ensure that it is, as far as possible, 'comprehensive and complete'. In the 'reflective phase', the practitioner uses those narratives to develop experiential knowledge and theory, and to begin to reflect on how that knowledge might be translated into action. The role of the facilitator in this phase is crucial, since Kim pointed out that it is extremely difficult for the practitioner to be objective about her successes and failures in translating theory into action. Finally, the 'critical/emancipatory phase' involves a detailed critique of practice (where the term 'critique' is employed in Habermas' sense of the emancipation from self-deception through increased self-knowledge), which is ultimately a critique of the practitioner herself.

For Kim, then, reflection starts in the world and ends in the self. Furthermore, the beginning reflective practitioner might remain in the initial descriptive phase for some time, until her critical faculties are well enough developed to progress to the reflective and, ultimately, the critical/emancipatory phases. This developmental model of reflection to some extent answers the criticism put forward by Mackintosh (1998) that 'if reflection is identified as being compatible with the ability to perform as a hypothetico-deductive thinker, it is unlikely that all nurses will be able to meet these requirements'. This assumption was based on the work of Cavanagh *et al.* (1995), Richardson and Maltby (1995) and Burrows (1995), which demonstrated that the majority of first- and second-year students could not perform higher-level reflective skills. This, of course, is only to be expected, since in the previous chapter we identified critical reflection specifically with advanced practice. However, if Kim's model is used developmentally, then novice reflective practitioners can begin with simple descriptive reflection and gradually progress to the more complex levels under close supervision and guidance.

Although Kim offers a useful model of reflection, it was designed first and foremost as a research methodology and therefore has a detailed and complex philosophical underpinning which some practitioners might perceive as confusing and unnecessary (see, for example, Usher and Bryant, 1989; Ottman, 1982). However, Borton (1970) has produced a similar but much simpler developmental model that is eminently suitable for use with even novice reflective practitioners, in which the practitioner is encouraged to ask herself three questions. Firstly, she asks the question 'What?', which encourages her to describe the situation that she wishes to reflect on. Borton's 'What?' stage is therefore very similar to Kim's descriptive narrative phase. Secondly, she asks the question 'So what?', which prompts her to build a personal theory from her description of the situation. This is similar to Kim's reflective phase. Finally, she asks the question 'Now what?', which encourages her to plan an active intervention based on her theory, and which is similar to Kim's critical/emancipatory phase. However, whereas

FURTHER READING

Kim's model of reflection is based on the work of the critical theorists (sometimes referred to collectively as the Frankfurt School). Under the leadership of Jurgen Habermas, critical theory developed initially out of Marxism and has a very overt agenda for social change through education. One of the earliest models of reflection based on critical theory came from the Marxist Paulo Freire, who saw the reflective process as a means of identifying and freeing oneself from false consciousness, and ultimately as a revolutionary tool. This approach was further developed by educationalists such as Carr and Kemmis, particularly in chapter 5 of their book *Becoming Critical*; by Mezirow, who saw the outcome of reflection as being a 'perspective transformation'; and by Stephen Brookfield, for whom reflection involved uncovering and challenging the power structures that 'undergird, frame, and distort educational processes and interactions'. Critical theory will be revisited in Chapter 7 when we explore action research, but for now, you might wish to look at:

Brookfield, S. D. (1995) *Becoming a Critically Reflective Teacher*, San Francisco: Jossey-Bass.
Carr, W. and Kemmis, S. (1986) *Becoming Critical*, London: Falmer.
Freire, P. (1972) *Pedagogy of the Oppressed*, Harmondsworth: Penguin.
Habermas, J. (1974) *Theory and Practice*, London: Heinemann.
Mezirow, J. (1981) 'A Critical Theory of Adult Learning and Education', *Adult Education*, **1**, 3–24.

Kim's model has its foundations in the philosophical work of Habermas and the critical theorists, Borton's framework is based on the simple and pragmatic needs of the practitioner to describe, make sense of, and respond to a real-life situation.

The more advanced or philosophically-minded practitioner is encouraged to explore critical theory as a model for reflection through the further reading suggested above. However, for now, we shall look at an example of how Borton's rather simpler framework can be used to structure the process of reflecting on a clinical situation. In this example, a critical care nurse became very upset when a patient with whom she had formed a close relationship was deemed not suitable for resuscitation, and she disputed the consultant's decision in a heated discussion in front of the patient. She later reflected on how she had dealt with the situation by using Borton's framework.

What happened?
I become very angry at the way in which the consultant took a life-and-death decision about this patient without any consultation with the staff who knew him

best. I tried to put across my point of view, but she refused to listen. I eventually lost my temper and shouted at her in the middle of the ward. At this point, she stormed out.

This is the initial descriptive stage of the reflective process, in which the practitioner is reconstructing the situation from her own perspective. Reflection-on-action has sometimes been criticised for not being objective (Reece Jones, 1995), but it is important that this descriptive reflective stage remains firmly in the subjective realm, since this provides the practitioner with the opportunity to explore her own personal emotions and perceptions of the situation. This descriptive reflection is eminently suitable for the novice, and even if the process terminates at this early stage, the practitioner will have been re-connected with her thoughts and feelings about the situation so that she can begin to learn from it.

So what am I to make of this?
First, I shouldn't have lost my temper. The consultant probably felt just as uncomfortable as I did about the decision, and dealt with it by asserting her authority. Although I was right to feel angry, I shouldn't have reacted in the way I did. Perhaps I could have told the consultant how angry I was feeling rather than expressing my anger in front of the patient. She might have responded to rational agrument, but by becoming angry, I simply gave her the excuse to storm out. I can see now that any chance of rational communication was blocked by our highly charged emotional states.

This second theory-building stage takes the practitioner beyond her earlier descriptive reflection, since she is not only reflecting on her thoughts and feelings, but learning from them. In the above example, the nurse is learning not only about the situation, but also about herself and (perhaps) about the consultant. Furthermore, she is beginning to develop a theory about how her reactions might have adversely influenced the situation, and about how she might have acted differently. Even if the process stops at this second stage, the nurse has achieved some valuable insights and is likely to behave differently the next time she encounters a similar situation.

Now what can I do to make the situation better?
Now that I am feeling calmer, I think that I should make an appointment to see the consultant. We need to talk about the situation sensibly. I may not be able to change her mind, but I owe it to myself and to my patient to give it my best shot. I also need to let the consultant see that I am a professional practitioner and that my opinion counts for something.

Although the second stage was action-oriented in the sense that the practitioner might learn from the situation and act differently the next time it occurs, this final stage seeks to respond *reflexively* to the actual situation that is being reflected on. In the above example, the nurse has learnt not only to deal with the consultant differently in the future, but also attempts to resolve the ongoing problem in the light of her reflections on the situation.

 REFLECTIVE WRITING

Now think of a situation from your own practice that you feel was left unresolved, and attempt to reflect on it by using Borton's three questions.

How useful did you find it? Which was the easiest question to answer? Which was the hardest? At which of Borton's stages do you usually reflect? Write down what you found most difficult about the process.

One of the problems with both Borton's and Kim's models is that little attention is paid to the finer details of reflection. Although each of the models offers a useful framework for structuring critical reflection on the macro level, inasmuch as they both suggest a number of stages through which the focus of reflection-on-action might develop, they say little about the ways in which reflection might be conducted and facilitated within each stage of the process, that is, with the micro-structure of critical reflection.

■ The micro-structure of reflection-on-action

A number of writers have attempted to provide detailed guidelines or frameworks for reflection-on-action. Some of these frameworks view reflection as an educational activity and are aimed primarily at students and novice practitioners, some are action-oriented and are aimed at more or less autonomous practitioners, and some are aimed more at helping the practitioner to gain access to her inner cognitive and emotional states. As far as we are aware, there has been no work carried out on comparing these frameworks, and in the absence of any objective criteria your choice is best made according to your own personal needs and preferences. We shall therefore briefly discuss three frameworks which have been designed to help with the process of reflection-on-action, and offer you the opportunity to explore and experiment with them.

☐ A practitioner's framework for reflection

This framework was developed by Sarah Stephenson, a staff nurse at the John Radcliffe Hospital in Oxford, as part of her degree studies. As she pointed out,

Table 2.1 A practitioner's framework for reflection (after Holm and Stephenson, 1994)

Choose a situation

Ask yourself:

- What was my role in this situation? Did I feel comfortable or uncomfortable? Why?
- What actions did I take? How did I and others act? Was it appropriate?
- How could I have improved the situation for myself, the patient, my mentor?
- What can I change in future?
- Do I feel as if I have learnt anything new about myself?
- Did I expect anything different to happen? What and why?
- Has it changed my way of thinking in any way?
- What knowledge from theory and research can I apply to this situation?
- What broader issues, for example ethical, political or social, arise from this situation? What do I think about these broader issues?

'Unlike writing an essay, there are no definitive rules on how to reflect. No one method is universally correct' (Holm and Stephenson, 1994). She therefore went about constructing her own set of cue questions, primarily as a tool to structure her reflective writing (Table 2.1). As you examine this framework, think carefully about the extent to which it addresses the issues that are pertinent to you as a practitioner. In particular, you might wish to consider the level of Borton's developmental model at which you usually reflect, and the extent to which Stephenson's guidelines meet your needs at that level.

The strength of this framework lies in its grounding in the real-life practice of a real-life staff nurse. Its strength, however, is also its weakness, since if no one method of reflection is universally correct, then Stephenson's guidelines are unlikely to meet all of your own unique and particular needs. Nevertheless, they provide a very useful starting point from which you might wish to make your own modifications as you become more experienced in reflection-on-action.

☐ A facilitator's framework for reflection

The second framework to be presented takes a different but equally valid perspective. Whereas Stephenson offered cue questions that had been constructed out of the experiences of the reflective practitioner, Chris Johns started from the perspective of the facilitator of reflection (Table 2.2). Thus:

> My careful recording of the dialogue that took place between myself and practitioners within the first two years of guided reflection as part of my doctoral study enabled me to look back and analyse the patterns of interaction. (Johns, 1998)

As before, consider how and to what extent Johns' guidelines meet your developmental needs.

Table 2.2 A facilitator's framework for reflection (after Johns, 1998)

Write a description of the experience.
What are the significant issues I need to pay attention to?

Reflective cues

Aesthetics	What was I trying to achieve? Why did I respond as I did? What were the consequences of that for:
	• the patient? • others? • myself?
	How was this person(s) feeling? How did I know this?
Personal	How did I feel in this situation? What internal factors were influencing me?
Ethics	How did my actions match with my beliefs? What factors made me act in incongruent ways?
Empirics	What knowledge did or should have informed me?
Reflexivity	How does this connect with previous experiences? Could I handle this better in similar situations? What would the consequences be of alternative actions for:
	• the patient? • others? • myself?
	How do I *now* feel about this experience? Can I support myself and others better as a consequence? Has this changed my ways of knowing?

The strength of Johns' cue questions is their grounding in systematic observations (using Strauss and Corbin's grounded theory methodology) of actual guided reflection sessions. In addition, he borrowed the epistemological basis for his framework from Carper's (1978) four patterns of knowing (adding a fifth pattern of 'reflexivity'), which are themselves well-researched and which will already be familiar to many nurses. Furthermore, Johns has started to break down his reflective cues in even more detail. Figure 2.2 shows a grid for considering the cue 'What internal factors were influencing me?'

Clearly, Johns' cue questions build into a very comprehensive framework for structuring reflection-on-action which many experienced practitioners will find useful. However, you might wish to consider the extent to which his fifth 'way of knowing' of 'reflexivity' really is reflexive. Certainly, if the reflection is conducted after the situation has been resolved, then it might be appropriate to ask, as Johns

Expectations from self: • obligation/duty • conscience • beliefs/values	Negative attitude towards the patient/family?	Expectations from others: • in what way?
Normal practice – felt I had to conform to a certain action	**What factors influenced my actions?**	Loyalty to staff versus loyalty to patient/family?
Fear of sanction?	Time/priorities?	Anxious about ensuing conflict?

Figure 2.2   Grid for considering the cue 'What internal factors were influencing me?'
(after Johns, 1998)

does, about how a similar situation might be handled in the future. If, on the other hand, the situation is still developing, the practitioner might well feel the need to explore how it could be taken forward. Unfortunately, Johns makes no provision for making changes to an ongoing experience.

☐   An educator's framework for reflection

The third framework to be considered is from the educationalist Graham Gibbs (Figure 2.3). You will notice that his cue questions are arranged in a circular format reminiscent of Kolb's learning cycle, and that the cues are rather

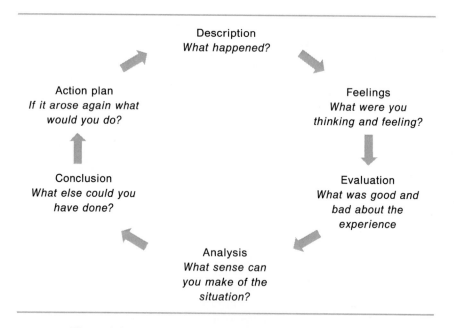

Figure 2.3   An educator's framework for reflection (Gibbs 1988)

general and unspecific. This has the advantage of giving the framework a more generic feel, although some (particularly novice) reflective practitioners prefer the added direction afforded by the previous frameworks. As you examine it, think about whether the lack of structure improves or inhibits your reflection-on-action.

This is very clearly an educational framework, and although it appears at first sight to be action-oriented, closer examination will reveal that it is, in fact, firmly grounded in *learning* from experience rather than in attempting to *change* the experience itself. Thus, although the framework appears to be cyclical, there is no reflexive path back to the action from which the learning is derived, and in common with Johns' framework, the 'action plan' asks the practitioner how she would act *if the situation arose again* rather than how she will resolve the current situation.

 DISCUSSION POINT

Choose one of the above frameworks that you feel you can work with, preferably one that you have not used before. Now employ your chosen framework to reflect (either in writing or in your head) on an issue that you feel is unresolved, or which you think might have been handled better. The issue could be practice-related, organisational or interpersonal. If you prefer, you could choose an issue from home rather than from work.

Now find a colleague who has had experience of a different framework. Take turns to discuss the usefulness of your chosen frameworks in relation to:

- the appropriateness to the issue being reflected on;
- your learning from the situation;
- the extent to which your model is likely to improve your practice in the future;
- the extent to which it is likely to improve *this* situation.

Remember that you are discussing the usefulness of the framework rather than the issue that you were reflecting on, which you might wish to keep confidential.

Following from the Discussion Point [above], you might find that the main failing of your chosen framework was on the final issue of changing the current situation. Indeed, none of the frameworks really attempts to resolve the situation that is being reflected on, although Stephenson does at least address the question of what knowledge the practitioner might apply to it. This lack of reflexivity (what the practitioner learnt from the experience is not translated into action to improve the on-going situation) might be appropriate when reflection-on-action is being employed as a learning tool with trainee practitioners. However, the advanced reflective practitioner whom we described in the previous chapter is concerned not only with learning from the situation, but with improving it. Furthermore, she does not wish merely to practice in a better way the next time she encounters a similar situation, but to improve the current situation. Having asked herself Borton's first two questions of 'What?' and 'So what?', she wishes to complete the reflexive sequence with 'Now what?'

■ A framework for reflexive practice

The advanced practitioner therefore requires a *reflexive* framework which addresses both the macro and the micro levels of reflection, and which pays particular attention to Borton's final action-oriented question of 'Now what?'; that is, which focuses not only on what has been learnt from reflection-on-action, but on how the situation might be made better. We therefore wish to offer a framework for the advanced reflexive practitioner that uses Borton's model as its macro structure, and fleshes it out with questions taken from all three of the sets of guidelines discussed above (Figure 2.4).

The first thing to note is that what we are presenting is a simple framework rather than a model. We are making no claims that it is a representation or description of the process of reflection; it is merely an ordered set of cues through which the practitioner might structure her reflective thoughts. Secondly, it is a generic framework that can be employed to structure internal, spoken or written reflections either alone, with a facilitator, or in a group. Because it is generic, it might not meet your specific needs, and the cue questions are therefore intended to be open to change and revision for different practitioners in different situations.

You will see from the arrows at the top of the framework in Figure 2.4 that it is both sequential and cyclical. In other words, it presents an ordered sequence of stages or levels, the last of which reflexively returns to the first. At the first level, the practitioner initially reflects on the situation in order to describe it. She then reflects again at the second deeper level in order to construct personal theory and knowledge about the situation, that is, to learn from it. At the third level, she plans how she might improve the situation through her actions, reflecting on their consequences. However, her actions will hopefully bring about change, and so she then returns to the initial descriptive level of reflection in order to work though the sequence again with the transformed situation. Furthermore, the cycles can continue until the situation is resolved.

☐ Level 1: descriptive reflection

As we noted earlier, some critics have pointed out that most practitioners do not reflect at this deeper level, and that some will probably never progress further

Descriptive level of reflection	Theory- and knowledge-building level of reflection	Action-oriented (reflexive) level of reflection
What ...	**So what ...**	**Now what ...**

... is the problem/difficulty/reason for being stuck/reason for feeling bad/reason we don't get on/etc., etc.?	... does this tell me/teach me/imply/mean about me/my patient/others/our relationship/my patient's care/the model of care I am using/my attitudes/my patient's attitudes/etc., etc.?	... do I need to do in order to make things better/stop being stuck/improve my patient's care/resolve the situation/feel better/get on better/etc., etc.?
... was my role in the situation?		... broader issues need to be considered if this action is to be successful?
... was I trying to achieve?	... was going through my mind as I acted?	
... actions did I take?		
... was the response of others?	... did I base my actions on?	... might be the consequences of this action?
... were the consequences	... other knowledge can I bring to the situation?	
• for the patient? • for myself? • for others?	• experiential • personal • scientific	
... feelings did it evoke	... could/should I have done to make it better?	
• in the patient? • in myself? • in others?	... is my new understanding of the situation?	
... was good/bad about the experience?	... broader issues arise from the situation?	

Figure 2.4 A framework for reflexive practice

than the concrete thinking required for descriptive reflection. These novice reflective practitioners might therefore remain at the first level, at least until their thinking has developed sufficiently for them to be able to begin to construct personal knowledge and theory out of their experiences. Despite not progressing past the first level of reflection, these practitioners will nevertheless benefit from consciously considering their practice in a structured way, from thinking the process through, and from exploring their feelings and those of the other people involved in the incident.

Case example
What is the problem?
I am a community psychiatric nurse (CPN) working with a client who has difficulty relating to other peope since his wife died nearly two years ago. He wishes to get out of the house more, but does not know how to go about it.

What was my role in the situation?
I felt that I needed to make things better for him by offering practical help and advice.

What was I trying to achieve?
I was trying to respond to the client's wishes by getting him more involved in the outside world.

What actions did I take?
I made practical suggestions, for example, to join clubs, take up evening classes, place an advertisement in the personal column of the local newspaper, etc. I even offered to accompany him to social events.

What was the response of others?
There were no others involved in the situation.

What were the consequences?
None of my suggestions worked, despite the client's best intentions.

What feelings did it invoke in the client?
He said that he felt he had let me down.

What feelings did it invoke in me?
I felt as though I had failed him, and that my counselling skills were lacking.

What was good/bad about the experience?
I felt as though I had built a strong relationship with him. However, there were no positive outcomes despite our best efforts.

In the case example [above], it is important that the CPN begins to look at her own feelings and those of the client. Both parties seemed to be quite comfortable with the stalemate situation, which had been continuing for some time. It is only once the CPN realises that they both appear to be content to continue in a situation where each claims to be feeling bad, that she will be motivated to explore it further.

☐ Level 2: theory- and knowledge-building reflection

More advanced practitioners will find it beneficial to think not only about what happened, but also about *how* and *why* it happened; that is, about the underlying processes and dynamics of the situation. At this second level of reflection, they will be prompted to think not only about the theory and knowledge which they (perhaps unconsciously) applied to the situation, but what other knowledge and theory they *could* have applied. In other words, they will be encouraged to reflect on how the situation could have been handled differently.

Case example
So what does this tell me?
Firstly, I need to accept the fact that we are getting nowhere, and that my counselling intervention does not appear to be very effective.

So what was going through my mind as I acted?
It is very difficult to recall exactly what I was thinking as I made suggestions to the client. Part of me seemed to realise that whatever I said would make no difference, but another part thought that this didn't really matter, as I was builidng a good therapeutic relationship with him.

So what did I base my actions on?
I thought at the time that I was following a model of counselling, but I can see now that perhaps I was acting in my own interest rather than the client's.

So what other knowledge can I bring to the situation?
My personal knowledge of this client suggests that he was very close to his wife, but that he didn't socialise very much, apart from with one or two close friends. My previous experiences of similar situations tell me that I sometimes become stuck with clients and find it difficult to move forward. In one particular case, my manager suggested that I stopped working with the client. My scientific knowledge tells me that this is not uncommon in counselling situations. The theory of transactional analysis suggests that we might be caught up in a 'game' in which each of us is getting a pay-off from failing to make progress with counselling. Some theorists also suggest that the counsellor should resist making direct suggestions to the client.

So what could I have done to make it better?
I should perhaps not have become so obsessed with trying to solve my client's problem for him. Perhaps it is not even the real problem.

So what is my new understanding of the situation?
Despite the fact that we appear to be making little or no progress, the client continues to want me to visit, so perhaps he is gaining something from it, even it if

is not what we set out to achieve. Perhaps I am providing all the social contact that he needs, and so he is (perhaps unconsciously) deliberately ensuring that we continue with the counselling sessions by failing to make progress. On the other hand, perhaps my repeated failure to help him is giving him a (much needed) feeling of superiority over me. Perhaps it is also in my interest not to succeed with this client. It is possible that I find the sessions safe and comfortable, and that I am secretly worried that if they are successful then I will have to move on to work with other less familiar clients.

So what broader issues arise form the situation?
I need to stop and reflect on my therapeutic relationships, and in particular, to consider whether I am really meeting my clients' needs. I was a little shocked when I realised that I have been here before with other clients. Perhaps I need more supervision with my counselling work.

The CPN appears to have learnt some important lessons from this second knowledge-building level of reflection. In particular, she has recognised a recurring pattern in her counselling work, and has made a decision to seek more supervision in order to prevent such difficulties from arising again. In some situations and for some practitioners, this will be as far as the reflective process can take them. Perhaps the situation has been resolved; perhaps it has moved on and it would be inappropriate to revisit it; or perhaps the practitioner does not have the autonomy or the authority to act on the situation. Even so, she will have learnt not only about herself and the way in which she dealt (or not) with the situation, but also how she might deal differently with similar situations when they next occur.

☐ Level 3: action-oriented (reflexive) reflection

However, in some cases the practitioner will have the opportunity to return to the situation with the intention of improving it, and this is where a reflexive framework for reflection-on-action can make its greatest contribution to practice.

Case example
Now what do I need to do in order to stop being stuck?
There are a number of ways that I could move this situation forward. If I am holding the client back, I could simply stop working with him and suggest that he is discharged. This action might give him a greater incentive to build up new and healthier relationships outside of counselling. Alternatively, I could confront the client with my theory so that he also recognises that we are stuck in a rut, or I could simply stop making suggestions to him and see how he reacts.

Now what broader issues need to be considered if this action is to be successful?
If the client is discharged, I need to consider alternative support mechanisms that

are less likely to induce overreliance on the system. If I confront him, I need to be prepared for his response, which is likely to be one of denial. Finally, if I simply stop making suggestions I will need to be prepared for criticism and rejection. Perhaps I need to talk to my supervisor in order to explore these options, and how I might handle them.

Now what might be the consequences of this action?
I would hope that the client might recognise that we have been playing games and move on. However, he might be unable or unwilling to accept the need for a change in our relationship and respond by demanding a different counsellor, or even by discharging himself. I also need to consider my own possible reaction to a change in our relationship, since I also appear to be gaining something from it.

In the case example [above], the CPN has a number of options that she can pursue, and clearly, her reflection-on-action is likely to have a direct impact on her practice. Furthermore, once the planning has taken place, the consequences of the action anticipated and thought through, and the action implemented, the CPN will have to return to the descriptive level of reflection to consider the newly transformed situation in a true reflexive cycle.

 REFLECTIVE WRITING

Return to the situation from your own practice that you reflected on earlier using Borton's three questions. Now repeat the exercise using the framework for reflexive practice that we have just outlined.

Once again, think about the following:
How useful did you find it? Which was the easiest level to reflect at? Which was the hardest? At which level do you usually reflect? Did the addition of the cue questions to Borton's model make it easier or more difficult to use? Why?

■ Conclusion

In the first chapter of this book we explored the idea that knowledge and theory can arise out of practice as well as being applied to it, and suggested reflection-on-action as a means whereby the healthcare practitioner might begin to build up her own body of experiential 'know-how' and 'know-that'. In this chapter we have examined some of the ways that the practitioner can begin this process of reflection-on-action, and concluded by offering a framework to guide her through the different levels of reflection. As we stated at the start of the chapter, there are two aspects to exploring the issue of how to reflect, and having suggested some generic frameworks we will now move to examine some of the more specific ways in which those frameworks can be enacted.

 REFLECTIVE WRITING

Now turn back to the aims which you identified at the start of the chapter. To what extent have they been met? Write a paragraph outlining the scientific and experiential knowledge you have acquired through reading this chapter and doing the exercises. Write a second paragraph identifying any aims which you feel were only partially met or not met at all. Now divide your page into three columns. Head the first column 'What I need to learn', and make a list of any outstanding issues which you would like to learn more about. For example, you might wish to find out more about one of the frameworks for reflection that we discussed in this chapter. Head the second column 'How I will learn it', and write down the ways in which your learning needs could be addressed, for example, through further reading, through attending study days, or through talking to other people. Head the third column 'How I will know that I have learnt it', and try to identify how you will know when you have met your needs. You might, for example, set yourself the task of successfully using the framework to reflect on your day at work.

You have just written your second learning plan for this book. We will be asking you to write one at the end of each chapter.

Chapter 3

Reflective writing

■ Introduction

In the first two chapters of this book you have been invited to engage in 'reflective writing' exercises. You have probably looked at these, picked up a pencil and tackled the exercises (or not!), but did you actually stop to think about the *processes* of what we have been asking you to do, or have you simply engaged in the writing as learning exercises without considering that the act of writing itself may well be enabling you to learn?

We discuss many different strategies and approaches to critical reflection in this book, from individual contemplative reflection, to reflection with others; from structured reflection through various different models, to reflection as a research strategy for uncovering knowledge. In this chapter we explore the value of written reflection, that is, of deliberately using strategies of writing as a way of reflecting and as a way of learning from our experience. Writing can, of course, be used together with any of the strategies discussed in other chapters; what we hope to establish here is the added value that can happen when you decide to write reflectively as well as, or in addition to, verbal and contemplative reflection.

People often ask us 'why write?' There seems to be a widespread reluctance amongst clinical practitioners to create written records of the ways in which they practice, let alone writing about practice as a way of reflecting and learning from it. Much of this reluctance arises from the fundamental way of working of most practitioners: by our very nature and self-definition we are 'doers', we act out our professionalism by doing a job. Our primary form of communicating with others is verbal: we talk to each other, we talk to our patients, clients and families. This verbal communication is part of the way in which we practice; it is very often embedded within the culture of our practice and so we are usually comfortable with our verbal skills. We are practitioners as a result of practising. Why, then, do we need to write about it? What is the purpose and what may we get out of it?

Our main aim in this chapter is to explore how critical reflection can be developed through the process of reflective writing. We will discuss what we mean by reflective writing and explore how writing in itself can be seen as a process for learning; in particular, exploring the ways in which writing may help us to develop critical thinking skills and lead to knowledge creation. We will look at some of the barriers to writing and how these can be overcome. Finally, we will discuss different ways of writing reflectively and how these may be used on an individual, group and perhaps even wider basis.

41

The aims and objectives of this chapter are:

1   to explore the ways that reflective writing is used and to look at the benefits of reflective writing as a learning tool;
2   to explore various strategies for reflective writing as a means of critical reflection and of developing critical thinking;
3   to help you to explore ways of writing reflectively within your professional role, your personal development and to benefit client care; and
4   to help you plan to use reflective writing within a professional portfolio.

 REFLECTIVE WRITING

Think carefully about our aims for Chapter 3. Now think about your own practice and how these aims might contribute towards developing it. For example, can you think of any ways that reflective writing may help you to explore a problem you have in practice? Think about your use of writing over the past few years – in what ways have you learnt about yourself and your practice as a result of this writing? Do you have to communicate through writing in your work? What would you like to do to make this more effective? Finally, do you have to keep a professional portfolio for any reason? Do you use reflective writing in any way within this?

Based on our aims above, write down some of your own, both in terms of what you hope to know and what you hope to be able to do after reading Chapter 3. We will return to your aims at the end of the chapter.

■   What is *reflective* writing?

In using the term *reflective writing*, we are referring to the processes involved in writing that can be utilised as means in themselves to help us learn from our experiences. Thus, reflective writing involves engaging in and completing the reflective cycle using the processes of writing as an instrument to help you learn. Reflective writing differs from other forms of writing only in that it has one primary purpose: it is undertaken for the specific purpose of learning; to enable us to come to a different, or deeper, understanding of whatever we are reflecting on. Thus, using a model of reflection such as those to be found in this book, or using some other sort of strategy which enables you to describe, analyse and evaluate your experiences and to write them down, are useful (if not essential) in helping you to write reflectively.

This essential feature of reflective writing is often overlooked when we start on the process, which may explain why many of us find it difficult to write reflectively. Much of the advice given by educators, in journal articles and even by professional bodies, tends to focus on the descriptive and emotional stages of reflective writing without sufficient emphasis being placed on the evaluative and restorative elements. As a result, many people have been disillusioned by their experiences of trying to write exercises such as critical incident analyses or reflective journals, because the links between the components of the experience and the learning to be achieved are not made. Many others have been put off reflective writing as a result of rules being externally imposed, concerning *what* you are expected to write about, and *how* you are supposed to write it; requirements to 'bare your soul' and make public what you would prefer to keep private; and the worries about writing things down that may have professional consequences, such as exploring instances of malpractice, naming clients and colleagues, or drawing attention to deficits in care.

For reflective writing to serve the purpose of helping you to learn, it is vital that you set the parameters or rules for the writing, and that you are in control of the whole process. Part of being successful as a reflective writer is that you are able to select from the array of models and structures available, or even create your own strategies, and that you feel comfortable with what you are writing and have control over who sees it. Also, part of this is that you control the product of the writing; it is up to you to decide who, if anybody, sees your writing, and no-one can force you to make public what you have written. Your first ventures into reflective writing may have been to satisfy requirements for courses or for portfolio completion. Despite the interpretations that are often put on these, neither dictates the content of your writing; you can make choices as to what to use in illustration or evidence that you have achieved the requirements of, for instance, learning outcomes or criteria for the professional body.

Thus, the success of writing reflectively, as with any other reflective activity that you will meet in this book, is in completing the reflective cycle. It is often neither the subject nor the content of what you reflect on that is necessarily important, but its analysis in terms of what can be drawn out in understanding and learning. We see reflective writing as one way of doing this, as one tool in the kit bag, which will suit some people and not others, just as many of the techniques throughout the book will have more appeal to some of us than others. This suggests that there is something different involved in the process of writing things down; something that will not happen if reflection remains verbal or within our head. What might that be?

We have seen, then, that the very act of writing is thought by many to be a learning activity in its own right. However, for some of us, unless we have taken the time to think about it, our experiences of writing are locked into our past educational experiences or our need to write within the confines expected in our professional role: we learnt to write *for* other people, and we write *what* others want us to write in the *style* others expect. For example, think of the difference between writing an academic essay and writing a letter to a friend. In other words, we *learn-to-write* through the processes of socialisation and teaching. We learn the externally imposed rules of writing for other people, which is not necessarily, and in fact is often the complete opposite of, the notion of *writing-to-learn*, which is at the heart of reflective writing.

REFLECTIVE WRITING

Think back to the last time that you decided to write about something – it may have been a letter, a shopping list, a report for work, some client records, etc. Draw a line down the middle of your page. On the left hand side, try to answer the following questions:

1 What did you write?
2 What was the purpose (why did you write it)?
3 How did you decide what, and what not, to write?
4 How did you decide on the order of what you wrote?
5 How did you organise or structure what you wrote?

On the right-hand side of the page, try to think about the 'why' questions – why were you writing, and why did you include some things and leave others out? Why did you order it in this way? Why did you organise what you were writing in this way?

Now, try to think a bit deeper about the process of writing itself and why you decided to write rather than commit to memory. Did the act of writing as a mental activity enable other things to happen? For instance, if writing a shopping list, did you remember, for some reason, other things to add to your list that you weren't intending to get or which you had 'forgotten'? If you were writing a report on a client, did you start to make connections between things that you hadn't previously seen before?

We will ask you to use your answers to this exercise as we work through the rest of the chapter.

These two concepts, identified by Allen *et al.* (1989) as *learning-to-write* and *writing-to-learn*, can be seen as fundamental to why many of us do not see the value of writing reflectively. Our previous experiences of writing have probably been rooted in providing some sort of evidence to others that we have learnt something, as opposed to the process being useful to us personally in helping us to understand through a creative process of writing for ourselves. Table 3.1 shows the features of these two concepts, and further exploration of them may help us to understand in more depth just why the idea of writing is so difficult for some of us to embrace.

The chances are that your past experiences of writing, at least throughout your formal education, are located within the *learning-to-write* framework. On the whole, we wrote what we thought others wanted us to write. For instance, we would re-write from textbooks in order to show a teacher that we had read (but not necessarily understood or learnt) the material; or we would write an

Table 3.1 A comparison of the assumptions of the two concepts learning to write and writing to learn (adapted from Allen *et al.*, 1989: 7)

Learning to write	*Writing to learn*
Students can successfully learn content whether or not they can write well	Writing is a process through which content is learned or understood (as opposed to memorised or reported)
Writing and thinking involve different skills. Each can, and perhaps should, be taught separately	Writing skills are primarily thinking skills (competence in one is inseparable from competence in the other)
Knowing something is logically prior to writing about it	Writing is a process of developing an understanding or coming to know something
Writing is a sequential, linear activity which involves the cumulative mastery of components like sentence construction or outlining	Writing is a dialectical, recursive process rather than linear or sequential
Communication is the main purpose of writing. Written work is a product in which the student reports what he or she already knows	Higher order conceptual skills can only evolve through a writing process in which the writer engages in an active, on-going dialogue with him or herself and others. Learning and discovery are purposes as important for writing as communication
The student's audience is most often assumed to be the instructor	Different disciplines utilise different conceptual processes and thus have different standards for writing. Students can best learn writing within their own disciplines while writing for real, concrete audiences

exam paper or essay which yet again involved a repetition of theory or knowledge, to prove that we could remember it. At times you may have written an essay asking you to discuss ideas, or analyse, or even be creative, but this is most likely still to have been at someone else's instigation rather than defined by you. Moreover, your success would have been dependent upon you correctly decoding the unseen rules about what was being asked of you. For example, how many times have you slaved over an essay, only to have it returned with a disappointing grade and the comment 'You haven't answered the question'? The main assumption of this concept is that thinking and writing are essentially different, and indeed, that writing is a means to an end, not the end in itself.

You will also have been 'taught' the rules of writing as a formal process for communication. These rules become so ingrained that it is difficult for us to conceive of writing that we can understand if it doesn't follow them. This is illustrated when we are faced with writing in languages which are not our own, or in media that are different from our usual way of working, such as poetry or metaphor. Not only are we taught what to write, but also how to write it, and the writing therefore becomes the medium for communication, but not the message. As a byproduct of this, we gain ideas about writing being right or wrong which influence us throughout our lives. This idea of writing as right or wrong is amazingly persistent for most people, and acts as a barrier for us when attempting to start writing reflectively. If your only writing has ever been for public consumption, and if this has been judged in some way, then it is difficult to conceive of taking control of that writing and seeing it as value free, that it is by you, for you, and that no-one else's judgement matters. In our work as educationalists and facilitators of reflective writing, one of our most challenging tasks is helping people to overcome the anxiety that makes them ask 'Am I doing it right?', or 'Is this what you want?'.

DISCUSSION POINT

Think back to your schooldays. Try to describe to a colleague your attitude to writing as a child. Why did you write? Who did you write for? How did you learn what was 'right' and 'wrong' about your writing? Think about the messages that your childhood experiences have given you about the value and purpose of writing that you have carried with you into your adult life.

Now think about your professional education. Did this reinforce those previous experiences of writing, or enable you to develop different skills? Discuss this with your colleague.

What is your attitude to writing now?

■ Reconceptualising writing

The right-hand side of Table 3.1 proposes a different concept of writing, one where the process of writing in itself is a seen as a way of learning. The assumptions underpinning this concept are that writing and thinking go hand in hand, that writing evolves from thinking, and that creativity arises from thinking about and doing writing. Furthermore, it is suggested that understanding comes from writing, that we learn as a result of interacting with the subject matter, and that in the process, this material becomes transformed into 'knowing'. Thus, the very process of writing is not seen as a passive activity directed by others, but is in itself dynamic, leading to new connections being made and new understanding occurring.

The last three features in the table are particularly important to our concept of reflective writing, in that they acknowledge the individual nature of writing for the person. In effect, they lift writing above the basic idea of writing for others, and transform it into a way through which we can combine thinking and writing in a dialogue with ourselves and others, and to develop our own understanding and create knowledge out of our experience. If we return to the discussion of knowledge that was presented in Chapter 1, we can see that this idea of writing as being creative in itself fits into the model of knowledge acquisition very comfortably (Figure 1.6), in that experiential practical knowledge may become experiential theoretical knowledge through the process of writing about it reflectively.

Now look back to what you wrote in your reflections on the last piece of writing that you did. The last questions asked, were to think about what happened as a result of the process of writing; whether you added something to your shopping list that was not previously there, or whether you began to see something in a different light as a result of writing the incident down. This provides an illustration of the *transformative* nature of writing when viewed from the *writing-to-learn* perspective; the act of writing in itself adds to the way in which we view our experiences. So, to return to our earlier question: *What is it about writing that adds something to our reflective processes?*

☐ Features of writing

☐ *Writing as a purposeful activity*

Firstly, writing is a purposeful activity. We always write for some purpose, even if it is simply a note for the milkman. Moreover, it is impossible to concentrate on writing whilst trying to do something else. As a result, we have to give the whole of our attention to writing; no other thoughts can be going on in our heads at the same time other than very simple things such as 'Do I need another cup of coffee?' The combination of thinking and translating those thoughts into writing involves complex mental and physical processes that force us to focus on the task in hand. In order to do this, we need to dedicate special time to writing, and for some of us this involves almost ritualistic behaviour, such as having to have our writing space organised in a particular way, having completed certain other tasks before sitting down to write, or even simply a matter of having the right number of pencils, our favourite pen, or our own computer to write with. The consequences of this are that when we write, we make a commitment to both the content and process of what we are writing. When writing reflectively, this commitment becomes all important, in that we need a stimulus or a purpose for doing it, and very often this arises from within ourselves and our practice.

☐ *Writing as a way of ordering our thoughts*

Secondly, writing forces us to impose some sort of order to the content of what we are writing. However, this order needs only to make sense to ourselves; it does not have to be an imposed order acceptable to others unless we are deliberately writing for an audience, such as an essay, a book chapter, or a piece of work for which we have been given a structure. This notion of order for writing is often quite intimidating, and for some it is a complete anathema and inhibits them from writing because yet again there is a fear of getting it 'wrong'. However, if we try to put aside the notion of a 'received' order that will please someone else, and think instead about what our own needs are, we can see that we always have some sort of order to what we write, even if we do not consciously decide on it initially.

 DISCUSSION POINT

Return again to your answers to the questions about the last time you wrote. You will probably be able to see that, quite unconsciously at the time, you wrote with a clearly defined purpose, and that you imposed an order on what you were writing.

With a colleague, discuss where this order came from. Did it just happen, or did you make decisions about how to structure your writing?

Whilst a structure might well appear out of the ether, it is more likely that you were responding to some internal rules that make sense to you, or that have arisen as a result of your previous experiences, and that help you to feel comfortable with your writing.

The process of writing not only helps us to find a structure for its content, but in choosing an order to the points, it helps us to prioritise and identify what is important and what is not of such significance. This happens because the speed of our writing is limited to the speed at which we can record our thoughts. This slows us down, and we go through a process of mentally sifting and pulling out what we feel are the most important things to write down. We cannot write at the speed at which we think, or even at the speed at which we talk, and so writing reflectively is going to be very different in content and structure to the way that we reflect when talking to others or contemplatively to ourselves. In fact, this has three distinct advantages.

Firstly, in writing things down we are forced to acknowledge issues that may be ignored if we are carrying on a conversation or reflecting inside our heads. Secondly, we can put a hierarchical order to issues that are significant to us, rather than to how they are seen by other people. Thirdly, this enables us to work through these issues as we have identified them, rather than being sidetracked away to other things. These make reflective writing an extremely personal process and one which, unlike contemplative writing where we may get stuck going round and round in circles in our head, enables us to work systematically through a process of reflection.

☐ *Writing as a permanent record*

This leads us to the third feature of writing that distinguishes it as a reflective strategy: writing creates a permanent record that can be returned to and reconsidered. Why is this important? The act of writing helps us to remember things, not only those which we think we have forgotten, but also things that may be hidden or overlaid by others which take priority. In trying to recall things that have happened to us and recount them verbally, we are selective in what we remember. This is the problem of hindsight bias, for which other forms of reflection have sometimes been criticised (Reece Jones 1995). Very often we are convinced that we have remembered every detail, yet others who were also there at the time might say 'Yes, but, do you remember this too . . . ?', thereby jogging our memory and filling in another piece of the jigsaw puzzle picture. Think too about the times that you have tried to teach someone else to do something; a skill, or even some theoretical knowledge. It is often only when you try to explain something to another person that you realise whether you really know it or not. In writing things down, we record what our memory allows us to remember at the time. This might be close to the event, or at some time distant, and creates at least one account of the event that can be used in the future for reflective activity. This original description can act as a memory jogger the next time you read it, when more or different details and explanations of what has happened occur to us. As a result of the time and space created, we are often able to take a different perspective on the event and see it in a different way by filling in more information, or considering it in the light of new or alternative experiences and knowledge.

The four excerpts which follow come from a student's reflective review of her experiences in a supervision group over a period of two and a half years. The first was written when the group had only been together for a short time, and the last excerpt presents a view of where her experiences of the group have taken her in terms of her learning about herself.

Excerpt one

The first clinical supervision session was unfortunate. There were comments passed during this, what could be termed as a psychological experiment, which culminated in an hour of uncomfortable silence interspersed with two of us asking for structure and being told by other members that we were trying to control. Since then, the meetings have been somewhat stilted and awkward but I will wait and see what transpires next semester. There certainly has not been any learning achieved yet. A new Learning Outcome for semester two is to critically explore models and beliefs regarding supervision thereby realising its relevance to my learning from this course.

Excerpt two

Unfortunately the group dynamics remain rather difficult within the supervision groups with two who are controlling, one who wishes structure but is being told she is controlling, one who views us all with what would appear to be disdain, and others who try to contribute but with little enthusiasm. I am afraid I remain in the latter group. I find difficulties in attending for that hour with work commitments and often arrive tense and rushed. I am trying to change my beliefs regarding the group but by the time I have recovered from the rush to attend and have settled in, the time has passed and the end leaves me feeling the same way. The atmosphere for me does not encourage the in-depth reflection and analysis I was hoping for; however, I am beginning to realise what a powerful tool for clinical practice this style of supervision could be.

Excerpt three

The supervision group has remained unhelpful, however one member had expressed the desire to leave the course. Due to this four of us decided to meet fortnightly to give her and ourselves support and encouragement in completing the assignments. It was interesting to meet in such a forum where all of us felt that we should have taken more responsibility to change the structure of the group instead of playing the victims. I now realise the power and support that such a group can bring where the environment feels safe. Although the meetings were dedicated to academic achievement rather than practical issues, it could be seen how that type of meeting would be uniquely powerful in supporting practitioners to reflect and analyse practice.

Excerpt four

Over the last four semesters there has been learning; however, it has not always been achieved in the way I was expecting. What did have an enormous impact on me was the Practice Development through Supervision unit. I have learnt so much from writing the assessment concerning my contribution to the group, and what started out as very negative has become a learning experience. The supervision assignment highlights how what I believed was an equivocal experience due to other people's attitudes and beliefs, actually was failing to realise that I had just as much responsibility as other members of the group to make the sessions work for all of us. It is always easy to blame other people when things go wrong, which often occurs in professional practice. The sessions made me realise the importance of understanding other people's perspectives. I do not perceive that the supervision sessions were anything other than dire, yet they made me realise the need for that model in professional practice. Due to the unfortunate group dynamics, I did not utilise the groups for any of my experiences in clinical or educational practice, but the importance for structured reflection in practice was obvious to me through the meetings that other practitioners have their own points of view which should be aired if a cohesive team is hoped for. Changes in practice to evidence-based and effective practice can only come about when each professional from each profession acknowledges each other equally. The supervision group was made up of specialists from different fields and each had a different perspective, but it was clear that after all we are all wishing to provide the same high-quality service to people in our care ... With the poor group dynamics and the frustration with the clinical supervision groups, I became a victim rather than taking the responsibility to ask for help and take control of my own education. This has resulted in a lot of wasted opportunities for learning and for the support that I craved.

The permanent record illustrated in these extracts, by writing incrementally as an experience developed over time, illustrates how we can look back and learn from events in the past. Of course, we are able to do this at any time by mentally recalling events; however, what these excerpts show quite clearly is that this person's perspective on the experiences actually changes over time, and it is unlikely that this observation can occur if contemporaneous records are not made at the time that the events are unfolding. It is easy to reconsider with hindsight, and certainly this student can put her experiences of the past into the perspective of the present. However, what she would have omitted if she had not written as she went along were the features of the experience that are no longer significant in the present. By writing them down, she can reflect on how the totality of the experience has brought her to her current ways of understanding the learning that has been achieved.

In writing, we allow ourselves the time to put things aside and return to them when we are ready to deal with them. We 'capture the moment' and can then return to it at our leisure. One student, who had started to use reflective writing on his computer to help him work through difficult issues at work, said that an advantage in writing things down was that it made him deal with them, unlike being able to ignore them if they were in his head. He said that once they had appeared on paper there was a constant reminder, and this acted as a prompt to sort them out, and that to some extent this was a hidden effect of writing; it acts as a conscience so that you cannot conveniently forget things; indeed, that they may turn out to be the key to a problem that you have not yet found.

☐ *Writing as a way of making connections between ideas*

The process of writing can, in itself, be seen as a creative one. Very often, we sit down with the intention of writing one thing, with a plan of some sort, and end up with something different from what we had envisaged. Our mind takes us down certain paths as a result of considering the material in front of us at that particular time, and it helps us to make an alternative, and sometimes unexpected, sense of what we are seeing. Thus, we may make connections between pieces of information that in the past we had not contemplated. The writing process helps us to *integrate* disparate information-sets into new combinations, enabling us to take a different perspective on an issue. These four features of writing are summarised in Table 3.2.

Table 3.2 Summary of the features of writing

Writing as a purposeful activity
  Provides a focus for thinking about an issue
  Sharpens our focus or explicitness of ideas through deliberate word choice
  Identifies key or important points
  The active nature of writing promotes critical thinking
  Interacting with material is a key variable in learning from writing

Writing as a way of ordering our thoughts
  Creates an order that is logical to us
  Helps to stop chaotic thinking
  Identifies priorities
  Identifies multiple elements of the issues
  Helps us to sort out what is important from what is not
  Aids understanding by analysis
  Aids development of critical thinking

Writing as a permanent record
  It 'captures' the moment
  Helps us not to forget important elements of an experience
  Allows time for contemplation
  Allows perspective to change over time
  Allows reflection and consideration

Writing as a way of making connections between ideas
  Gives a rounded picture
  Helps to integrate previously separate and unconnected pieces of information
  Helps to integrate theory with practice
  Aids personal insight
  Helps us to see things differently
  Helps frame action

■ Strategies for writing

Having looked at what reflective writing is and how it can help us to critically reflect, we now move on to explore some writing strategies that we might employ. It is important to remember that no single strategy will suit everyone, that there is no right and wrong to reflective writing, and that the adoption of a technique that is contrary to one's own personality, learning style and inclination is likely to be doomed to failure from the start. So, perhaps one way to start in identifying a writing strategy is to reflect on ways that we have written in the past.

REFLECTIVE WRITING

Have a look back at the answers you gave to the first reflective writing exercise in this chapter. In particular, think about what they say about the way that you usually go about writing.

Now make a list of all of the different types of writing that you can remember doing. This includes not only writing in an educational context, but writing for pleasure or for the purpose of communicating with others.

Which of these forms of writing did/do you enjoy, or get satisfaction out of the most? Try to write down the reasons why these are at the top of your list.

Now consider your approach to writing: What is your motivation for writing? Does it come from inside of you; are you intrinsically motivated, do you feel that you *have* to write for some reason that is driving you? Or are you extrinsically motivated; does the stimulus to write come from outside, maybe for reward, or for work, or for other people such as course work for lecturers?

☐ Finding a writing strategy

Understanding how and why we write enables us to select ways of writing that may help us in reflecting. Sharples (1999) suggests that writers can be divided into 'discoverers' and 'planners' according to the two broad approaches that they take to their writing. Discovers, he says, are:

> driven by engagement with the text. For them, self-understanding arises from writing. They may prefer to begin by scribbling out a draft that reveals their thoughts to them. Then, they often rework their text many times, reading and revising until it 'shapes up' to the constraints of the task and audience. The rhythm of their writing is often one of long periods of engaged composing, followed by extensive revision. (Sharples, 1999: 112)

In contrast, planners:

> are driven by reflection. For these people, writing flows from understanding. They spend a large proportion of their time on exploring ideas and on preparing mental or written plans. The plans guide composing and when there is a mismatch they either edit the text or revise the plan. Their rhythm of composing is, typically, one of rapid alternation between engagement and reflection, continually making minor adjustments to keep plan and text in harmony. (Sharples, 1999: 113)

It is, of course, rare that we would all fall neatly into one category or the other. However, you may recognise some of the characteristics that you listed in the last reflective writing exercise from these descriptions. But how will this help with our own writing? By recognising the ways in which we have approached writing in the past, we may be able to anticipate ways in which we can make writing work for us; equally, we may be able to evaluate particular ways of approaching writing and make a reasoned decision that they are not for us. This is very important in being comfortable with your writing, in choosing to write rather than being compelled to write because you are expected to. By understanding your own relationship with writing, you are more likely to view it as a positive way of learning, rather than as something that is imposed upon you by an outside force.

Sharples (1999) goes further in his identification of writing styles by citing a study by Wyllie (1993) which looked at student and academic writers and attempted to classify them by the strategies they used as writers (Table 3.3). The table illustrates what we all really know at heart: that different people approach writing in different ways. But sometimes we need reminding of this, such as when others appear to effortlessly sit at a word processor, or with pen and paper in front of them, and write thousands of words, while the rest of us are making just one more cup of coffee, or putting another load of washing on the line just to put off the moment when we have to sit down in front of an empty screen and do something with it! The different strategies that Wyllie identified may help us to understand further about the creative processes that we use in writing, and to accept that we can all be equally successful in writing provided that we find a method that suits us, rather than attempting to conform to one that someone else imposes.

 REFLECTIVE WRITING

Earlier in this chapter we asked you to consider your previous experiences of writing, why you have written in the past, and what your attitude to writing has been, and is now. The reasons for doing this will, we hope, be becoming clear to you.

What we would like you to do now is to focus on the types of writing that you have enjoyed in the past – those where you have gained some sort of pleasure or satisfaction, or where you can say that you have gained something from the experience of writing, even though the actual act of doing it may have been difficult for you.

Now recall those previous experiences, write down the features that made them rewarding, and plan some writing strategies that draw on these.

Understanding the reasons why you have enjoyed writing is important because you can plan to write reflectively in a style that suits you and with which you feel comfortable. For example, if you like a definite structure to your writing you may like to utilise one or more of the reflective strategies outlined in this book (see Chapter 2), such as those suggested by Chris Johns (1998) or

Table 3.3 Features of different strategies for writing (adapted from Sharples, 1999:116–17, from original work by Wyllie, 1993)

Writing characteristics	Watercolourist	Architect	Bricklayer	Sketcher	Oil painter
Overall type of writer	Planner	Planner (external)	Planner/discoverer	Discoverer/planner	Discoverer
Strategy for writing	Single draft of whole paper with minimal revision, usually sequential	Plan mostly before writing, then write, then review	Polish one sentence, paragraph or section before moving to the next	Rough plan, revise later	Jot down ideas as they occur, organise later, rarely sequential
Strategy for planning	Plan in head with broad headings	Detailed plan. Compose with broad headings	Type of planning depends on combination of strategies	Compose with broad headings	Compose with broad headings. Sometimes have a rough plan
Order of writing	Always sequential	Often sequential	Sometimes sequential	Sometimes sequential, sometimes jump about	Sometimes sequential, sometimes jump about
Starting writing	Rarely start easiest part first	Sometimes start easiest part first	Rarely start easiest part first	Occasionally start the easiest part first	Often start easiest part first
Revision strategy	Little revision – some changes	Revise a fair amount, mainly at sentence level	Fair amount of revision, mainly spelling, grammar and re-sequencing	Much revision, mainly meaning and sequence changes, and sentence level	Much revision, particularly meaning and sentence
Correction strategy	Tend not to correct	Rarely correct as they go, mainly on printout	Correct at both stages, but mainly later	Correct as they go, also later	Correct as they go, but mainly later
Strategy for reviewing work	Tend to review more on screen than other strategies	Tend to review on printout	Will review on screen, but prefer printout	Review on screen and on printout	Least tendency to review on screen, mainly printout
Relationship with screen	Don't find screen restrictive. Rarely lose overall sense of the text	Occasionally find screen too restrictive	Often find screen restrictive. Often lose overall sense of the text	Occasionally find screen restrictive	Occasionally find screen restrictive

Graham Gibbs (1988). This brings us back to whether you fall into the category of being a discoverer or a planner. For many people, the idea of writing to a prede-termined structure is what puts them off writing, because they find it difficult to reduce their experiences into categories. For them, the types of writing that fall into the 'creative' category are more likely to engage them. Similarly, you may find that one single strategy is not appropriate for all the times that you want to write, and it is useful to consider trying other ways of writing that appear to be better suited to whatever it is that you are writing about.

It is important, however, to remember the reflective component as being a key issue here; that we are reflecting in order to learn and to enable us to take a different perspective. This is hard work, since we are deliberately deciding to explore our own reality and our own experiences, and at times this may be pain-ful or reveal things to us that have been hidden. Equally, there can be great joy in writing, such as in unlocking secrets that have puzzled us for some time, or when we learn things about ourselves and those around us that we like and can celebrate.

☐   Finding something to write about

Initially, finding a subject for writing can be one of the hardest hurdles to over-come. In terms of reflective writing, we need to find a stimulus to write, and to write about something that will enable us to learn. One of the terms for that 'something' is a *critical incident*. To some extent, this is an unfortunate term for those engaged in healthcare, because the word 'critical' has particular associa-tions with life-threatening crises or dramatic events. However, if we see critical as meaning 'important' or something that has significance for us in some way, we can start to refocus what we see as a *critical* incident. Similarly, for an event or an occurrence to be seen as an incident, we would logically have to be able to describe it; it would need to be an event that had boundaries that we could define, and certain actions or activities that went on within it that could be encap-sulated. Many of the structured strategies for reflection that you will meet in this book are based on the concept of the critical incident. The classic definition of a critical incident was phrased by John Flanagan:

> By an incident is meant any observable human activity that is sufficiently com-plete in itself to permit inferences and predictions to be made about the person performing the act. To be critical, an incident must occur in a situation where the purpose or intent of the act seems fairly clear to the observer and where its consequences are sufficiently definite to leave little doubt concerning its effects.
> (Flanagan, 1954: 327)

This definition arose from Flanagan's own work as a psychologist with the Amer-ican Air Force. It is useful in enabling us to identify episodes that fulfil these criteria so that a concrete description can be written and explored reflectively.

This suggests, however, that critical incidents need to be relatively small or minor occurrences. For many of us who write reflectively, the topics of our writing are wider than single definable incidences, such as relationships with our clients or colleagues, the whole of the history of dealing with one particular patient (see for instance Johns' work (2000: 96–107) using written reflective accounts from a nurse's journal), designing a curriculum, or a complete experience at work; the list is endless. To some extent these can be regarded as critical incidents because, for whatever reason, they can be seen to fulfil the first set of criteria in Flanagan's definition. However, they do not readily comply with the criteria in the second sentence, which imply that there are easily definable and finite consequences or actions. Many of the reflective writing strategies used within education focus almost exclusively on the use of critical incidents, and this is where many practitioners will experience reflective writing for the first time. It is undoubtedly an extremely useful technique when used to identify and explore experiences that can be described in Flanagan's way, but limiting ourselves to critical incidents may narrow the reflective focus for our writing.

A second way of identifying the subject of our writing can be found in Atkins and Murphy's (1993) work, which suggests that there are three stages to the reflective process (summarised in Table 3.4).

Table 3.4 Atkins and Murphy's (1993) stages of the reflective process

Stage 1	An awareness of uncomfortable feelings and thoughts
Stage 2	A critical analysis of the situation, which is constructive and involves an examination of feelings and knowledge
Stage 3	Development of a new perspective on the situation

The first of these is where the stimulus for reflection occurs, and is identified as:

> An awareness of uncomfortable feelings or thoughts. This arises from a realisation that, in a situation, the knowledge one was applying was not sufficient in itself to explain what was happening in that unique situation. (Atkins and Murphy, 1993: 1189)

Whilst, undoubtedly, much reflection is stimulated by unpleasant or uncomfortable feelings, this one sentence has pervaded the notion of reflection in nursing to such an extent as to provide a negative connotation to the whole process. Many practitioners have been introduced to the reflective process through the idea that reflective practice arises solely from things that have caused discomfort. Of course, nothing can be further from the truth! We tend to build on success, and in the past many of us unconsciously repeated actions and ways of working that had been previously successful, and avoided ones that had not. The overt use of reflective processes, and of critical reflection as a whole, is to enable us to learn deliberatively from our experiences and to enable us to identify action that can be taken in the future.

Thus, reflective writing does not need to be restricted to identifying critical incidents that have caused us to feel uncomfortable. Rather, reflection is concerned with anything that happens to us that *we want to write about for some reason.* It is not necessarily the subject that is the key here; it is the fact that we want to write about it! Hence, it may be very useful to commit problems to paper, particularly those that tend to get stuck in our head and which we go over and over in a seemingly unrelenting spiral. But these are by no means the majority of our experiences, and in fact most of our time is spent in positive activities that are very successful.

So, to return to the question that we started this section with: what do we write about? The simple answer is that we can write about anything that has happened to us. Perhaps a more pertinent question, however, is how do we select from those experiences so that we are not attempting to catalogue the whole of our day? For

REFLECTIVE WRITING

Close your eyes and think back to yesterday. Briefly scan in your mind the whole day and review all of the things that happened to you. Now, write down the 10 things that stand out as the most important to you.

Why did you write these things down as opposed to all of the other things that happened to you? What is significant about these 10 that separated them out from the other things that you did?

Look at your list more closely. Have you imposed some sort of value system on these experiences that isolate the activity from the experience of it? For instance, did you write 'I went to work' because it has social and economic significance, or did you write about an experience at work that had emotional significance?

Look back at your list again, and think about it with a different focus. This time, think about the emotional content of the experiences, and delete any that don't involve some sort of feelings about them. Now replace these with the equivalent number of experiences. For instance, you may replace 'Went to work' with 'I bought an ice-cream and sat for five minutes in the sunshine relaxing to eat it.'

Now you have a different list, and one that probably has a special significance for you as a person, rather than you as an individual playing a combination of different roles that impose sets of rules on you. Take each one of these experiences separately and try to write down why they are significant for you, what the emotional component of them is, and what you have learnt about yourself as a result of them.

us, the key to answering this question concerns the significance of the experience within our daily lives. If something is important to you for whatever reason, then it is worth writing about. In fact, it is likely that you will *want* to write about it! Taking this approach frees us from the rules imposed by others on our writing. We learn to write for ourselves, and in so doing, we *use* writing as a means of self-discovery.

Of course, it is unlikely that we would be able to write in this way every day, but if writing becomes a way of life, it can be a habitual technique for exploring and experiencing our world. What we do need to be able to do, though, is to shed many of the externally imposed rules and regulations that we have learnt about writing as a result of our past experiences, and view writing for ourselves as value-free (unless we choose to impose values) yet valuable to us; to use styles and strategies for writing that are comfortable for us and suit the need for which we are writing. Reflective writing can be in any style that we want it to be, unless we are writing for other people who have defined a style for us. In the next section we briefly look at different styles and strategies for writing, all of which can be used for writing reflectively if the other stages of the reflective cycle are superimposed on them.

■ Styles and strategies for reflective writing

We have all received the less than helpful advice that the best way to start writing is to simply sit down and do it! Unfortunately, as a strategy, this is probably correct, but there are ways of doing it that are less threatening than simply being faced with a blank screen or piece of paper. Our intentions in the previous sections were to help to understand the processes of writing and to come to an awareness of previous writing experiences so that they can be used to facilitate writing in the future. We cannot reiterate too many times that there is no one right way of writing; the only correct way is the way that works for you. However, the styles and types of writing which follow may help to get you thinking about some possible strategies that you can utilise.

☐ Analytical strategies

We have called these analytical strategies because the process of analysis and synthesis is integral to the process of writing. These strategies have in common the notion of objectivity and attempting to stand back from an event whilst acknowledging the personal and emotional commitment. The style of writing alternates between description, recognition of the features of the event, analysis, exploration and synthesis. It is perhaps characterised by dialogue, or having a conversation with oneself in which argument and counterpoint are proposed and written.

☐ *Journal writing*

This is perhaps the commonest analytical strategy to be found in the professional and educational literature and is probably the easiest place to start writing, in that a journal kept specifically for one's own personal and private use overcomes all of the barriers about judgement and other people having access to our writing.

The term 'journal' used here incorporates what other authors may call diaries or logs, and the purpose of these is for the writer to record, in some way, things that are significant to her. Many people, such as Johns (1998), advocate structured reflections, and any of the models presented in this book can be extremely useful. When experimenting with journal writing it is worth bearing in mind the processes and features of writing that we discussed earlier. For instance, can we use the features as a mental checklist, or even as a physical design to enable us to structure our writing as we progress?

However, it is worth attempting to incorporate physical structures into the journal that allow us to return to the entry, re-read and annotate it with further thoughts. One way of doing this is advocated by Holly (1984), when she suggests that we start a new page for each entry, and write the description of the incident on the left-hand page, with the right-hand page being dated for the reflective analysis and writing. This enables the writer to return to the entry at a later date and add further entries to develop the reflection. The journal then becomes a dialogue with ourselves as we return to it, up-date and add to it as a record of our work. Journals rarely contain the physical evidence to support the learning being identified, and indeed this is not the primary function of the journal. Rather, the journal is intended to provide a medium for the writer to have a conversation with herself where issues can be explored within the safety of her own boundaries.

☐ *Critical incident analyses*

Many writers choose to build up a series of case studies using critical incident technique. This is often combined with a strategy for reflection that breaks the incident and the reflective cycle down into separate sections and uses key prompts to direct the analysis. It also has the added advantage of freeing the writer from creating her own analytical strategies, but can be inhibiting for those who do not think in the way asked of them by the predetermined structure. The key to using critical incident analysis is that the reflective cycle is completed in terms of defining strategies for action or reflecting on the new insight that has taken place.

☐ *Dialogical writing*

This is a form of writing where the writer consciously sets out to have a conversation with herself, proposing ideas and counter-ideas in a series of questions and answers, or through graded discussion that is moved forward through the writing.

☐ *Making a case*

Although similar to dialogical writing, the purpose of this is to create an argument that will persuade another person of the value of the viewpoint. This, in many ways, is very close to an academic writing style

☐ Creative strategies

These techniques separate out the descriptive, personal and emotional components from the analytical and reflective. They are classed as creative because they involve using the imagination and transforming experience away from the rational ways of analysis that characterise the above group, and move the writer into imagination and metaphor as a way of creating insight and facilitating learning. Often, the artefact produced is not a descriptive account, but may be a reworked account of the experience that is used separately for reflection and analysis after its creation.

☐ *Writing the unsent letter*

Have you ever written a letter and then never sent it? An unsent letter can perform some very useful functions in enabling us to write in a style that is far-removed from the analytical styles of the previous strategies, and provides us with a way of capturing emotions and feelings in their rawest forms. Unsent letters are often used where experiences have been particularly painful, and in order for the writer to explore them, she needs first to draw on the cathartic effect of pouring emotions onto paper. The unsent letter technique seems to be very effective when the imagined recipient of the letter is the person who has caused the problem; for instance, an incident with a colleague or manager, a difficult client, or a teacher who appears to have been unreasonable. What is unlikely to be recorded in this technique is a description of the event in any linear form, if it is there at all. Nor is it likely that the whole event will be conveyed to the reader.

The advantage of this technique is that the writer can literally write exactly what she thinks to the imagined recipient of the letter, yet there is safety in the knowledge that it will not be sent. At times, we have experiences that are so painful emotionally that we are not able to explore them rationally close to the time that they occur. Using the unsent letter to record feelings and emotions can be a way of taking the first step of creating some sort of permanent record of the event, which will stimulate memories when it is re-read at a later date. However, it may also have the effect of enabling the writer to start to deal with those emotions simply through the process of writing them down on paper.

☐ *Writing to another person*

This is really a variation on the above strategy, but instead of imagining writing to the person involved in the event, the writer writes as if telling another person with whom she is familiar, be it a friend, a relative or even a respected teacher. This technique enables the writer to put her own point of view, but this tends to be modified by the imagined effect or authority of the recipient. It is more likely that this type of letter will include a description of what has happened, or it may include ideas and propositions from the writer that take a dialogue forward.

☐ *Writing as the other*

With this technique, the writer attempts to put herself in the place of the other person in the event, and tell the story from her point of view. This can be useful in attempting to get a person to move beyond barriers that are preventing her from analysing a situation, particularly if the writing is facilitated by using key questions. This can be supplemented by the writer writing about the event first from her own viewpoint, and then from that of another, or even from all of the players in the interaction. Whilst it is impossible to 'get inside someone else's head', the activity of attempting to see an event from a different point of view often enables insight to develop.

☐ *Story telling*

In this technique, the writer writes as if creating a story for an audience, either to be read aloud or to be read silently. In this way, the unconscious thoughts that we were not aware of at the time of an experience can be brought to the fore and acknowledged. Metaphor can be used to recreate the experience, where the writer is able to impose her perspective on the account. Examples of this strategy may include giving the key players fictional names that reflect how the writer sees them, or imputing motive on to players where they cannot have had access to this.

☐ *Poetry as reflective writing*

Poetry is perhaps the archetypal style of creative writing, where the features of writing reflectively as having meaning for ourselves is most acutely obvious.

☐ Writing reflectively with others

Most of the writing we do is as individuals, writing of, from or about ourselves. However, reflective writing techniques can also be used for writing publicly with others. We are all familiar with written artifacts that have several contributors, such as a newspaper, or a set of patient records; these are built up from individual contributions, and the sum total of these tells a story that is more than any one of the writers may have known. As a result of more than one person writing from their own perspective, the subject of their writing becomes rounder and fuller.

Think of the possibilities of this approach for reflective writing. We already see jointly authored papers and books (and indeed this book is such an example, where three people have contributed from their own expertise and experience and produced a final product that includes much more than any one of us could have envisaged); but the techniques and models of reflective writing can also be used by people working together to explore phenomena or incidents in many ways, and with varying outcomes.

Any of the models of reflection explored in Chapter 2 or others presented throughout the book, are just as suitable for joint writing as for use by an individual. For instance, Kim's model could be used by two people to explore an incident that happened to both of them, and may help to resolve any difficulties between them as a result. The writing aspect of it is important in that equal weight would be given to both people's 'stories' so that a full picture would emerge. Similarly, a joint record could be made of a supervisory relationship, with both supervisor and supervisee contributing to the same document from their own perspectives. This would provide all of the advantages of writing over discussion, and indeed it could even be used for supervision at a distance which would be entirely through written dialogue.

Reflectively writing can also be used incrementally with a group of people who work within a team, or who come together for a specific purpose. Imagine, for instance, the painstaking work that is done by a ward team looking after a long-term patient. In addition to the records used in documenting care, the team could create a living book for that patient in which views are recorded on treatments and approaches to care; breakthroughs described, new paths taken, and so on. In this way, nursing knowledge would be documented as it is created, with evidence and records of alternatives and issues as they arise. A similar approach can be taken for new initiatives or changes in an environment, particularly where it is difficult for all members of the team to get together to explore the issues between them. In this way, views can be built up through an ongoing dialogue, with all members having the opportunity to put their point of view and have it acknowledged.

These are only a few suggestions for the ways in which reflective writing can be used in the public domain between two or more people. Many others that can add richness to writing reflectively are possible, which could contribute towards the creation of knowledge from experience.

 DISCUSSION POINT

Are there any issues in your work environment that you feel would be suitable for a collaborative reflective writing approach? Discuss with your colleagues how issues that appear to be stagnant could be moved forward by providing a book for people to record their ideas and thoughts in, and to record progress made.

FURTHER READING

All of these techniques are developed further elsewhere. Chris Johns' work typifies journal writing, and is particularly useful for providing guides for structured reflection. Similarly, Ira Progoff and Mary Holly have made useful contributions to strategies for reflective writing in journals.

Holly, M. (1984) *Keeping a Personal Professional Journal*, Victoria: Deakin University.
Johns, C. (2000) *Becoming a Reflective Practitioner*, Oxford: Blackwell Science.
Progoff, I. (1975) *At a Journal Workshop: The Basic Text and Guide for Using the Journal*, New York: Dialogue House Library.

■ Reflective writing in professional portfolios

Many healthcare professions now require their members to keep a professional portfolio in order to demonstrate evidence of their regular updating and professional development. For many of these professions, such as nursing, midwifery, health visiting, occupational health and physiotherapy, there is an expectation that reflective writing will be utilised to explore learning experiences and to show how they are informing and being incorporated into practice. An essential and critical difference between a portfolio *per se* and the strategies of reflective writing, is that a portfolio is designed and constructed to portray a picture of its creator and, as such, is likely to be open to public scrutiny in some form. Whilst reflective writing may well be included in and form an essential part of a portfolio, it behoves the writer to make clear decisions as to what part of the portfolio is selected for others to read.

Portfolios are usually created for a specific purpose, such as course work, as a record of practice, and so on. As such, specific criteria are published as to what the portfolio should contain. It is usual that the content needs to provide evidence of the owner of the portfolio meeting the stated criteria. In educational portfolios, these will usually be phrased as learning outcomes or core constituents such as attendance certificates, job descriptions or records of work completed.

There are many articles and books detailing portfolio construction and compilation, along with advice from professional bodies, and it is therefore not appropriate to explore this issue here. However, what we would like to explore further here is the way that reflective writing can be used within a portfolio to provide evidence of learning and development of the person in relation to their professional role.

We have seen from the previous two chapters that much of the literature on reflection, reflective practice and ideas about knowledge arising from practice is located in the world of education. Authors in the professional and academic press

FURTHER READING

Jasper discusses the role of portfolios in professional practice in two articles which aim to set the context of portfolio development as a dynamic strategy for practice and personal development:

Jasper, M. (1995) 'The Potential of the Professional Portfolio for Nursing', *Journal of Clinical Nursing,* **4**, 249–55.

Jasper, M. (1998) 'Using Portfolios to Advance Practice', in G. Rolfe and P. Fulbrook (eds), *Advancing Nursing Practice*, Oxford: Butterworth Heinemann, chapter 15.

The following books all provide clear ideas and strategies for portfolio development.

McGrowther, J. (1995) *Profiles, Portfolios and How to Build Them*, London: Scutari Press.

Moon, J. (1999) *Learning Journals. A Handbook for Academics, Students and Professional Development*, London: Kogan Page.

Morton-Cooper, A. and Palmer, A. (2000) *Mentoring, Preceptorship and Clinical Supervision: A Guide to Support Roles in Clinical practice*, 2nd edn, Oxford: Blackwell Scientific Publications.

Palmer, A. (2000) 'Freedom to Learn – Freedom to Be: Learning, Reflecting and Supporting in Practice', in D. Humphris and A. Masterson (eds), *Developing New Clinical Roles: A Guide for Health Professionals*, London: Harcourt Health Sciences.

report on reflective strategies used with students, and there is also a plethora of individual accounts of reflective writing in practice. These often make the connection between theories of reflection and real-life examples, but little attention has been paid to the processes of reflective writing within the reflective cycle, or to how practitioners use writing within their own practice when it is not required of them as part of a course. It seems to be assumed that writing will occur, but scant attention is paid to how to do it, or to how practitioners are actually doing it when they are not monitored or facilitated in some way.

One study (Jasper, 1999) that has attempted to explore how experienced nurses use reflective writing, offers evidence that writing does indeed provide professionals with a vehicle for exploring their practice, for identifying experiential learning and for developing their knowledge base as a result. Using a grounded theory methodology, Jasper used data from a total of 37 nurses from a wide variety of disciplines to identify how reflective writing was used within their portfolios as part of their professional practice. The emergent theory is represented in Figure 3.1, and comprises a core category supported by four sub-categories.

DISCUSSION POINT

Think about your own portfolio (assuming that you have one – if you haven't you may like to use these questions to think about how you might construct one). Now, with a colleague, discuss:

- Why you keep a portfolio.
- What you have got in it.
- How you have structured it.
- Why you have structured it in this way.
- How you use reflective writing in your portfolio.
- How you use the learning achieved within your practice.

The core category, which was called *developing evidence of accountable professional practice*, resulted from exploring the relationships between the sub-categories, and appeared to be the central motivation for these nurses to write reflectively. The driving force, initially, for reflective writing was the professional body's (the UKCC) requirement for a personal profile (or portfolio) recording professional development and competence triennially. Although this provided the primary motivation for portfolio compilation, the practitioners interviewed identified a

Professional development
Developing a knowledge base
Evidence of professional practice
Evidence-based practice

Critical thinking
Making connections
Organising thoughts/structure
Taking a new perspective on issues
Exploring issues

**DEVELOPING EVIDENCE OF
ACCOUNTABLE
PROFESSIONAL
PRACTICE**

Personal development
Developmental tool
Learning from experience
Cognitive, deliberative process
Developing analytical skills

Outcomes for clinical practice
Moving care forward
Delivering the best patient care

Figure 3.1 A model of the way that experienced nurses use reflective writing in their professional practice (Jasper, 1999)

multitude of other reasons for keeping these personal records, all of which consisted of reflective writing of some form in addition to functional record keeping of such artefacts as course attendance certificates and qualifications. All participants expressed a desire to provide a record of their professional practice, of decision-making and knowledge acquisition, of personal development, and of moving forward in their learning and expertise. This was founded on the need to have evidence of their work as professionals and to provide evidence in terms of their accountability for their practice. This is illustrated in the following interview extract with a staff nurse:

> I think that if you're writing it down and you're doing it properly you can't help but get a clearer understanding of how you practice as a nurse. And I think that clarity, particularly nowadays, is important, because you do have to be able to account for what you are doing. You can't just stand up in a coroner's court, or anywhere else, and say 'Well, that's the way we've always done it', because someone is going to say 'Why have you always done it that way?' You can't say 'in my clinical judgement'anymore because someone will say 'What did you base your judgement on ... ?'

This suggests that these nurses had recognised, and could actively engage in, reflective writing as an essential part of their practice. Moreover, the whole process of writing reflectively was seen to be the primary way that they learnt as a result of, and about, their practice.

The four sub-categories in Jasper's theoretical model are useful as ways of exploring both the content of reflective writing within portfolios, and the learning and development that it encourages. Furthermore, the model has been used within clinical management teams to structure group and individual reflection, as a framework for clinical supervision, and to focus individual reflective writing within portfolios. A closer look at the four sub-categories illustrates how the reflective writing strategies, and the strategies for reflection presented in this book, can be focused for the individual practitioner around their clinical practice.

☐ Professional development

Professional development may well be our overt reason for reflective writing. For the majority of nurses, midwives and health visitors there is a professional requirement to maintain a portfolio that documents the achievement of the criteria for triennial registration with the professional body (the United Kingdom Central Council for Nurses, Midwives and HealthVisitors at the time of writing). Writing within a portfolio can provide concrete evidence of creating and adding to a knowledge base, thus enabling us to demonstrate evidence-based practice and illustrate professional development. As professional development is central to our competence as practitioners, it is important that we clearly identify, within our portfolio, just how we have developed and how this contributes to our practice.

Similarly, reflective writing can be utilised to document developments in professional practice in a linear fashion, which not only provides evidence of accountable practice, but also acts to present to the reader with a picture of the way that *this particular practitioner* executes their professional role. The example below offers an excerpt from a nurse's portfolio as an illustration of this professional development. The bringing together of all the separate elements is unique to this nurse's portfolio, since whilst the service development in itself may have been documented, there would have been no other permanent record of the professional knowledge and skills that this nurse has achieved as a result of writing about this experience.

Case example: establishing a new service of nurse-led heart failure outpatient clinics

I stood there naked, no uniform to proclaim my nursing identity, no working base, no place within the hospital structure and no established role. All the rights of access and the support of institutional systems that allowed me to function as a Cardiac Care staff nurse were withdrawn when I left the Trust to commence a new role as Heart Failure Nurse Advisor, employed by an independent healthcare company. As I sought an empty desk at which I could begin to establish a base, I looked through the windows into the Cardiac Care Unit that was so familiar to me and felt a surge of mixed emotions. The excitement and pride that my hard spadework to obtain funding for this new role had finally borne fruit was tempered by this sense of nakedness and isolation. In addition, I was also aware of vestiges of the anger and disappointment that had previously threatened to overwhelm rational thinking when informed that, from the day of commencement of this new post, I would merely have the right to enter the building to work, the Trust 'would have no further interest in me'.

Over the course of the succeeding eight weeks I started to organise this new service for a particular patient group. Centred around thrice weekly nurse-led outpatient clinics, the administrative mechanisms normally employed to bring patient, healthcare professional, medical notes and other resources together at an arranged time and in a suitable clinic environment were unknown to me. My first task therefore was to navigate myself through these various systems to seek out relevant information and the personnel in possession of the necessary authority to 'permit' me access to their administrative support services. However, as the administration was to be my responsibility I considered that the clinics would not constitute a great increase in demand upon the resources of the various department; a point clarified in the few necessary requests for help. However, in the refusals I received lay the suggestion that this was, in fact, the overriding concern. I assumed the managers would, in turn, have to account to their own superiors for any accommodation they afforded my clinics. Not to be thwarted, through the medium of developing relationships with the personnel who carry out the duties upon which I hoped to prevail, I gained sufficient information and advice to develop an action plan to meet the needs of department heads and myself. In this way, one by one, I finally negotiated sanction and support for my requirements.

As I critically reflected on my planning and actions during these experiences a common element became apparent. My learning had taken a new direction towards knowledge of management and working processes together with related budget and resource constraints. In each circumstance, it was this new under-standing that allowed me to explore ways to negotiate the support I needed.

During this time, I was reading commentaries on the critical social theory *Knowledge and Human Interest* in which Habermas (1978) proposes that an individual's understanding of his function within social systems is shaped by the prevailing mechanisms, cultures and traditions in that society. Such structures serve to maintain the interests of those in positions of influence but militate against the fair and active participation of individuals who uncritically find these power bases acceptable. In this domain, Habermas (1978) believes that knowl-edge serves an emancipatory human interest for, through critical self-reflection, the individual becomes aware of the composition of these structures and how they impose unreasonable barriers. Thus, knowledge is emancipatory for through its acquisition the individual may also identify ways to challenge such a constraining status quo.

As summarised here, these concepts did indeed help me make sense of my feelings and my actions. I recognise how I drew on this knowledge to negotiate agreements that not only facilitated my active participation in previously alien social structures, but enhanced the building of productive working relationships. These learning processes not only served my primary interest to secure an effec-tive clinic service, but the endeavour of setting up the clinics resulted in a confi-dence in my new abilities and, indeed, I felt emancipated by the whole experience.

Finally, my name is gradually becoming synonymous with the service; I am earn-ing a nursing identity. New working relationships continually develop; I am gaining a support network. The naked and isolated view of myself is transformed to that of someone who values her new professional identity and colleague group. I once felt anger at the words 'the Trust will have no further interest in you' but I now appreciate that the person who uttered these words probably had insight into the pitfalls awaiting me and intended to alert me to the work ahead. Now rid of the handicap of negative feelings, I can move on to focus on developing the quality of the service and to finding effective ways to demonstrate its benefit to patients and the organisation.

☐ Personal development

Alongside professional development demonstrated through the writing process, there often occurs a concurrent personal development as we gain insight into our-selves, our values and the ways in which we work. It is as if writing is a develop-mental tool used to facilitate the maturation and insight that arises from learning from experience. The process of writing is a cognitive, deliberative one that engages the person in organising thoughts in a new way in order to make sense and learn from them. The above example equally demonstrates the learning and development about herself that this nurse developed through writing about her experiences.

This is one of the areas of reflective writing within portfolios that worries people the most, particularly if they feel that others will be reading the work and making judgements about them as people. This is an entirely rational fear and is linked to the fact that in reflective writing we are asking people to look inside themselves and explore the very core of their emotions, values and feelings, with the added stress of committing it to paper. Indeed, as Atkins and Murphy (1993) identified, to be successful reflective practitioners we need to have developed certain qualities in terms of open-mindedness and motivation, as well as having acquired the skills of self-awareness, description and observation, critical analysis and problem-solving, synthesis and evaluation. It is by being prepared to rise to the challenge of exploring our practice, of being willing to rise above the safety of established theory and knowledge, and unpick events and incidents with the purpose of learning from them, that we develop as people.

☐ Critical thinking

As we saw earlier, the reflective writing process is a way of making connections between previously disparate pieces of information, of developing ways of organising or reorganising thoughts, and of exploring issues and structures so as to be able to take a new perspective on them. Indeed, many writers see the reflective process as key to developing critical thinking, and reflective writing in some form as a crucial process of enabling it to happen. Critical thinking is regarded as one of the ways that practitioners make decisions about their practice, and developing the ability to think critically is now an essential component in the majority of educational programmes.

But what do we mean by critical thinking? Critical thinking has been defined as:

The process of purposeful, self-regulatory judgement; an interactive reflective, reasoning process. (Facione, Facione and Sanchez, 1994: 345)

Despite the shortness of this definition, critical thinking is recognised as a complicated, complex and intricate process that involves problem-solving, reasoning in considering opposing viewpoints or competing theories, and an attitude of inquiry. Ennis (1985) suggests that in addition to these processes, critical thinking also involves making decisions related to how to act or to believe. Table 3.5 summarises the characteristics of a critical thinker identified by the American Philosophical Association (Facione, 1990), and Brookfield (1987).

In short, critical thinking is about weighing up all the possibilities for action and being able to make a reasoned and rational choice. Kintgen Andrews (1991)

Table 3.5   Features of a critical thinker (adapted from Facione, 1990; and Brookfield, 1987)

The ideal critical thinker is	Critical thinkers are people
• habitually inquisitive • well-informed • trustful of reason • open-minded • honest in facing personal biases • prudent in making judgements • willing to reconsider • clear about issues • diligent in seeking relevant information • orderly in complex matters • reasonable in the selection of criteria • focused in inquiry • persistent in seeking results which are as precise as the subject and the circumstances of inquiry permit (after Facione, 1990)	• engaging in productive and positive activity • viewing their thinking as a process rather than an outcome • varying in their manifestations of critical thinking according to context • experiencing triggers to critical thinking as positive or negative • feeling comfortable with the emotive as well as the rational elements of the critical thinking process (after Brookfield, 1987)

suggests further that critical thinking is a process of metacognition, of thinking about thinking, whilst Paul suggests that the practice of *dialogical* reasoning:

> plots two or more opposing points of view in competition with each other. Support for each view, and the raising and countering of objections, is integral to the process. (Paul, 1996, cited by Boychuk Duchscher, 1999)

The nurses in Jasper's (1999) study all identified the process of writing as facilitating critical thinking because it invited them to explore their experiences from different viewpoints. One nurse described the new understandings he came to and the justification for his decision-making in the following excerpt:

> something like the business with the flower remedies that we had to refuse to administer. I actually went back and did 28 hours research over two days, produced the stuff necessary for case conference and reflected on the whole incident because it was very unpleasant; it was what I would consider to be a very unpleasant critical incident which I had to justify to myself first of all. I think without the process of writing it I'd be in trouble, I wouldn't be able to defend the decision. For instance, I can now quote regulations from the guidelines for the administration of medicines but it doesn't . . . so I actually like going back to the original thing.

The components of critical thinking have been identified by Brookfield (1987) as:

☐ *Identifying and challenging assumptions*

This means ensuring that you write down the assumptions that you made in relation to an event that you describe. These assumptions may be the knowledge or theory that you used, particular paradigm cases that you can remember, or experiential learning. In addition, you may be using information from your client or their family, written records, or verbal clues that have been passed on by others. Remember also to consider what you take in through your senses: what you see, smell, feel by touch or hear. Perhaps there was an emotional reaction or component to the event that also contributes to your perception of the situation. The description of events that you make needs to be as accurate a record of what happened as possible so that you can identify the assumptions that you made.

☐ *Recognising the importance of context*

Our actions are never context-free; we all work within the confines of our experiences of the world, time and the places that we have lived. These ultimately interfere and affect the way that we see others. Exploring the context of events and acknowledging the limitations of our perceptions enables us to think more analytically, and therefore critically. Writing these down provides us with a way of objectifying our experiences; we are able to stand outside of the experiences as personal and view them from a different perspective.

☐ *Exploring and imagining alternatives*

Critical thinking involves being able to compare and evaluate different solutions to problems or to consider events in order to uncover new and different ways of perceiving the world. Brookfield (1987) suggests that this involves:

> coming to realise that every belief we hold, every behaviour we cherish as normal, every social or economic arrangement we perceive as fixed and unalterable can be and is regarded by others as bizarre, inexplicable, and wholly irrational.

It is salutary to remember that other people will not 'see' things and events in the same way that you do. Two people will rarely give the same description of an event, even if they were standing next to each other when it happened. Hence, features of an event that you see as important or significant may not be the same for other people. This is understandable when you set each person's perception within the context of her own life experiences. Writing enables us to explore and imagine alternative viewpoints by providing us with structures and questions which challenge our previous way of looking at things.

☐ *Reflective scepticism*

Being sceptical protects us from accepting 'universal truths' or that there is only ever one explanation for an event or one way of looking at it. Developing scepticism leads us to question and seek alternative answers, and may lead ultimately to the development of new understandings by encouraging us to reject previously accepted explanations.

The concept of critical thinking can be developed through writing by overtly using these components as a check list, and by auditing our entries against them. In turn, this may well lead on to *creative* thinking, where not only can we justify and defend our actions, but we may also develop new understandings and perspectives on a situation, or come to understand a past event in a different light. As one nurse said:

> I think creative thinking is actually taking the bits of knowledge that you already have and producing something entirely new from that; that you come forward from what you already know. I think you develop by recognising the infinite combinations of little bits of knowledge, little pockets of knowledge.

The processes of writing discussed earlier in this chapter, the need to create a space for writing and to treat it as a deliberative activity, provide the mechanisms for facilitating the development of critical thinking. The physical activity of structuring and restructuring or seeking explanations and new ways of knowing, leads us to look for unique explanations in themselves that may direct action and affect outcomes for our clients.

REFLECTIVE WRITING

Read the earlier account of setting up a new service of nurse-led heart-failure outpatient clinics.

Now write your answers to these questions:

* What elements of this experience would you say demonstrate professional development?
* What elements demonstrate personal development?
* What elements demonstrate the development of critical thinking?
* Has this resulted in new ideas or new understanding taking place?
* What are the likely impacts on clinical practice?

Now choose a piece of reflective writing of your own and apply the same questions to it.

☐ Outcomes for clinical practice

What characterised the respondents in Jasper's (1999) study was a desire to deliver the best possible care to their clients, whether these were patients, residents or students. One aim of reflective writing was to move practice forward in some way through using all three of the previous categories. For instance a nurse teacher said:

> up until the point where I committed it to writing I guess I wouldn't have been able to articulate it in the way I am now. I might have felt I was learning something, but the writing process means I am able to be clearer in my own thoughts to the end that if I was in a similar situation again I would be able to reflect on professional judgement.

It is clear that practitioners are learning about their practice as a result of writing, and that this learning transforms into action for patient/client care. Not only can we clearly see the development of ideas and solutions through writing, we can see the way that this will be enacted in a practical context.

 REFLECTIVE WRITING

Now turn back to the aims which you identified at the start of the chapter. To what extent have they been met? Write a paragraph outlining the scientific and experiential knowledge you have acquired through reading this chapter and doing the exercises. Write a second paragraph identifying any aims which you feel were only partially met or not met at all. Now divide your page into three columns. Head the first column 'What I need to learn', and make a list of any outstanding issues which you would like to learn more about. For example, you might wish to find out more about improving your practice through action research. Head the second column 'How I will learn it', and write down the ways in which your learning needs could be addressed, for example, through further reading, through attending study days, or through talking to other people. Head the third column 'How I will know that I have learnt it', and try to identify how you will know when you have met your needs. You might, for example, set yourself the task of successfully conducting a small action research project into your own practice.

Chapter 4

Clinical supervision

■ Introduction

As we discussed in Chapters 1 and 2, there are a variety of ways in which we can acquire the knowledge and skills necessary for critical reflection. We have already explored reflective writing as one such approach, and in this chapter we present clinical supervision as a structure for reflective practice and as a forum for practice development and knowledge acquisition. Whilst reflection is an activity that can be undertaken alone, the process of guided reflection through clinical supervision enables the practitioner to see beyond herself, thereby extending her personal interpretations to include other viewpoints.

During the course of this chapter we will describe more fully the concept of clinical supervision and its relationship to reflective practice. In addition, we will discuss a number of modes and models of clinical supervision which can act as frameworks for the facilitation of critical reflection. Finally we will outline some of the practicalities of implementing clinical supervision in practice. The aims of this chapter are:

1 to help you to reflect on your experiences of giving and receiving supervision in a variety of roles;
2 to enable you to reflect on the personal, professional and practical factors involved in the implementation of clinical supervision;

 REFLECTIVE WRITING

Think carefully about our aims for Chapter 4. Now think about your own practice and how these aims might contribute towards developing it. For example, what are the current guidelines regarding clinical supervision in your own institution? If you are already engaged in clinical supervision, either as a supervisee or a supervisor, how does it enable a critical evaluation of practice? If you do not have access to clinical supervision, how would you go about finding an appropriate supervisor?

Based on our aims above, write down some of your own, both in terms of what you hope to know and what you hope to be able to do after reading Chapter 4. We will return to your aims at the end of this chapter.

3   to outline and discuss the necessary conditions for effective clinical supervision; and
4   to help you to evaluate the role of clinical supervision in your current practice situation.

■ Clinical supervision

☐   The development of clinical supervision in nursing and the helping professions

Whilst clinical supervision is a relatively new concept in most branches of nursing, it has long been an established part of practice in other helping professions such as counselling, psychotherapy, social work and midwifery. Hence, much of the established literature dealing with the theory and practice of clinical supervision has emerged from within these disciplines (Hawkins and Shohet, 1989; Holloway, 1995; Kadushin, 1992; Casement, 1985). Historically, the notion of supervision evolved from the psychoanalytic work of Sigmund Freud in the 1920s, who advocated that supervision should become a formal requirement for trainee analysts. In 1951 Carl Rogers, the pioneer of person-centred therapy, expanded this idea to include all active counsellors and psychotherapists, that is, all those with a caseload, regardless of whether or not they were qualified. Since then, clinical supervision has evolved rapidly, and a number of modes and models have been integrated into the disciplines of counselling and psychotherapy as a compulsory prerequisite not only of training, but also of post-qualification practice. The current emphasis of clinical supervision in counselling and psychotherapy is on the process of the relationship as opposed to patient outcome (although patient care is always an important consideration), with specific interest in the use of the self as a therapeutic tool.

Supervision in social work also took its lead from Freud's original model of caseload supervision, although more recently, and in light of new developments and policies surrounding child protection, it is examining other more suitable alternatives, including process models. Clinical supervision has been an important part of midwifery practice for many years, although it has always had more of a managerial orientation by being linked to appraisal systems and disciplinary procedures (Bond and Holland, 1998).

Although clinical supervision is a fairly recent development in nursing, it is well accepted in some branches of the profession such as mental health and health visiting where, theoretically at least, it is part of everyday work. Practitioners working in the field of mental health probably engage more directly with the skills of counselling and psychotherapy in their everyday practice, and so it is not surprising that models of clinical supervision in mental health arenas draw upon the tried and tested approaches from within counselling and psychotherapy. However, whilst it is well accepted and widely acknowledged to be part of mental health nursing, there is evidence to suggest that, in fact, it is not well established in practice (Butterworth *et al.*, 1998; Farrington, 1995). In addition, where it is practiced, it is not always actively linked to critical reflection or innovations in practice (Bond and Holland, 1998).

Initial interest in clinical supervision in general nursing developed as a direct result of two notable publications, namely the *Vision for the Future* document (DOH, 1993b) and the Faugier and Butterworth (1994) position paper on clinical supervision. The Allitt inquiry did much to raise the issue of professional standards in the public arena, and the *Clothier Report* (DOH, 1994) subsequently highlighted the necessity for adequate standards of supervision, training and education. The UKCC (1996) responded to these documents by issuing a position paper advocating the implementation of clinical supervision within nursing and recognition of the importance of its role and contribution towards ensuring safe, effective care delivery through the process of lifelong learning. Despite being increasingly included in trustwide strategies, and the continued belief by many that it is being successfully undertaken in clinical practice, it is still not a reality in many areas of health care (Butterworth *et al.*, 1998; Bond and Holland, 1998; Farrington, 1995). Furthermore, where clinical supervision *is* implemented, it is patchy and there is still some debate about the practicalities of creating a clinical supervision process which addresses the needs of all parties concerned, including professional bodies, practitioners, managers and consumers. So why is it that so many practitioners are so resistant to clinical supervision?

 DISCUSSION POINT

What does the term clinical supervision mean to you? What are the feelings evoked in you when you think about being supervised? Make a note of any anxieties or concerns you may have.

Think back to situations in which you have either been supervising someone or have been supervised by someone yourself. Examples might include caring for younger children, babysitting, learning a new skill such as driving, or taking an exam. Try to think of a positive example of supervision and a negative example. What skills did you/your supervisor employ in each situation? What did you find helpful about being supervised? What was not helpful?

With a colleague, share your previous experiences and your current understanding of the term 'clinical supervision' in your current work situation and attempt to come up with your own definition, relating your discussion to the wider context of health care. If you are already in clinical supervision, you might also like to reflect on these experiences.

The literature on clinical supervision is filled with anxieties, misconceptions and misunderstandings, although it appears that one of the greatest causes of anxiety relates to the perceived lack of power ascribed to the supervisee (Kohner, 1994). Bond and Holland (1998) link this to the emphasis on the managerial component of supervision, although the UKCC (1996) quite clearly indicates that clinical supervision is not the exercise of overt managerial responsibility, nor is it a system of formal individual performance review.

Historically, the profession of nursing is well known for its defensiveness around the issue of building intimate relationships. Research undertaken by Isobel Menzies-Lyth (1988) in the late 1970s and early 1980s described this anti-emotional climate in nursing, highlighting the behaviour of nurses within social organisations and, in particular, their coping mechanisms. She discussed the difficulty of establishing professional relationships and both the fear of, and the desire for, control within personal, collective, social and organisational defence

---

 FURTHER READING

The emotional labour of caring is something that is now being given a great deal of attention in the nursing press, and much is written about stress and burnout in the caring professions and how health care professionals can learn to cope with their own feelings. Projects have also been started to examine caring for the carers. Writers still find that the work of Menzies-Lyth is central to their own argument, and it is cited as seminal in the development of patient centred care as opposed to task oriented care (MacGuire, 1998). Whilst most books on clinical supervision comment on these issues, Menzies (1970, 1988), Ersser (1998) and Dawson (1998) provide an in-depth exploration of the notion of self as carer.

Briant, S. and Freshwater, D. (1998) 'Exploring Mutuality in the Nurse–Patient Relationship', *British Journal of Nursing*, **7** (4) 204–211.

Dawson, P. (1998) 'The Self', in S. Edwards (ed.), *Philosophical Issues in Nursing*, London: Macmillan – now Palgrave, ch. 9.

Ersser, S. J. (1998) 'The Presentation of the Nurse: A Neglected Dimension of Therapeutic Nurse–Patient Interaction?', in R. McMahon and A. Pearson (eds), *Nursing as Therapy*, Cheltenham: Stanley Thornes, ch. 3.

MacGuire, J. (1998) 'Tailoring Research for Therapeutic Nursing Practice', in R. McMahon and A. Pearson (eds), *Nursing as Therapy*, Cheltenham: Stanley Thornes, ch. 9.

Menzies-Lyth, I.E.P. (1970) *The Functioning of Social Systems as a Defence against Anxiety*, London: Free Association Books.

Menzies-Lyth, I.E.P. (1988) *Containing Anxiety in Institutions: Selected Essays*, London: Free Association Books.

mechanisms. A number of authors argue that many of Menzies-Lyth's research findings still hold true today, and link anxiety and defensiveness with resistance to clinical supervision (Bond and Holland, 1998; Briant and Freshwater, 1998).

There are any number of other reasons that might explain the apparent lack of enthusiasm for clinical supervision, not least the argument for the lack of resources and finance, and also to some extent the difficulties with the term itself. This is a significant problem, for in order to influence the potential success of an implementation programme, it is first essential to establish ownership of clinical supervision. The common purposes, functions and aims of supervision must be discussed and agreed, providing all concerned with an opportunity to discuss any anxieties, clarify misconceptions and confusion, and to concur and determine an appropriate way forward.

☐   Defining clinical supervision

Various attempts have been made to describe and define clinical supervision. The *Vision for the Future* document outlined clinical supervision as:

> a term to describe a formal process of professional support and learning which enables practitioners to develop knowledge and competence, assume responsibility for their own practice and enhance consumer protection and safety of care in complex situations. (DOH, 1993: 3)

The most commonly referred to definition of clinical supervision in the literature, and the one that has most widely been adopted, is that of Faugier and Butterworth:

> an exchange between practising professionals to enable the development of professional skills. (Faugier and Butterworth, 1994: 9)

Other definitions contain elements of the purpose of clinical supervision as identified in the UKCC (1996) position statement, emphasising standards, quality of care, patient safety and protection:

> Clinical supervision is a designated interaction between two or more practitioners, within a safe/supportive environment which enables a continuum of reflective, critical analysis of care, to ensure quality patient services. (Bishop, 1998a: 8)

Some writers highlight the value of supporting of the practitioner and the role of learning from experience, for example:

> Clinical supervision is a regular, protected time for facilitated, in-depth reflection on clinical practice. It aims to enable the supervisee to achieve, sustain and creatively develop a high quality of practice through the means of focused support and development. (Bond and Holland, 1998: 77)

They go on to say:

> The process of supervision should continue throughout the person's career whether they remain in clinical practice or move into management, research or education. (Bond and Holland, 1998: 77)

What all of these definitions have in common is that they acknowledge the dynamic nature of the shared experience in the process of clinical supervision. Some qualify this by adding the desired environmental characteristics, safety and support, but not all of them relate clinical supervision directly to the notion of reflection.

☐   Clinical supervision and reflective practice

This chapter assumes that reflective practice is at the heart of clinical supervision. This does not mean that supervision is dominated by the use of a reflective model, but rather that effective clinical supervision always involves critical reflection by the supervisee and, indeed, by the supervisor. Clinical supervision therefore provides an environment within which critical reflection can be fostered (Johns, 1993).

Some writers argue against reflective practice being an integral part of clinical supervision. Fowler and Chevannes (1998), for example, suggest that reflection may be inappropriate for some practitioners, thus compromising the success of supervision itself. They believe that this is especially true for those

 REFLECTIVE WRITING

How often do you share your thoughts and experiences of professional practice with others? Identify both formal and informal situations in which this process takes place.

Spend some time thinking about the benefits of reflecting on your practice with the guidance of another professional. Perhaps you can think of a specific time when you have talked to someone about a particular work situation. Did this help, and if so, how? Write a paragraph outlining what you think you gain from sharing your practice with another person. Also make a note of any concerns that come to mind.

Write a brief paragraph stating what you want from clinical supervision.

Now complete the following statements, clarifying as many of your hopes, expectations and fears as you are able at this time.

• When I come to supervision I hope I will . . .
• I expect I will . . .
• I am afraid I will . . .

more inexperienced practitioners, whom they feel have a lack of knowledge and experience to draw upon to make sense of practice. The thrust of Fowler and Chevannes' argument is founded on the earlier work of Benner (1984), which has since been criticised, adapted and developed, not least by Benner herself, thus calling into question the fundamental basis of their argument. Although there might be a case for arguing that reflection is (initially) alien to the usual way of thinking some practitioners, we would agree with writers such as Binnie and Titchen (1995) that the functions and tasks of clinical supervision are inextricably linked to the development of critical reflection, such that what clinical supervision offers is a formalised structure within which reflection can take place. Fitzgerald is in agreement, stating:

> It is my belief that it is within these types of supervisory relationships that reflection plays an important role in the clinical supervision process. The use of a reflective framework facilitates a structured approach to the agenda of the supervisory meeting and helps to maintain the focus on practice whilst enabling a questioning approach. (Fitzgerald, 2000: 155)

What is clear is that in order to manage the implementation of clinical supervision effectively, there needs to be a mutual definition and expectation so that both supervisors and supervisees can achieve ownership of the programme and

---

 FURTHER READING

There are a number of papers that explore the relationship between clinical supervision and reflective practice. Yegdich (1999) provides a good overview of some of the myths surrounding clinical supervision, and includes a short piece about reflective practice. In the second edition of *Reflective Practice in Nursing*, there is a new chapter written by Mary Fitzgerald that examines the arguments for and against critical reflection as an integral part of clinical supervision.

Fisher, M. (1996) 'Using Reflective Practice in Clinical Supervision', *Professional Nurse*, **11** (7), 443–44.

Fitzgerald, M. (2000) 'Clinical Supervision and Reflective Practice', in C. Bulman and S. Burns (eds), *Reflective Practice in Nursing*, 2nd edn, Oxford: Blackwell Scientific, ch. 5.

Fowler, J. and Chevannes, M. (1998) 'Evaluating the Efficacy of Reflective Practice Within the Context of Clinical Supervision', *Journal of Advanced Nursing*, **27**, 379–382.

Yegdich, T. (1999) 'Clinical Supervision and Managerial Supervision: Some Historical and Conceptual Considerations', *Journal of Advanced Nursing*, **30** (5), 1195–1204.

appreciate its value and importance both to themselves, to the organisation and for their patients. Achieving ownership will not only help to allay some of the anxieties but also ensure clarity of information in relation to the choice of modes and models. It is to this task that we now turn our attention.

☐   The supervisory relationship

It is widely accepted that the success of clinical supervision is highly dependant on the quality and effectiveness of the supervisory relationship (Kohner, 1994). In addition, as we have already indicated, there is a prevalent view that the supervisor should not be the supervisee's manager, although on occasions this might be difficult to avoid (Fitzgerald, 2000; Van Ooijen, 2000; Bond and Holland, 1998; UKCC, 1996). So who can be your supervisor? A supervisor might be a peer, a more experienced professional, an external facilitator, or a manager who is not directly responsible to you, but should be someone who shares a similar vision to yours of the intent and emphasis of clinical supervision (Johns, 1998).

How do you choose your supervisor? If you go back to the previous exercises in this chapter, in which you explored what has been helpful for you in the past when you have been supervised and your list of hopes, expectations and fears about supervision, you might find that these will help to identify the sort of person you are looking for. Ideally, this should be someone who can offer you challenge as much as support, someone you feel you can work with personally and professionally, whom you have respect for, and who can help you to develop in areas that you know are lacking (Proctor, 1986). Often, someone from a different discipline can help you to see things from a wider perspective by challenging the embedded norms of your everyday practice. Other points that may influence your choice of supervisor might be age, gender and cultural factors. Choosing the person you would want to be your supervisor is important, but there are also practical issues to consider such as convenient timing, shift patterns, appropriate

DISCUSSION POINT

With a colleague, spend some time discussing the advantages and disadvantages of the following:

- Individual supervision
- Group supervision
- Peer supervision
- Managerial supervision
- Multidisciplinary supervision
- Supervision with an allocated supervisor

venues and your willingness to be flexible. Where possible, we would suggest that you find a venue for your supervision which is away from your usual work area, and where you are less likely to be interrupted and perhaps able to speak more freely. However, if this is not practical it is important to find an environment within which you feel safe. When choosing your supervisor it is worth bearing in mind their training and experience and any specific interests they carry which will act as a background to the work you do together.

Another aspect of your decision is what particular mode of supervision you would prefer, given that you have a choice. When selecting a particular form of supervision it is important that you are clear about what is available, who makes the decision, and how and why it is made.

■ Modes of supervision

The literature often presents conflicting and confusing ideas about the modes and models of clinical supervision. The *model* of supervision refers to the theoretical and philosophical underpinnings of supervision and the way in which this informs the work, and these issues will be discussed later in the chapter. The *mode* of clinical supervision refers to the practical ways of operationalising the process itself, such as individual, group, peer or managerial supervision. There are benefits and limitations to each mode of supervision, both for the individual and for the organisation.

Organisations often prefer groups for reasons of efficacy and cost effectiveness, and this is something that will be addressed in detail when we outline the theory and practice of group supervision in Chapter 5. However, individual or one-to-one supervision is often the first choice for beginning supervisees, especially those who experience difficulty with self-disclosure and/or find groups threatening. One-to-one supervision has the benefits of allowing the supervisor and supervisee not only to concentrate their attentions on the development of the working alliance, but also has the added advantage of giving the supervisee more time.

In contrast, peer supervision emphasises the role of self and peer assessment as a resource for ongoing professional development. A peer group is one that consists of people who judge themselves to be at an equal level to each other, and in which all members of the group are supervisees and supervisors, all are deemed competent, and where feedback is based on shared expertise and collaborative partnerships in what might be termed a hierarchy amongst equals (Bond and Holland, 1998; Heron 1981). Peer supervision may also take the form of one-to-one supervision in which the time is shared between the two individuals. A list of the key characteristics of individual, group and peer supervision is outlined below.

☐ Individual

• This form of supervision has the advantage of the continuity and intimacy of the one-to-one relationship which may enhance the professional development of the practitioner.

- The process and feedback inevitably depends upon the supervisor's style, ethical and theoretical preferences.
- Feedback will be limited to that of the supervisor. An issue for the supervisee is how to compensate for this bias, and to that end the supervisor's task is to encourage the supervisee to use a broad range of additional professional resources.

☐ Group

- Case material can be used in such a way that provides a learning opportunity for the whole group.
- It is crucial to the function of the group to establish ground rules and to discuss equal access to supervision.
- There is potential for the group to be used as a resource for feedback processes and the creation of a variety of perspectives.
- The size of the group can affect the success of the supervision.

☐ Peer

- Supervision acts as a resource for ongoing professional development and support.
- It is based on mutual feedback and shared expertise.
- It provides a hierarchy amongst equals through collaborative partnerships.

Having decided upon a mode of supervision which is both agreeable and practical, it is important to ascertain the model to which you and your supervisor feel most closely aligned to.

■ Models of supervision

☐ Building a relationship

A number of theoretical and philosophical models have been developed to inform the basis on which the tasks, functions and responsibilities of clinical supervision are derived. Each model views the helping relationship from a different perspective, outlining a framework which influences the way that clinical supervision, the supervisor and the supervisee are perceived. Many of these models are drawn from the field of counselling and psychotherapy, and have been adapted to nursing and other health related professions, although there is an ongoing debate regarding the extent to which supervision is didactic or therapeutic in orientation. Although models can guide the practice of supervision, your choice is heavily dependant upon your own beliefs and values and your own understanding of the purpose of clinical supervision.

We will briefly outline four of the main models in this chapter: the psychodynamic, the humanistic, the cognitive-behavioural and the systemic. The first two models pay more attention to the intrapersonsal relationship and how this effects the interpersonal life of the practitioner, the patient and the supervisor, whilst the second two models focus on the wider interpersonal life of the supervisor/ supervisee and the effects of this on their working context. All four models have something to offer the practice of clinical supervision, and differences between them are largely a matter of emphasis.

☐ The psychodynamic model

Sigmund Freud was the creator of psychodynamic thinking, and although his theories and concepts have been modified and developed over many years, the central tenets remain unchanged. Psychodynamic theory perceives human behaviour as being governed by unconscious factors, with psychodynamic counselling offering ways of tapping into the unconscious through the analysis of dreams, resistance and transference. Transference occurs when patients express feelings toward the practitioner that they originally felt for parents or significant others. These feelings can be present in any situation but are likely to be exaggerated or evoked in cases where the patient is vulnerable, for example in the course of physical illness and subsequent admission to hospital. Countertransference occurs when the practitioner carries feelings consciously and unconsciously as a result of the relationship.

From the psychodynamic perspective, the therapeutic relationship is characterised by distance and formality, with the enforcement of clear boundaries and an explicit contract. Hence, in the psychodynamic approach to supervision, the discussion may focus on the approaches to the nurse–patient relationship and the management of transference, ways of resolving countertransference reactions and understanding how these reactions may be used as a therapeutic tool. It is also thought that the dynamics of the relationship between the nurse and the patient is reflected in that between the supervisee and the supervisor, hence the parallel process is of central significance to the psychodynamic supervisor (Jacobs, 1996).

In supervision, an understanding of the parallel process can be obtained by analysing the interaction between transferential and countertransferential relationships as these are reflected in the supervisory relationship. At a basic level the supervisor is interested in the transfer of feelings, thoughts and behaviours from one relationship to another, and the responses that might occur as a reaction to these. The processes of transference and countertransference may be an important feature in allowing the nurse to respond positively to situations rather than to react against them, thereby providing opportunities for insight and learning. Detailed explanations of these processes can be found in other texts (Casement, 1985; Jacobs, 1991), but we shall illustrate them here with a simple example (Figure 4.1).

86

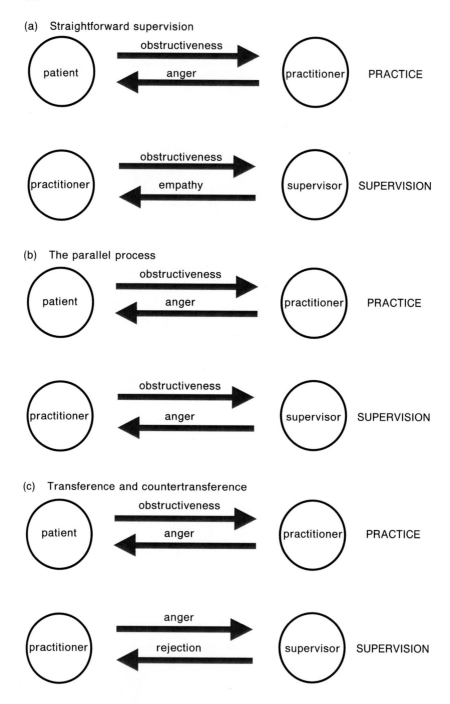

Figure 4.1 The dynamics of supervision

Imagine a physiotherapist working with a particularly resistant patient who is obstructing all of her interventions, and to whom the physiotherapist responds with anger. In the straightforward supervision session illustrated in Figure 4.1a, the practitioner relates her frustration at the situation (and indeed at the patient) to her supervisor, who responds by showing empathy and perhaps by making some constructive suggestions.

As we have already described, a number of writers have noticed the way in which the emotional content of the practice situation is often mirrored in the supervision session. In this case, the practitioner might quite unconsciously find herself displaying the same obstructiveness towards her supervisor as the patient displayed towards her (Figure 4.1b). It is the job of the psychodynamic supervisor to recognise this parallel process and deal with it appropriately, either by confronting the practitioner with her behaviour, or else by responding in the same way that the practitioner responded to her patient in the practice situation, in this case with anger. This latter intervention is particularly powerful, since the practitioner now finds herself in the same emotional situation as her patient, and can experience at first hand how it feels to be confronted with anger by someone who is supposed to be helping her. The danger, however, is that the supervisor might fail to recognise what is happening, in which case she might become enmeshed in the situation and not be able to use it constructively.

Another potential pitfall is that the practitioner might unconsciously transfer the feelings she has towards her patient onto her supervisor. In this case, she might find herself becoming angry with her supervisor for no apparent reason, and blaming her for the problems she is having with her patient (Figure 4.1c). The supervisor can deal with this transference in the same way that she dealt with the parallel process, that is, either by confronting the situation or by using it constructively in order to help the practitioner to work through her anger. As with the parallel process, the danger lies in the supervisor not recognising the transference reaction and responding to the anger, perhaps by feeling rejected, rather than working with it. This process of becoming enmeshed in the feelings and responding emotionally rather than recognising them and responding cognitively is called countertransference.

As well as providing a mechanism for understanding the affective component of the supervisory relationship, the psychodynamic approach also offers a model for strict boundaries and clear contract setting, whilst recognising that the contract is dynamic and can be reviewed at any time. In addition, practitioners may also be offered the opportunity to examine their defense mechanisms and how these might be supporting or impeding their practice, which goes some way to attending to some of the issues previously discussed, particularly those concerning emotional closeness (Briant and Freshwater, 1998; Menzies-Lyth, 1970, 1988). Practitioners can find the psychodynamic way of working uncomfortable, as the emphasis is on the role of self and knowing self in relation to other, and demands that the practitioner acknowledges their uncaring as well as caring, leading to a potential shift in self-image.

☐   The humanistic model

The humanistic model of supervision has its roots in person-centred or humanistic psychology, which was founded by Carl Rogers, and which is the basis of what is known today in nursing as patient-centred care. The humanistic model recognises the capacity of the person to know what is right for herself, emphasising the notion of learning through self-directedness, and has influenced the development of educational theories leading to the evolution of experiential learning (Brandes and Ginnis, 1985; Rogers, 1969).

According to Rogers, the core conditions of empathy, genuineness and respect (unconditional positive regard) are necessary and sufficient conditions for effective individual development (Rogers, 1991), and the humanistic or person-centred supervisor seeks, through those core conditions, to communicate trust and respect for the supervisee. The process of supervision is developmental and may start with the supervisee being highly motivated but anxious, fluctuating between autonomy and dependence on the supervisor, and between feeling overconfident and being overwhelmed. The learning that is facilitated by the supervisor's quality of presence, as communicated in the core conditions, enables the practitioner to develop trust in both herself and her supervisor. As this happens, she becomes increasingly more able to know and assert her beliefs and values, and to experiment with a wide range of responses both in supervision and in practice.

We can see, then, that one of the major benefits of this approach is the emphasis that it places on autonomy and responsibility, concepts that are crucial to autonomous and accountable practice. The humanistic model of supervision therefore has much to offer nursing practice, for example, the notion of empowering the client and allowing her to direct her own care, and to trust that the client knows what she needs.

However, there are a number of difficulties and limitations to the humanistic model. Firstly, because it places great emphasis on the co-participatory nature of the relationship and the non-judgemental approach to the supervision of practice, it is essential that the supervisor is not hierarchically linked to the supervisee, and it would not be acceptable to have your manager as your supervisor. However, there is inevitably a judgmental element to clinical supervision, and this might raise difficulties for the uncritical application of the humanistic model to nursing practice, since whoever supervises is still professionally accountable and may be concerned about elements of practice which present ethical dilemmas. Finally, the supervisor who works within a humanistic model will be expected to have a willingness to challenge and to be genuine as a sign of respect for herself and for the supervisee, and this in itself can present a problem, since being willing and able to challenge is a challenge in itself, and perhaps not one that all supervisors are prepared to accept.

☐   The cognitive-behavioural models

The cognitive-behavioural models are action-orientated, with the emphasis on outcomes and tasks, thinking problems through, and identifying possible solutions and their consequences, resulting in less emphasis on the relationship and more focus on external factors (Beck, 1976; Bandura, 1969).

In the cognitive-behavioural approach to supervision, the discussion may focus on specific examples of the practitioner's irrational thinking and on teaching the techniques of problem-solving to enhance practice through the use of action-planning, goal-setting and a decision balance sheet. In addition, the supervisor may help the supervisee to identify external resources that might facilitate action. Supervision is seen as a working alliance, although the supervisor is often more directive and didactic in her enabling. A contract is set up and there is an expectation that it will be adhered to, and that the supervisee will do homework if agreed. This model is particularly helpful because it focuses on achieving outcomes, it is organisation friendly and it emphasises the action component of reflection. One of the limitations of this model is that the person of the practitioner can get left out, leading her to feel unmet and uncared for.

☐   The systemic model

The philosophy behind the systemic model is based on the notion that there are many possible ways of looking at reality and that there is no ultimate objective

---

 FURTHER READING

All of the models we have presented have something to offer the healthcare practitioner already in clinical supervision or just setting out. However, it is impossible to fully describe them here, and you might find the following texts useful in exploring one or more of the models further.

Bandura, A. (1969) *Principles of Behaviour Modification*, London: Holt, Rinehart & Wilson.

Beck, A.T. (1976) *Cognitive Therapy and the Emotional Disorders*, New York: International Universities Press.

Boydell, T. (1976) 'Experiential Learning', *Manchester Monograph No. 5*, University of Manchester, Department of Continuing Education.

Brandes, P.L. and Ginnis, P. (1985) *A Guide to Student Centred Learning*, Oxford: Basil Blackwell.

Holloway, E. (1995) *Clinical Supervision: A Systems Approach*, London: Sage.

Jacobs, M. (ed.) (1996) *In Search of Supervision*, Buckingham: Open University Press.

Jacobs, M. (1991) *Psychodynamic Counselling in Action*, London: Sage.

Rogers, C. R. (1969) *Freedom to Learn*, Ohio: Merrill.

Rogers, C. R. (1991) *Client Centred Therapy*, London: Constable.

truth. The emphasis of the systemic approach is on interpersonal relationships and communication rather than on the individual's intrapsychic life. Systemic models are interested in how organisations function and in examining the role of the individual in the group (Holloway, 1995).

The systemic model recognises that any supervisory intervention is influenced by the context, that is, the social background of the supevisee and the patient, the organisation within which supervision is taking place and the professional discipline within which the practitioner is working. The main concepts of the systemic model are hypothesising, circularity and neutrality. Hypothesising is based on the belief that there are multiple versions of reality and that any individual's view of reality is informed by their beliefs and experience. In supervision there is always the risk that either or both the supervisor/supervisee will treat their hypothesis as true rather than as one of many possibilities, which limits the potential for seeing new and different hypotheses within supervision. Hypothesising in practice and supervision will be discussed further when we explore reflection-in-action in Chapter 6.

■ Frameworks of supervision

Whereas the modes and models of supervision provide the setting and philosophy, we also need a framework in order to give structure to the supervisory relationship. The frameworks for supervision fall broadly into three categories: structural, developmental and goal-oriented.

□ Structural frameworks

The cyclic model developed for counselling by Page and Woskett (1994) provides a structured sequential model with five phases, each subdivided into a further five (see Figure 4.2). This comprehensive model provides the supervisor with a flexible set of guidelines which are designed to be used in an integrative way as opposed to a rigid framework to be adhered to. The guidelines enable the supervisor to develop both herself and her supervisee in a professional manner, viewing the supervision process as one of dynamic movement rather than being static, with change regarded as fundamental both to the practice of supervision and to clinical practice.

As we can see, each of the five phrases in this framework offers guidance as to how to conduct a supervision session, making explicit the necessary tasks. This structural type of approach can be very helpful for the beginning supervisor and, indeed, for the novice supervisee. Many frameworks of reflection are presented in a cyclical format (see Chapter 2), and can therefore run parallel to Page and Woskett's structural framework of supervision. In addition, there are research processes that also follow a similar approach, which will be discussed in Chapter 7.

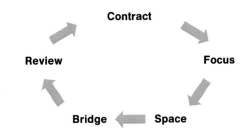

Contract	Focus	Space	Bridge	Review
Ground rules	Issues	Collaboration	Consolidation	Feedback
Boundaries	Objectives	Investigation	Information-giving	Grounding
Accountability	Presentation	Challenge	Goal-setting	Evaluation
Expectations	Approach	Containment	Action-planning	Assessment
Relationship	Priorities	Affirmation	Client's perspective	Recontracting

Figure 4.2   A sequential model of supervision (adapted from Page and Woskett, 1994)

☐   Developmental frameworks

Developmental approaches originate in developmental psychology, and not surprisingly they emphasise the educational functions of clinical supervision, moving from the child through the adolescent and young adult to maturity (Stoltenberg and Delworth, 1987). In these models, the supervisee is seen to move from a place of felt novice to perceived expert during the course of her supervision (Benner, 1984).

Hawkins and Shohet's (1989) process framework is one such developmental approach, in which emphasis is placed on the development of the supervisory alliance as a way of encouraging and empowering the supervisee. This framework is helpful in enabling the practitioner to identify and celebrate her progress.

☐   Goal-oriented frameworks

One of the most widely quoted frameworks for supervision is that of Proctor (1986), whose goal-oriented framework focuses on the formative, normative and restorative tasks of supervision. The task of the formative educational function includes monitoring, teaching and consulting for lifelong learning and professional development. The supportive restorative function involves containment and holding with the purpose of alleviating the emotional labour of nursing,

	Known to self	Not known to self
Known to others	OPEN SELF Increased via clinical supervision	BLIND SELF Discovered via clinical supervision
Not known to others	HIDDEN SELF Revealed and explored via trust and confidence in clinical supervision	UNKNOWN SELF Decreased via clinical supervision

Figure 4.3 Clinical supervision and the Johari window (Heath and Freshwater, 2000, adapted from Lufe, 1969)

whilst the normative function includes examining the organisational issues, including ethical dimensions, the code of practice, administrative functions, standards of practice and quality control. This framework is useful in that it offers professional guidance (in the normative function), challenge (in the formative function) and support (in the restorative function), hence recognising the need for balance between these elements.

As with the models discussed earlier, all of the above frameworks have something to offer the supervisory alliance, and the flexible practitioner will be able to utilise and adapt aspects of several frameworks within a dynamic situation such as supervision. What all the frameworks have in common is the requirement for self-reflection and developing self-awareness as part of becoming a reflective and effective practitioner.

One well-known framework that encompasses this notion of becoming self-aware in practice is the Johari window (Figure 4.3). As can be seen from the figure, our awareness is expanded as we take the risk of disclosing some of our 'hidden' areas and by being receptive to feedback from others about our 'blind spots'. For this level of self-disclosure to occur there need to be certain boundaries in place to ensure the safety and trust of the supervisee. It is essential that these boundaries are discussed in the first session of supervision as part of the contractual negotiation.

□   Contracting

In setting up clinical supervision, it is essential that the boundaries of the supervisory relationship are established through the explicit drawing-up of ground rules via a mutually negotiated contract. The contract is made as explicit as possible between all interested parties, not only to encourage ownership but also to allow individuals to make an informed choice about the relationship they are embarking on. This initial session is also helpful in encouraging individual practitioners to reflect upon their beliefs, needs and values, so the process of reflection begins immediately.

REFLECTIVE WRITING

What would you need to have in place in order to embark upon a supervisory alliance?

Make a list of items that you would want to discuss with your supervisor/supervisee when negotiating your working contract.

Some of the things you might want to consider in negotiating a clear contract include:

- openness on both sides;
- preparation requirements (i.e. what does the supervisor expect you to do prior to a supervisory session?);
- awareness of the value of supervision as a resource;
- development of good working skills as the most important aim of the relationship;
- focus (which is always the working effectiveness of the supervisee);
- accountability;
- responsibility of the supervisor;
- awareness of supervisee's level;
- agreement on needs and appropriate material;
- practical matters including time boundaries, venue and confidentiality.

Confidentiality is something that often concerns supervisees. This is not surprising, since we have already seen that there is considerable confusion around the differences and similarities between supervision, line management and professional discussion with colleagues.

■ The dynamics of the supervisory relationship

☐ The role of the supervisor

Many writers have attempted to detail the fundamental features of the role of the supervisor (Fitzgerald, 2000; Johns and McCormack, 1998; Faugier and Butterworth, 1994; Faugier, 1992). Writers talk about the supervisor having a willingness to facilitate learning in others whilst being open to learning about themselves, and it is thought to be essential that supervisors have a willingness to undertake self-assessment and that they should not only have training in supervision but should also be in supervision themselves (Kohner, 1994). This is crucial if the supervisor is going to role model one of the fundamental purposes of supervision to their supervisee, that is, to look at the intention behind the intervention. Some authors are of the opinion that many of the skills required for the role of clinical supervisor can be equated with the skills of the effective practitioner (Johns, 1998; Fowler, 1996).

DISCUSSION POINT

Looking back at your previous writing which identifies your hopes, expectations and fears regarding clinical supervision, think about choosing your own ideal supervisor. Discuss with a colleague the specific skills and qualities of the ideal supervisor.

Now spend some time together reflecting on these qualities and the ways in which you meet them.

The supervisor's preferred relationship model, her definition of supervision and her supervisory styles heavily influence the role of the supervisor, as we can see from the styles described below:

☐ *Constructive*

The supervisor is very helpful, which has obvious benefits in the early stages of supervision, but if continued this style can eventually lead to the supervisee feeling smothered. When using the developmental approach, the supervisor needs to be aware of when it is appropriate to allow the supervisee to walk on her own even if there is a risk of falling.

☐ *Authoritative*

The supervisee feels like her work is constantly under a microscope, and experiences the supervisor as picky. The supervisor may recognise that she has perfectionist tendencies which might be useful at times, especially when considering the normative function of supervision, but may be offputting in the early stages of supervision when the task is to build a safe trusting relationship. This style can be linked to managerial supervision.

☐ *Didactic/consultative*

The supervisor focuses on the educational components of information-giving and providing the supervisee with the benefit of her wisdom and experience. Again, this can be very important at all stages of the supervisory work and is especially helpful at the beginning for the novice supervisor. However, the supervisor can forget that the supervisee is also a teacher and has her own wisdom. This style might be likened to mentorship/preceptorship.

☐ *Amorphous*

The supervisor is not really present for the supervisee, she is without shape and appears invisible in her interventions. The supervisee can feel unsupported and unheard due to a lack of boundaries; developmentally the supervisee needs to be held and contained. Perhaps the first phase of Page and Woskett's framework has not been established, and the relationship is missing. However, it can sometimes be important for the supervisor to be more in the background, especially when the supervisee is sophisticated, although the supervisor would usually be making a conscious choice to hold back.

☐ *Unsupportive*

The supervisor is present but offers little or no supportive interventions; challenges are cold and punitive with a hint of authority about them. Challenge is important but the timeliness of interventions is crucial and always in relation to the stage of the supervisory alliance. Unfortunately, this style of supervision can feel too much like clinical practice to the practitioner, where she is often left feeling unsupported.

☐ *Therapeutic*

The supervisor concentrates on the personal needs of the supervisee, moving into a counselling role and overstepping boundaries. There is a fine line between this style and Proctor's restorative function, and whilst therapeutic input can be part of the work, the boundaries between counselling, therapy and supervision need to be made clear.

☐ *Detective*

This style of supervision focuses on trying to find the cause of problems and lay blame. The supervisor feels that she has to get to the bottom of things and understand the complete story, hence detail is important. The supervisee can feel like she is under oath and under investigation.

☐ *Reflective/facilitative*

The reflective supervisor draws upon a facilitative style that incorporates her own experience and insight but that also permits her to include herself as a professional learner. Interventions are supportive, including the use of feelings and cognitions, but are also probing and challenging. Some of the skills of the effective reflective supervisor are outlined below.

☐ Skills of reflective supervision

The effective reflective supervisor knows when it is appropriate to make a particular type of intervention using:

☐ *Listening and responding skills*

- Ability to use various forms of questions to elicit further information and to stimulate reflection.
- Ability to respond to the supervisee using a variety of skills including clarifying, summarising, reflecting and accepting.
- Ability to use clear questions focused on the supervisee's professional context.

☐ *Reflexive skills*

- The ability to recognise your own skills and the impact that these have on the supervisory interaction, which presupposes a certain degree of self-awareness.
- The ability to check your own ideas, preconceptions and hypotheses and the effect of these on supervision.
- The ability to evaluate the effects of your approach to supervision on the supervisee and the supervisory relationship.
- The ability to be flexible in your approach to supervisory methods, style or mode in order to be a more effective supervisor.

☐ *Observing skills*

- Recognising progress and acknowledging it with the supervisee.
- Identifying areas for further development.
- Observing the strengths and weaknesses of the supervisee and of the supervisory relationship.
- Noticing recurrent themes or patterns in your work with the supervisee and between the supervisee and their clinical practice.

☐ *Transparency*

- The skills to use self-disclosure appropriately.
- The ability to be open about your way of working.
- Being open about your own opinion without imposing it on the supervisee.
- Being able to justify reasons for interventions made.
- Ability to reflect openly on the specific emphasis of supervision.

☐ *Feedback*

- Being able to stay with the supervisee's fear and anxieties.
- Ability to give positive feedback without appearing patronising.
- Responding to the supervisee in a non-judgmental manner based on the belief that the supervisee is acting in the best way she can at that moment and is also willing to learn.

☐ *Sensitivity to wider social issues*

- Being aware of and being able to respond sensitively to power differentials.
- Being aware of the social context within which the supervisee is operating and the influence of this on the supervisory relationship.

- The ability to stimulate the development of the supervisee's skills within the working context.
- Noticing the influence of the supervisee's social background, belief systems, norms and values on the supervisory relationship and the wider working context.

☐ *Creativity and flexibility*

- The skills to be able to create and offer a variety of different methods and techniques for reflection

It would be impossible for every supervisor to achieve every skill on this list in every session of supervision, and it is important for her to acknowledge that she is also in the constant process of reflection-on-action and, as such, aspire to be what Winnicott (1971) might have termed the 'good enough supervisor' (Heath and Freshwater, 2000).

☐ The role of the supervisee

The supervisory alliance also makes certain demands of the supervisee, who also requires skills to fulfil her responsibilities. Supervisees are required to be proactive in the relationship and to realise that they have an equal part in monitoring and evaluating the supervisory alliance (Kohner, 1994). In preparation for supervision, the practitioner is expected to reflect upon practice incidents prior to the session, perhaps doing a 'mini-supervision' through critical reflection to sharpen her awareness of the issues for discussion. This not only encourages the supervisee to develop the skills of reflection-on-action, but also gives the responsibility for setting the supervisory agenda to the supervisee, so that the available time can be used to best advantage.

Supervisees can engage in a variety of exercises to enhance their capacity to adequately prepare for supervision, some of which you have been doing as you have moved through this text, such as reflective writing, using a model of reflection, and gathering further information to inform your decision-making.

☐ Barriers to success

Bishop (1986) recently carried out a survey to explore the level of implementation of clinical supervision within trusts across England and Scotland. Whilst the majority of respondents were engaged in some form of clinical supervision (which incidentally they valued highly), this was not without its difficulties and in many places it was only partially implemented. Reasons given for the lack of stratified policy and uniform implementation of supervision included lack of money for time and staff training, misunderstandings regarding the role of the clinical supervisor, increasing workload pressures, and lack of managerial commitment. It would seem that the success of clinical supervision is heavily influenced by the commitment of the manager and the organisation as well as the individual practitioners (Farrington, 1995; Kohner, 1994). It is therefore crucial that all levels of staff within an organisation, including managers, have access to adequate information and education regarding the purpose of clinical supervision and reflective practice, so that informed decisions can be taken in order to mobilise the necessary resources.

Individual practitioners also need to reinforce their verbal commitment to critical reflection on practice through clinical supervision through their actions, since clinical supervision requires an investment of time and energy before the short-term and long-term benefits can be fully actualised.

 REFLECTIVE WRITING

Now turn back to the aims which you identified at the start of the chapter. To what extent have they been met? Write a paragraph outlining the scientific and experiential knowledge you have acquired through reading this chapter and doing the exercises. Write a second paragraph identifying any aims that you feel were only partially met or not met at all.

Now divide your page into three columns. Head the first column 'What I need to learn', and make a list of any outstanding issues which you would like to learn more about. For example, you might wish to find out more about improving your practice through clinical supervision. Head the second column 'How will I learn it' and write down the ways in which your learning needs could be addressed, for example through further reading, through attending study days, or though talking to other people. Head the third column 'How I will know that I have learnt it', and try to identify how you will know when you have met your needs.

Chapter 5

Group supervision

■ Introduction

It is probably true to say that clinical supervision has become a victim of its own success. Not only are growing numbers of individual practitioners beginning to recognise the benefits of good supervision, but more and more organisations are introducing it as an institutional requirement. However, whilst many managers and practitioners are fully aware of the benefits of supervision and wish to introduce it into their clinical areas, they are often hampered by a lack of resources, including insufficient time, not enough trained and experienced supervisors, and a shortage of money to pay for outside supervision. The solution that more and more individuals and organisations are turning to is some form of group supervision.

We have already discussed the principles of supervision in some depth, and so in this chapter we will focus on groups and the particular issues involved in supervising and being supervised in group settings. Our aim is therefore to enable you to learn more about the theory and practice of group supervision, and in particular to reflect on your experience of being in groups of all kinds. More specifically, our aims for this chapter are:

1   to help you to reflect on your experiences in groups from a variety of different theoretical perspectives;
2   to enable you to plan and organise a supervision group;
3   to enable you to reflect on your personal attributes as a group facilitator; and
4   to outline and discuss the basic skills required to safely and competently begin facilitating a supervision group.

 REFLECTIVE WRITING

Think carefully about our aims for Chapter 5. Now think about your own practice and how these aims might contribute towards developing it.

Based on our aims above, write down some of your own, both in terms of what you hope to know and what you hope to be able to do after reading Chapter 5. We will return to your aims at the end of the chapter.

■ Groups and group supervision

Hawkins and Shohet (1989) have identified a number of advantages of supervision in groups. First is the very issue that we identified above as contributing to the growing popularity of group supervision, that is, the economies of scale. As they point out, however, 'ideally group supervision should come from a positive choice rather than a compromise forced upon the group and supervisor' (Hawkins and Shohet, 1989). Other advantages that they discuss include opportunities for peer support and peer feedback, access to a wide range of life experiences of other members, the possibility of employing action-based techniques, and the opportunity to learn about group process and group dynamics from first-hand experience. They also highlight a number of possible disadvantages of group supervision, including being less likely to mirror the individual work which the supervisee might be conducting with patients (see our discussion of the 'parallel process' in the previous chapter), a preoccupation with group dynamics to the exclusion of doing any supervision, and the fact that there will inevitably be less time allocated to each individual than in one-to-one supervision.

Hawkins and Shohet make the important distinction between group and team supervision. Whereas in group supervision the group will have come together solely for that purpose, team supervision 'involves working with a group that has not come together just for the purposes of joint supervision, but have an inter-related work life outside the group' (Hawkins and Shohet, 1989). They point out that there is a crucial difference in supervision needs between teams that share work with the same clients, for example ward-based nurses, and groups of practitioners who have their own individual clients, or who share clients with other practitioners who are not in the supervision group. We will consider this in more detail later in the chapter.

They also discuss peer supervision, that is, supervision with one or more other practitioners where no-one takes on an overt group facilitation role. Again, they highlight advantages and disadvantages, but their main concern would appear to be the danger of game-playing without realising what is happening. Games can and do take place in most groups, but the advantage of a facilitated supervision group is that one of the jobs for which the facilitator is trained is to identify when games are occurring and to deal with them or point them out to the group members. In addition to the problem of game-playing, we would add the difficulty and possible danger which an unfacilitated group faces of not recognising the potentially damaging impact of group dynamics.

A compromise might be to share the facilitation role between the group members, so that a different member facilitates the group at each meeting. Bond and Holland (1998) recognise this as a viable option, but point out a number of disadvantages, including a lack of authority and a lack of facilitation skills. We shall return to this issue shortly, but for now we will simply state that unfacilitated peer groups can result in a great many problems, and we would be very reluctant to recommend this model of group supervision.

Whilst recognising the important distinctions between facilitated groups, teams and peer groups, we have chosen to explore differences between groups in terms of function rather than structure. We have therefore distinguished between intrapersonal group supervision, interpersonal group supervision, and transpersonal group supervision.

Intrapersonal group supervision (groups which focus on the processes *within* the individual) can best be described as individual supervision with an audience. In this model, the supervisor works individually with each group member in turn while the rest of the group looks on. Clearly, it has the advantage of requiring no special facilitation skills over and above the skills of individual supervision, and, arguably, there is much to be learnt simply from observing the supervisory encounter, even for members who are not involved in supervision at that moment. If the intention behind establishing group supervision is purely a resource issue, then this is a model that is simple to set up and can provide supervision to an entire team of practitioners at very little financial cost. However, Bond and Holland (1998) do not recognise this as a form of group supervision, stating that 'they might as well be a queue of people waiting outside the flimsily partitioned office of a clinical supervisor, eavesdropping on what's going on'. Furthermore, they do not even view it as cost-effective, adding that 'it is a time-consuming way to provide one-to-one clinical supervision'.

Interpersonal group supervision (groups which focus on what happens *between* individuals) utilises the group members as a resource. Whereas the intrapersonal group model places the supervisor clearly in the role of expert, the interpersonal model recognises that group members also have the skills and experience to offer supervision to one another. The role of the facilitator is therefore concerned less with direct supervision than with enabling and empowering group members to supervise each other. This approach is a more efficient use of resources, and as well as receiving supervision from a number of different individuals, the group members also gain some experience of supervising others under the watchful eye of the facilitator. The interpersonal model comes closest to the definition of group supervision offered by Bond and Holland (1998) of 'three or more people who come together and interrelate cooperatively with each other towards their common purpose of giving and receiving clinical supervision'. Although this is the most common model of group supervision, it views the group as nothing more than the sum of all the possible combinations of personal interactions, and so neglects some important aspects of group development and group dynamics.

Finally, transpersonal group supervision (groups which look *beyond* the individual) views the group as being more than simply the sum of all the inter- and intrapersonal group events. Rather, the group is seen as having a separate identity that is different from the sum of all its parts; the group, in effect, has a life of its own. We can therefore talk about 'the group' and 'group life' as if the group was a person. Indeed, some models of group development and group processes are analogous to human development from birth to death, with childhood mischiefs, adolescent identity crises and adult productivity, leading to the wisdom of old age. This model, in which the group takes on a life of its own, might account for such phenomena as group hysteria and 'lynch mobs', where the group behaves in ways that none of the individuals who comprise the group would ever dream of doing.

The group facilitator therefore has a dual role in such a group. On the one hand, she has some kind of supervisory function, either directly or indirectly by facilitating group members to supervise each other. On the other hand, she also has a responsibility for maintaining and developing the group life, for working with 'the group' as an individual entity separate from the individuals who comprise it. Groups that follow this model are sometimes called t-groups or training groups, since one of their functions is to provide the group members with experiential learning about group dynamics. Because this transpersonal model has an educational component, it is particularly useful for new supervisors and group members who are interested in learning about groups by reflecting on their own practice. However, we would recommend that new facilitators who are planning to employ this model initially work with a skilled and experienced co-facilitator.

 DISCUSSION POINT

Try to relate the above models to some of the groups of which you have been a part. These might include family groups, social groups, work-based groups and activity or recreational groups. For example, your ward handover might resemble an intrapersonal group in which each nurse reports on her patients in a one-to-one interaction, with other team members looking on in silence. Or it might function more like an interpersonal group in which each patient is discussed by the whole team, with everyone interacting with everyone else. Similarly, your family might resemble a loosely configured collection of individuals or it might function as a unified whole, as a transpersonal entity in its own right. You might, for example, find yourself saying things like 'my family believes in X' or responding as a family in ways that you would never do as an individual.

With a colleague, try to identify one group of each of the three types and discuss how they might function differently. For example, what would be the benefits and disadvantages if your intrapersonal ward team adopted an interpersonal model?

■ Group development and group dynamics

The best, perhaps the only, way to learn about group supervision is to take part in a group as either a supervisee or a facilitator. In an ideal world, you should gain experience of the former before embarking on the latter, and even then it is essential to ensure that your own practice of group facilitation is itself closely, expertly and regularly supervised by someone with experience (and preferably training) in group work. Despite the ethos of this book of learning from reflection on our practice, it is necessary to acquire some basic theory before starting. The reason for this, as we shall see, is that a great deal of what happens in groups is covert: it happens beneath the surface, it is often disguised as something else, and it is sometimes carried out unconsciously. If, as a new facilitator, you are not directed towards what to look for, you may never find it.

If we are to think of the group as a single entity, as an individual in its own right, then we need to consider how this individual develops over time. Indeed, a number of theorists have noticed that groups behave differently at different phases of their existence, and have attempted to formulate a series of stages through which groups are thought to pass. Although most of these models were constructed to explain the development of therapeutic groups, they have been widely employed with groups of all kinds.

Probably the most well-known model of group development is that devised by Tuckman (1965), who identified four stages through which a group passes, namely forming, storming, norming and performing. Tuckman noticed from a review of over 50 published papers that when groups come together for the first time, they have certain tasks to perform before they can get down to whatever business they were established to carry out. The initial forming stage, when the group first meets, is characterised by anxiety and a lack of direction, and the group typically looks to the facilitator for leadership. However, in many groups, the facilitator would not see such overt leadership as part of her role, and so the group is ultimately disappointed and often rebels against the facilitator. This rebellion initiates the storming stage, in which the role of the facilitator, and sometimes the existence of the group itself, is questioned. During this stage, group members often vie for the leadership role and the reasons for the formation of the group can be totally forgotten in the struggle for power and control. The group eventually realises that, if any work is to be done, then the members must work together for the common good of the group. This is the norming stage during which support and cooperation develops, norms and rules are established, and group members begin to accept the facilitator's role. Finally, once all of these issues are resolved, the group enters the performing stage and begins its work.

Tuckman emphasised that not all groups pass through all four stages (some, for example, never reach the final performing stage), and neither do the stages always follow each other in a neat sequence. If a group is stuck or feels threatened, for example, it might regress to an earlier stage, just as a teenager who feels threatened might revert to thumb sucking or acting out. He also pointed out that, although the stages gradually follow-on from one another during the life of the group, they are also worked through during each individual group meeting.

Levine (1979) suggested a similar model based on sociograms, which are pictorial representations of the patterns of communication within the group. His parallel, inclusion and mutuality phases bear a strong resemblance to Tuckman's stages, and are also very similar to the stages suggested by Schutz (1958) of 'in–out', 'top–bottom' and 'near–far' (see Table 5.1).

These models can be useful in helping us to understand how relationships between group members grow and develop during the life of a group, and they are also invaluable for assisting the group facilitator to recognise and deal with general group dynamics such as scapegoating and subgrouping. For example, a group in its storming stage will tend to rebel against the facilitator, perhaps even going as far as accusing her of incompetence. By being aware of the stage at which the group is functioning and the issues it is trying to deal with, she can see scapegoating as a universal coping mechanism rather than as a personal attack on her facilitation skills. Indeed, she can reframe the attack positively as a sign that the group has progressed through the forming stage and is developing normally, in the same way that rebellion against parents and other authority figures is a normal sign of personal development during the teenage years.

 REFLECTIVE WRITING

Think back to when you joined a new group; for example, when starting a new course or beginning a group project. Try to reflect on the growth and development of the group, as well as its problems and setbacks, in relation to one of the three models of group development described in Table 5.1. Write a brief paragraph on each of the stages of your chosen model, focusing especially on how it felt to be in the group. For example, if you chose Tuckman's model, you might reflect on your feelings of anxiety and uncertainty during the forming phase, or on the jostling for leadership that might have occurred during the storming phase.

Although they are useful for charting the macrodynamics of the group, these models provide only a limited picture of the minute-by-minute changes in the microdynamics, and offer little insight into the underlying group processes that are shaping those developments. Models such as those offered by Tuckman, Levine and Schutz provide us with a useful 'growth chart' for the group in terms of milestones that we might expect it to reach at certain points in its development; they can, as we have seen, predict childhood dependency, teenage rebellion and adult cooperation, but they provide little help in dealing with the day-to-day traumas of living with a dependant child or a rebellious teenager. For that, we need a rather more sophisticated tool.

If, as we have suggested, the analogy of the group as an individual in its own right is an accurate one, then we might expect the group to function on both a conscious and an unconscious level in the same way as a person. Furthermore, by uncovering the unconscious motivations for conscious acts, we might start to understand the day-to-day microdynamics of the group.

Table 5.1 Three models of group development

Tuckman	Levine		Schutz
Forming Characterised by anxiety and dependence on the facilitator	*Parallel phase* Communications in the group run parallel to each other rather than across the group, and are usually directed towards the facilitator	Facilitator ○ ○ ○ ○ ← ○ ← ○ ←	*'In–out' stage* Characterised by dependency on the facilitator. Group members want to be accepted and loved by her
Storming Characterised by conflict, issues of leadership and rebellion against the facilitator. *Norming* Characterised by cohesion and trust. The group begins to develop shared norms, mutual support and co-operation	*Inclusion phase* Communications towards the facilitator decrease, and those between group members increase. Fluctuating pairing and subgroupings occur. There are struggles for power and control	Facilitator subgrouping	*'Top–bottom' stage* Characterised by conflict and the struggle for control. The facilitator is rejected and alliances form between group members
Performing Characterised by working on the task. The group becomes self-sufficient and functions independently of the facilitator	*Mutuality phase* All members of the group are included. Everyone is in touch with everyone else. Empathy deepens	Facilitator	*'Near–far' stage* Characterised by intimacy and the formation of relationships between group members

Wilfred Bion, who trained as a Freudian psychoanalyst, took just such an approach. For Bion (1959), the conscious life of the group, what he called the 'work group', is concerned with the task that it came together to carry out. In a clinical supervision group this task is, obviously, that of giving and receiving clinical supervision. However, he claimed that every group also has an unconscious life, and in this respect is what he called a 'basic assumption group', concerned with maintaining the group, with keeping it alive, and with responding to perceived threats to its integrity. In any group, then, what appears to be happening on the surface, the work that the group is doing, is not the whole picture. The group is also functioning on a deeper level, unbeknown to any of its individual members, according to the basic assumptions it is making about the world and the perceived threats coming both from inside and outside the group. As we have said, this 'group mentality' is held collectively by the group and is not usually present in the conscious minds of the individual group members. Furthermore, the group mentality might not correspond to the conscious mental states of *any* of the group members. For Bion, then, the group truly has a life of its own.

From Bion's experience of working with groups, he detected three basic assumptions that groups make about the perceived threats to their existence. Firstly, there is the basic assumption of dependency. For Bion, one way in which the group might unconsciously deal with perceived threats is by seeking a source of security, a 'magical' person who will supply all its needs, what Bion called a 'group deity'. The group usually turns to the facilitator to perform this function, with the assumption that when things are not running smoothly, the facilitator can make everything better. If the facilitator refuses to take on this role, the group might turn to another person, or indeed someone might nominate herself for the role which in turn can lead to rejection or scapegoating of the facilitator. Inevitably, however, the 'group deity' will not be able to meet the expectations of the group, and will usually end up by being rejected.

The second basic assumption is fight/flight, in which the group unconsciously attempts to deal with its problems either by attacking them head-on or by running away from them. This is a very 'black and white' group mentality in which all other solutions apart from fight or flight are rejected. Furthermore, the welfare of individual group members is of secondary consideration. In fight mode, the problems of the group might be projected onto a particular group member, who is then scapegoated; by attacking that particular person, the group believes that it can magically destroy the problem. In flight mode, individual members might be abandoned or even expelled from the group; by ignoring the problems of a particular person, it is believed that the problems of the entire group will disappear. The paramount concern is for the survival of the group rather than of its individual members, and this scapegoating or rejection can extend to the group facilitator if she is not seen to be mobilising the group to attack or coordinating its retreat.

The third basic assumption is pairing, in which the group behaves as if it will somehow 'give birth' to a saviour, who will then provide a redeeming 'big idea', through a teaming-up of two of its members (Bion's Freudian training is definitely showing here!). The pair can either consist of two group members or might include the facilitator, and is often interpreted by other group members as sexual in nature (which, considering its underpinning rationale of procreation, is hardly surprising!). Such pairings can be quite creative in the short term, but are largely unproductive since the group saviour is inevitably not forthcoming. It must be emphasised again that all of these basic assumptions are part of the *unconscious* life of the group, and the group members do not consciously and individually decide to act in a cruel or uncaring way to one another, anymore than you or I consciously decide what to dream at night.

To summarise, group supervision is sometimes employed as a more cost-effective alternative to individual supervision, but it is, in fact, something quite different and can offer far more than merely supervision with an audience. In particular, the transpersonal model regards a group as a living, thinking and growing entity that is more than, and other than, the sum of the individuals who comprise it. Not only do groups grow and develop over time, but also, like people, they need to reach a certain level of maturity before they are able to do any meaningful work. Furthermore, groups work not only on an overt conscious level, but also covertly and unconsciously, particularly when under threat. These unconscious group dynamics often manifest as individual pathologies, in which particular members (often the facilitator) are singled out for attack by the group as a whole. Left to their own devices, groups can cause distress to their members and often tear themselves apart.

 FURTHER READING

Most of the basic texts on group dynamics and group process are now rather elderly, but some remain as relevant today as when they were first written. Bion (1959) is that rare thing: a source book of major importance and influence that is also very readable even for the beginner to group theory. Bion's model is nicely summarised in Wright (1989), which also deals with Tuckman, Levine and several other theorists in a concise and informative way. Wright is also one of the few writers on groupwork with a nursing background. For the more advanced reader, Agazarian and Peters (1981) and Yalom (1970) both discuss group dynamics in considerable depth.

Agazarian, Y. and Peters, R. (1981) *The Visible and Invisible Group*, London: Routledge & Kegan Paul.
Bion, W.R. (1959) *Experiences in Groups*, London: Tavistock.
Wright, H. (1989) *Groupwork: Perspectives and Practice*, Harrow: Scutari Press.
Yalom, I.D. (1970) *The Theory and Practice of Group Psychotherapy*, New York: Basic Books.

The dangers of unfacilitated groups cannot be overstated. In this respect, you might like to think of group process and group dynamics as a useful tool for achieving specific aims, for example, as a pair of scissors. Like most tools, there are certain dangers in using it, although when used properly it can be extremely powerful. A new and inexperienced group can therefore be viewed as a young child with a pair of sharp scissors, who realises neither the full benefits nor the dangers of what she has in her hands. Unless properly supervised, there are bound to be injuries, either to the child herself or to whoever comes near her.

■ Establishing the group

The remainder of this chapter is concerned with the practical issues involved in setting up and facilitating a supervision group. Like most practical skills, group facilitation can only be learnt by direct involvement in a group, and most of the reflective exercises which follow assume that you are participating in some kind of group experience, either as a facilitator or as a group member.

A number of decisions have to be taken before you start your supervision group. Firstly, you need to decide on the basic model that your group will be following. Will it be an intrapersonal group in which you will conduct individual supervision with each group member in turn, an interpersonal group in which you will facilitate group members to supervise one another, or a transpersonal group in which your main focus will be on group process and dynamics? This is a major consideration that will influence almost every other decision you take, and so you should reflect on the three models very carefully before deciding which feels right for you.

☐ Issues of group membership

Your next decision concerns who will be invited to join the group. This might not be your decision to take, since the membership of supervision groups is often predetermined. For example, you might be facilitating a group for a specific and well-defined clinical team in which everyone is expected to attend. However, when you do have some control over group membership, there are several well-established criteria that you should consider.

Firstly, there is the issue of whether membership to the group should be open or closed. If your group is open, new members are able to join during the life of the group, and you might suggest or encourage members to leave before the group has run its predetermined course. The advantage of a closed group (that is, one with a fixed and constant membership) is that feelings of safety and group identity are established more quickly than if members are constantly coming and going. Furthermore, the group progresses more rapidly since it does not have to backtrack when a new member joins, either deliberately to explain the group rules to the new member, or unconsciously in terms of regression to an earlier stage of development. The main disadvantage of closed groups, however, is that all groups suffer from attrition; over the life of any group, people will leave for a number of practical, personal and psychological reasons, and so it is possible that the size of the group might become economically or functionally nonviable before the group has reached the end of its natural life.

This brings us to the next important consideration: that of optimum group size. Brown (1989) considered anything from three to 12 members to be the workable range for most groups, but pointed out that larger groups allow for the possibility of significantly more one-to-one relationships (three pairs in a three-person group compared to 36 in a nine-person group), a greater likelihood of sub-grouping, an increase in psychological freedom (with the increased possibility of quiet members being able to blend into the background), and more protracted problem-solving, but with better quality solutions. He went on to observe that different kinds of groups have different optimum numbers, with five to six being ideal for 'the more therapeutic person-centred type of short-term closed group' (Brown, 1989), whereas larger numbers are more appropriate for problem-solving, structured activities and open groups, where the tendency to sub-grouping can be used productively by dividing the group for certain tasks. Similarly, Nichols and Jenkinson (1991) observed that when numbers fall below six, the group usually adopts an intrapersonal model, or what they referred to as 'an observed personal counselling session'. In deciding on the number of members for your group, you should also take into account the almost inevitable dropout rate, and allow for two to three above your optimum number, especially in a closed group.

As well as deciding on the size of your group, you will also need to give some thought to its composition. Firstly, you will need to think about whether the group is to be composed of strangers who do not have any work or social contact outside of the group, or a team of people who work and/or socialise together. In groups where members already know each other, if existing relationships are open and positive then they will usually contribute positively to the group, whereas problematic and destructive outside relationships will inevitably lead to disruptions and possibly to problems, particularly in a new group. Similarly, some members of the group might well have an outside relationship with the facilitator, and this might prove difficult where there is a power differential in that relationship, for example, if the facilitator is the boss or the assessor of one or more group members (or vice versa).

Secondly, there is the issue of balance within the group. This is a particularly relevant issue for multidisciplinary groups, of groups comprised of different staff grades, or of groups whose members work with widely differing types of clients, but also applies to the age, gender and culture of group members. For example, should you aim for a homogeneous group in which all members are similar in the above respects, or should you select a heterogeneous group that aims for diversity rather than conformity? As you might imagine, there is no simple answer. Homogeneity is necessary for group identity and cohesion, for what Bion referred to as the tasks of the basic assumption group (see above), whereas heterogeneity is important for creativity and forward movement, what Bion referred to as the tasks of the work group. This is Redl's law of optimum distance, which states that groups should be 'homogeneous enough to ensure stability, and heterogeneous enough to ensure vitality' (Redl, 1951).

Expanding upon this, Bertcher and Maple (1977) argued that groups should be homogeneous on descriptive attributes such as age, gender and culture, and heterogeneous on behavioural attributes such as character type, extraversion/introversion and leader/follower characteristics. Clearly, such decisions might be out of your control, but a good rule of thumb is to try to avoid a group in which there is one person who is too far removed from all the others on any of the above attributes. Thus, do not include someone who is much older or younger than everyone else, a lone social worker in a group of nurses, or a ward manager in a group of support workers.

☐ Issues of time

Another important issue to be considered in establishing the group is that of time. Just as the membership of the group can be either open or closed, so too can its life-span. Open groups run indefinitely with no predetermined end point, although the life-span of open groups is often renegotiated at certain fixed intervals, such as every 20 meetings. It is possible to run a group of open life-span but closed membership, although it is likely that such a group will become smaller and smaller until it is no longer viable. It is more usual, then, for open life-span groups to have open membership (but not necessarily vice versa). Closed life-span groups can be of almost any length from six to 60 meetings, but you should be aware of allowing enough time for the group to progress through the early formative stages of development in order that there are enough remaining sessions for it to carry out its work. In general, short life-span groups tend to resolve issues of forming, storming and norming more quickly than longer life-span groups. For example, a six-session group might feel the urgency of time and be up and working after only two or three sessions, whereas a 20-session group might take the luxury of seven or eight sessions to resolve its forming, storming and norming issues.

The other major time issue is that of frequency and duration, of how often and how long the sessions should be. This issue might not be resolvable before the group commences, as most healthcare workers are busy people who can only spare limited time away from their work. In an ideal world, the importance of supervision will be recognised by someone in the organisation with budgetary control, and provision will be made for time out from clinical work or for paid overtime to attend supervision. However, in the real world of healthcare provision, the frequency and duration of sessions is best negotiated with the group members. Generally speaking, groups should last for at least an hour, although the length of intrapersonal groups, in which each individual member is given personal supervision in turn, will depend on the number of supervisees in the group. Similarly, if your group includes interactive exercises or other structured activities, then you might find that you need at least 90 minutes, and possibly two hours for each session.

The frequency of your group is equally negotiable, but, ideally, you should aim for meetings at least fortnightly, and preferably weekly. Some groups find that they can meet only monthly, and while this might be fine for training or therapy groups, busy practitioners barely have a day in which issues for supervision are not raised. Some of these issues might keep for a month, but many will require far more urgent attention. If a compromise has to be made, aim for shorter but more frequent meetings rather than longer but less frequent ones.

Finally, while still on the issue of time, you should not underestimate your own time commitment as a group facilitator. As well as the one hour per week (or whatever) during which you are actually facilitating the group, you should also allow time for initial planning of the group as a whole, preparation time for each session, time to review and reflect on each session, time for writing up notes (if appropriate) and, most importantly, time for your own supervision on your role as group facilitator.

☐ Other resource issues

We have already briefly mentioned the resources of your time as group facilitator and the time of the supervisees. Other staffing issues include a decision on the number of facilitators required (one is usual, but you might find that in a large group or where you aim to do work in subgroups, that you need some help), issues of time and money for your own training as a group supervisor, and possible payment for an expert in group work to provide your own supervision. This is all very costly, and if you (or your organisation) are considering group supervision as a cheap option to individual supervision, you should perhaps think again.

As well as staff resource issues, you also need to think about accommodation for the sessions. A quiet, well-ventilated and adequately heated room is the minimum requirement. Seating should be comfortable and, if possible, all the chairs should be of roughly the same design and arranged in a circle. You might also wish to provide some luxuries such as coffee-making facilities, as well as props such as flip-chart pads and pens for any written exercises and group brainstorms.

The location of the venue is also very important. For example, should the group be held in a room in the workplace where interruptions are possible, and which might have an emotional resonance for some of the supervisees, or should you opt for a less convenient but more neutral venue to which some of the group members might have to travel, and which might incur a hire cost? Connected to this is the issue of boundary protection, that is, the extent to which you are able to shut out the outside world and have a space that is truly your own for the duration of the meeting. Compromises are often necessary over the venue, but it is an extremely important issue, and you should strive for the best possible location.

■ Being a facilitator

Most of the research suggests that group facilitators are made rather than born. Successful group facilitation requires a combination of skills, values and attitudes that are partly acquired early in life, can partly be taught by reading or by attending courses, and are partly picked up on the job through experience. Clearly, neither this book nor any other can help you with the former; there are some skills, values and attitudes which have to be gained early in life, and if these are deficient, then you will probably never be a successful group supervisor. If, for example, you are overly domineering, do not listen to other people's points of view or are prejudiced against certain groups of people, then you should not be involved in group supervision; indeed, you should probably not be involved in healthcare at all. However, most group supervision skills and values can be learnt, and many of the caring and relationship-forming skills and attitudes that you employ as a health care worker are also applicable to group facilitation.

☐   Values and attitudes

Nichols and Jenkinson (1991) identified two important attitudes to be held by any group facilitator. Firstly, she must value and understand the nature of personal change and growth, and secondly she must be open to her own feelings and those of others. They posed five questions that any prospective group facilitator should ask herself:

- Do you know that you are aware of and open to the flow of feelings in your daily life – do others confirm this to be so?
- Are you able to say that you value your own feelings and allow their expression rather than striving to mask them?
- Are you able to share your feelings with a trusted companion without being defensive?
- Are you able to receive and experience the feelings of others in a relaxed, accepting manner without wanting immediately to placate, soothe or distract them from expressing feeling?
- Do you judge that if a person expresses or 'acts out' feeling in a group you will be able to allow this to unfold without a panicky need to take control and return to more matter-of-fact issues?

(Nichols and Jenkinson, 1991: 46)

 REFLECTIVE WRITING

Think carefully about each of the above five questions. Reflect on your own strengths and weaknesses and write a short paragraph on each, noting where you would have something to offer a group and where you need to do some personal work. Try to identify some possible sources of help with your areas of weakness.

If you can honestly answer 'yes' to all of the above questions (and few people can!), then you probably possess Carl Rogers' three 'therapeutic conditions' of empathy, genuineness and respect, which he claimed were necessary and sufficient to bring about therapeutic change in both individual and group work (Rogers, 1961). Empathy is the sensing of the feelings being experienced by the other person, and the communication of those feelings back to her. Genuineness means being yourself, not putting up a professional front or personal façade, and expressing to the other person exactly what you are experiencing from moment to moment. Finally, respect, or what Rogers sometimes referred to as unconditional positive regard, involves communicating a positive, acceptant attitude towards the other person, whatever she is expressing at the time. That is not to say that you should deny your own feelings of anger, revulsion, or whatever at what she is saying or doing, but rather that you accept and prize her as a person even though you might disapprove of her words or actions.

☐   Facilitation skills

As well as the above attitudes, there are also a number of skills related to group facilitation. Brown (1989) suggested that these skills can be exercised in four directions, namely facilitator–group member, member–member, facilitator–group and facilitator–external environment (Figure 5.1).

Facilitator–group member skills are employed when the facilitator needs to be able to communicate on an individual level, and are the most often used skills in the intrapersonal group model. They are also employed extensively in the first stage of group development (compare the diagram of facilitator–group member skills in Figure 5.1 with Levine's parallel phase in Table 5.1). Member–member skills are employed to facilitate group participants to communicate with each other. They are the most often used skills in the interpersonal group model, and also correspond to Levine's mutuality phase (Table 5.1). Facilitator–group skills recognise that the group also has an identity of its own, and are the

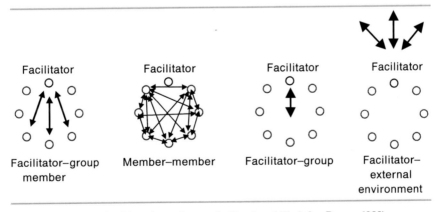

| Facilitator | Facilitator | Facilitator | Facilitator |
| Facilitator–group member | Member–member | Facilitator–group | Facilitator–external environment |

Figure 5.1   Directions of group facilitation skills (after Brown, 1989)

key skills in the transpersonal group model. Finally, facilitator–external environment skills acknowledge the fact that the group does not exist in a vacuum, and are utilised most often in the early stages of establishing the group, and also in the mature working stage when disclosures by group members might need to be communicated to, and negotiated with, the outside world.

Brown (1989) also distinguished between general and specific skills, where the former are the skills associated with group process (that is, with Bion's basic assumption group), and the latter are associated with the group task (that is, with Bion's work group). In our case, the skills necessary for the work group are those basic supervision skills outlined in the previous chapter, and so we will focus here on the general skills of group facilitation.

Brown identified four basic sets of general group skills, which he labelled group-creation skills, group-maintenance skills, task-achievement skills and culture-development skills. These titles are fairly self-explanatory, and correspond roughly to the skills identified by Wright (1989) of conducting, modelling, following, interpreting and analysing, and also to Nichols and Jenkinson's (1991) three key skills for group facilitation, namely observational skills, the ability to 'take it all in'; analytic skills, making sense of what you have taken in; and work skills, keeping the group focused on their aims and goals. These skills will be explored in more detail later in the chapter.

☐   Leadership styles

A final consideration for the facilitator of a newly-formed group is the leadership style that you intend to adopt. Much of the early research in this area identified three styles of leadership; namely, autocratic, democratic and *laissez-faire*. Lippitt and White (1953) found that democratic and autocratic leaders were both effective in task-achievement and productivity, but that a democratic style produced less dependence and resentment and greater satisfaction for group members. However, later studies suggested that the situation and function of the group are important variables, and that different leadership styles should be employed in different situations. Fiedler (1967), for example, distinguished between task leadership and group maintenance leadership, the former of which requires a more directive, cognitive and information-giving approach, whereas the latter requires a facilitative, empathic and affective approach. This model bears distinct similarities to Bion's work group and basic assumption group model discussed earlier, and suggests that the effective leader requires different skills at different points in the group's life.

Adair (1968) offered an expanded version of Fiedler's model, which included a recognition of the needs of individual group members as well as group needs and task needs, and claimed that it is the leader's role to recognise these three continuously fluctuating and overlapping sets of needs and orchestrate an appropriate response. In particular, he found that a democratic style is usually preferable, but when dealing with urgent task needs, a more autocratic approach is most effective and is often appreciated by group members. Bond and Holland (1998), writing specifically about group supervision, made a similar claim that group facilitators should move gradually from short periods of being directive early on, to a predominantly 'space-giving' model of facilitation in which the group members communicate and cooperate with very little intervention from the facilitator.

We have seen, then, that there are three essential prerequisites for group facilitation. Firstly, we need the right attitude. We should be open to and in touch with our own feelings and those of the group members, we should be honest in the expression of our feelings, and should be non-judgemental when group members express their feelings. Attitudes can be cultivated and changed, so we should not despair if we think that we do not live up to this ideal. Secondly, certain skills are required, including specific supervision skills and general group facilitation skills. The former were covered in the previous chapter, and the latter include the skills of maintaining and facilitating the group, of observing, interpreting and feeding back group content, and of dealing with group difficulties. All of these will be explored in more detail later in the chapter. Finally, it is necessary to be familiar with a range of leadership styles, particularly the democratic and the autocratic, and know when and how to employ them to maximum effect. These attitudes and skills cannot be attained by reading a book, and there is no real alternative to practical experience for the would-be group facilitator. As we discussed in Chapter 1, you can only gain experiential knowledge such as that required to facilitate a group by critically reflecting on the process of actually doing it.

■ Starting the group

There are two major tasks to be accomplished in the opening meetings of a new group: the first is to clarify the aims of the group, and the second is to agree on the ground rules.

☐ Aims

Some groups have very broad aims, such as personal growth and development, or for members to gain insight about themselves. Supervision groups, however, usually have clearly defined task aims as well as less explicit group and individual aims. We shall start by examining the aims of the group in relation to the task for which it was convened. It is clearly not sufficient merely to dismiss the task aim as to provide supervision for the group, since the aims of supervision are themselves broad and varied, and can, for example, be directed towards providing support for the supervisee, as a means to personal, group or institutional change, as a form of education, or as an approach to problem-solving.

As facilitator, your first task is to explore exactly why the group members have joined, and what they expect to gain from group supervision. It is likely that different members will be hoping to achieve different goals, and some negotiation will probably be necessary. You should also explore openly and honestly with the group the question of whose aims it has been established to meet, which might include those of the organisation, of the supervisees or of the facilitator. For example, it might be that the organisation has very specific expectations for the group as a whole, which have to take priority over the aims of individual group members. There is nothing intrinsically wrong with this, as long as those aims are explicitly stated, and no attempt is made by the facilitator to impose them covertly without the knowledge of the group members. If, on the other hand, it is being left to the group to negotiate its own aims, then this should be done as democratically as possible, so that all the group members feel that they can 'sign up' to what is decided, even if it was not exactly what they anticipated. For example, some members of the group might see the aim of supervision not only to deal with work problems, but also to address personal issues if they impinge on work. However, unless all members are willing to bring personal issues to the group, resentment will quickly develop on both sides, with some members feeling that others are not contributing fully, and some feeling that others are taking up valuable group time with irrelevant personal issues.

□ Ground rules

If the negotiation of group aims is the first task need of the group, then establishing the ground rules is the first maintenance need. The first and most fundamental ground rule that the group will have to establish concerns confidentiality. This is a particularly important issue for supervision groups of healthcare professionals, since there is not only the problem of what any group member (including the facilitator) does with personal information that other group members might disclose about themselves, but also of what they might disclose about clients and their treatment. Both of these problems have professional as well as ethical implications. For example, what are you to do if a group member discloses that she has a criminal record for theft? Alternatively, what if she recounts an instance of unprofessional conduct? In either case you have a professional duty (and perhaps a moral duty) to discuss these revelations outside the group.

Clearly, then, in a group of this kind, confidentiality cannot be absolute. Rather, the aim of the ground rule should be to establish the limits of confidentiality and to agree on the circumstances when the facilitator (or indeed, any other group member) might communicate information to people outside the group. It is vitally important that these circumstances are made absolutely clear to every group member, since this allows them to make an informed choice about what they disclose in the group. Similarly, if it appears that someone is about to make a disclosure that might need to be communicated outside the group, then the facilitator has a responsibility to remind her of the limits to confidentiality so that she can decide whether or not to continue with her revelation.

Fortunately, big disclosures of this nature do not arise very often, and it is the smaller day-to-day issues that are usually more pressing. Most groups establish a rule that, in general, these day-to-day issues are not taken outside of the group, although the boundaries between group business and non-group business are sometimes rather fuzzy. For example, a personal issue between two group members might be brought to the group for discussion. Does it then become a group issue that can no longer be discussed outside the group by the people involved? Such a rule would clearly be debilitating, and might prevent issues being brought to the group. The usual solution to this problem is not to ban discussion of issues previously brought to the group, but to have an agreement that, when such issues are discussed, those discussions will be reported back at the next group meeting.

Apart from a rule about confidentiality, other ground rules are largely a matter of individual choice. Bond and Holland (1998) give examples of ground rules relating to autonomy and choice, to speaking for oneself, to being non-judgemental, to group commitment and to reciprocity. For some groups, these rules are largely tacit, whereas other groups prefer to state them explicitly. The problem with tacit rules is that they only become an issue when someone violates one of them and then denies that such a rule exists. For this reason, probably the most important ground rule to establish is the one that says that all rules are open to renegotiation, and that new rules can be established any time that the group feels is necessary.

 DISCUSSION POINT

Most informal groups have tacit ground rules that are known to all the members but never explicitly discussed. With a colleague, think of a group of which you are both members (for example, a ward team) and try to uncover the unspoken ground rules of the group. What would be the benefits or problems of making them overt?

■ Running the group

In many ways, everything that we have discussed up to this point has been merely a preliminary to the real business of running the group. We have already touched on the question of what makes a good facilitator, and we shall now apply that to the broader issue of the group programme, which Brown (1989) has defined as 'what the group does as a means of trying to achieve its aims'.

□ The group programme

The major decision when deciding on the group programme is the degree of structure that you wish to impose. At one extreme, some groups are completely unstructured inasmuch as they are primarily 'talking groups' which focus on members discussing supervision issues with relatively little intervention from the facilitator. At the other extreme, some groups are so full of games, exercises and role plays that the structure is in danger of overwhelming the content, and there is little scope for responding to issues brought to the group by its members. A good compromise is to start the group with one or two exercises as a warm-up, and to use them as a springboard for raising supervision issues. This, of course, applies only to inter- and transpersonal models of group facilitation, since the intrapersonal model is not concerned with the group *per se*, but only with a collection of individual supervisees. However, the most important consideration is flexibility, and if someone comes to the group with a burning issue it would be rather insensitive to press on with your preplanned warming-up exercises, which would in any case hardly be needed.

Space does not permit a detailed discussion of the many warming-up exercises available to the group facilitator, but some source books are given below in the Further Reading box. When planning warming-up exercises, however, it is useful to bear in mind that they serve two functions. The first is to ease group participants into the session, to loosen them up in preparation for the real work of the group. These 'ice-breaker' games might involve name-learning exercises in the forming stage of the group and trust exercises later in the storming and norming stages. These ice-breakers are often frivolous in nature, and might involve some kind of physical activity such as calling out a person's name as you throw a ball to them, or guiding a blindfolded member of the group round the room.

The second function of these exercises is to get people talking about supervisory issues, and this usually entails either a talking or writing activity such as dividing into pairs and discussing something that happened at work, or carrying out a structured reflective writing task (see Chapter 3) and sharing it with the group. As we have already mentioned, these exercises are only necessary if nothing is immediately forthcoming from the group, and even then, some facilitators prefer to work with the ensuing silence rather than deliberately breaking it with an exercise.

Once the group is working, the aim of the facilitator is largely to ensure that it continues to work. We shall discuss how the facilitator manages this process with reference to Nichols and Jenkinson's three key skills of observation, analysis and work which we briefly mentioned earlier.

Observational skills are an important aspect of your job as facilitator, and involve not only taking in everything that is happening in the group, but also communicating your interest and attention back to the group members so that they feel valued and respected. In an intrapersonal group your observations will focus mainly on individual group members during your interactions with them. You will be attending not only to the content of what they are saying, but to their non-verbal behaviour and paralanguage; for example, their tone of voice, their posture, their facial expression and so on. In an interpersonal group your main focus will be on the communications between group members, with far less regard for content, which will be addressed mainly by other group members. You will be observing who is talking to whom, who is the focus of discussion and

FURTHER READING

There are a number of very useful and practical books on group games and exercises. Probably the most well-known is *Gamesters Handbook* by Brandes and Phillips, along with its sequel, *Gamesters Handbook Two*. These books offer a practical guide to facilitating games for social and personal development, and between them contain over 200 games, including some specifically aimed at group leaders. In a similar vein is Bond's *Games for Social and Life Skills*, which has an excellent collection of ice-breakers, self-awareness, social skills, communication and trust games, and is a good starting point for anyone new to group games. You might also wish to explore *Effective Use of Games and Simulation* by Van Ments and Hearnden, which includes games to promote change and address issues of conflict and prejudice, and *The Effective Use of Role-play*, also by Van Ments, which has useful chapters on setting up and running role-play exercises, on debriefing, and on other experiential methods such as psychodrama, sociodrama and encounter groups. Other books worth considering are those by Davison and Gordon and Thatcher and Robinson.

Bond, T. (1986) *Games for Social and Life Skills*, London: Hutchinson.
Brandes, D. (1984) *Gamesters' Handbook Two*, London: Hutchinson.
Brandes, D. and Phillips, H. (1979) *Gamesters' Handbook*, London: Hutchinson.
Davison, A. and Gordon, P. (1978) *Games and Simulations in Action*, London: The Woburn Press.
Thatcher, D. and Robinson, J. (1984) *Perspectives on Gaming and Simulation 8: Business, Health and Nursing Education*, Loughborough: SAGSET.
Van Ments, M. (1989) *The Effective Use of Role-play*, rev. edn, London: Kogan Page.
Van Ments, M. and Hearnden, K. (1985), *Effective Use of Games and Simulation*, Loughborough: SAGSET.

who is excluded, and you might attempt to record these observations as sociograms (which are similar to the diagrams in Table 5.1 and Figure 5.1). Finally, in a transpersonal group you will be observing neither individual members nor the interactions between them, but rather the 'group mood', that is, whether the group is relaxed, anxious, hostile or whatever. This requires a great deal of sensitivity and empathy, since the mood of the group is often far less tangible than the mood of its members, and might not, in fact, correspond to how any of the individuals who comprise it are feeling at the time.

Observation of what is going on in the group is not, of itself, sufficient for good facilitation, and you should also be attempting to make sense of the group behaviour. This involves the skill of analysis, and the question you should be asking yourself is: 'What is going on here?' In an intrapersonal group, your focus will be on each individual as you interact with them, and you will be offering an individual interpretation and analysis of their verbal and non-verbal behaviour. For example, you might notice that a particular individual appears anxious while she is relating what seems to be a relatively minor incident, and you will be making hypotheses about the unconscious reasons for her anxiety. In an interpersonal group, you will be attempting to understand the communications between group members, and asking yourself why certain patterns are being established, and why, for example, a usually popular group member is being ignored whilst a quiet member is the centre of attention. And in a transpersonal group, you will be attempting to make sense of the group mood in terms of the underlying basic assumption group, and asking yourself what is going on in the group unconscious.

Through using your skills of observation and analysis, you will then be able to facilitate the work of the group, that is, the task of supervision. In an intrapersonal group, this will involve a direct supervisory input with each member in turn. A facilitator who employs this model might start with a particular person, and work around the group one by one, or else allow the group members to self-select. There is often congruence between the style in which a group is facilitated and the way in which supervision is conducted. Thus, if she chooses to facilitate the group in an intrapersonal way, then it is likely that she will conduct supervision based on the same model. For example, if a group member brings to supervision a difficulty he is having with a work colleague, the facilitator would explore the problem predominantly from the intra-psychic perspective of the supervisee by examining difficulties he has with other people in general. At times, she might invite other members to comment on specific issues, but the supervision would come predominantly from the facilitator herself. Indeed, the term 'facilitator' is not particularly descriptive of this role, and 'director' or 'leader' might be more appropriate.

In contrast, the interpersonal group facilitator is, as her title suggests, very much involved in facilitating group members to share and communicate with each other, and it is likely that this philosophy will similarly extend to her model of supervision. In the above example, then, she would not only attempt to facilitate other group members to provide the supervision, but would conceptualise the problem in terms of the interpersonal relationship between the supervisee and her work colleague. The fundamental belief underpinning this model of facilitation is that group members have the skills, experience and knowledge to offer peer supervision, and the facilitator's job is to enable that process to happen. Her direct interventions in the supervisory process will therefore be limited to helping group members when they get stuck, to correcting dangerous or obviously wrong suggestions from other group members, and to ensuring that the group sticks to its business. For her, a successful group is one in which she says almost nothing, what Bond and Holland (1998) refer to as a 'space-giving' mode of facilitation.

The role of the transpersonal group facilitator is similar to that of the interpersonal facilitator, except that she is more likely to interpret work group issues in terms of the underlying basic assumption group, and to address them accordingly. In the earlier example of the supervisee who is having difficulties with a work colleague, she would conceptualise the issue not as a personal problem for the supervisee, nor as an interpersonal problem between the two protagonists, but as the symptom of an underlying problem in the staff team as a whole. She would therefore attempt to resolve the issue by drawing parallels between the unconscious life of the supervision group and that of the clinical team, and explore how problems in each might manifest in term of a conflict between two of the group members. Her aim is therefore not to intervene directly in the business of the work group, but rather to explore the unconscious motivations for the conscious work group decisions. A summary of these three positions can be found in Table 5.2.

As we pointed out earlier, a book such as this can only take you so far with your practice of group facilitation. It can provide you with what we referred to in

Table 5.2 Models of group supervision

	Intrapersonal	*Interpersonal*	*Transpersonal*
Observational skills	Observation of the verbal and non-verbal behaviour and paralanguage of individual supervisees	Observation of interpersonal patterns of communication rather than individual behaviour	Observation of the group mood and other aspects of group behaviour
Analytic skills	Individual interpretation and analysis of verbal and non-verbal behaviour	Analysis of communication patterns	Analysis of the group mood in terms of the underlying basic assumption group
Work skills	Direct personal supervision which focuses on the issues for the supervisee	Supervision by group members which focuses on the interactions between the supervisee and others in the work setting	Supervision by the group as a whole which focuses on parallels between the underlying processes in the supervision group and those in the work team

Chapter 1 as scientific theoretical knowledge in the form of models and theories, and to some extent with scientific practical knowledge in the form of guidelines for practice, based on those models and theories. However, you will only acquire the experiential practical knowledge that characterises the expert practitioner by actually facilitating a group. Furthermore, the experiential theoretical knowledge of the advanced practitioner only comes about by critically reflecting on your experience, preferably with a supervisor who is skilled and trained in group work.

 REFLECTIVE WRITING

If you are already part of a supervision group, either as a facilitator or a supervisee, write a paragraph about how you (or your facilitator) exercise the above skills. Does your group follow one of the above models, or is it more eclectic? What are the advantages and disadvantages of a 'pure' approach to facilitation rather than an eclectic mixture of all three?

☐ Group difficulties

It can be seen that with both the inter- and the transpersonal models the main work of the facilitator takes place when something is going wrong, and so we will now briefly consider some of the problems to which you might need to respond. Brown (1989) identified two possible causes of group difficulties. Firstly, individual members might find themselves in problematic roles, either of their own making or because of others. Individuals take on and reject roles throughout the life of the group, and sometimes these roles are positive and facilitate the development of the group, whereas at other times they impede the group. People tend to become stuck in a role for one of two reasons. Sometimes a role is imposed on them by the group in order to fulfil a group need, for example, the role of the scapegoat, who is the repository for all of the group's problems. At other times the individual adopts a role that serves a useful short-term purpose such as avoiding a painful situation, but which is harmful or restrictive in the longer term, such as the role of 'silent member' who might have withdrawn from the life of the group when under pressure but now finds it difficult to get back in. Other typical problematic roles include the 'group patient', who can always be relied upon to bring along her problems so that other group members are not forced to examine theirs; the 'group harmoniser', who smoothes over group conflicts so that difficult and painful issues are never properly dealt with; and the 'group jester', who turns difficult issues into jokes to avoid the group having to confront them.

DISCUSSION POINT

With a colleague, brainstorm some of the ways in which you might disrupt a group of which you are a member.

_____

Your list might have included some or all of the following:

- overt or covert criticism of the facilitator or other members;
- challenging the value of the group;
- staying silent;
- dominating the group;
- intellectualising;
- trivialising;
- scapegoating (or becoming the scapegoat);
- fidgeting, coughing, passing cigarettes or sweets;
- monopolising group time; or
- seeking help but rejecting all solutions.

The second cause of group difficulties identified by Brown is when the group as a whole becomes stuck in some way. Whereas individual problems are largely symptoms of issues between group members, whole group problems are usually indicative of disputes between the group and the facilitator. For example, when your group suddenly becomes quiet, apathetic, depressed or otherwise resistant, it is probably trying to tell you something, although if Bion is to be believed, it might not consciously know just what that 'something' is. If you feel under threat from your group, you should bear in mind the following guidelines:

- Don't be defensive when criticised.
- Don't put group members down (tempting though it might be at times!).
- Don't compete with leadership challenges.
- Build on support that exists in the group.
- Don't ignore the fact that the group is not working effectively.

The most important thing to remember, however, is not to take it personally. It is probable that the group is not unhappy with you as a person, but with your role as facilitator.

Most whole group problems, then, are concerned in one way or another with issues of authority and leadership, either with too much of it or with not enough, but whatever the problem the solution is usually the same and involves bringing the issues into the open so that they can be discussed. Once again the way that this is done will depend primarily on the model of group facilitation that is being employed. We will take the problem of a quiet group member as an example. In an intrapersonal group, the facilitator will address the individual with the problem, saying something such as: 'You seem to be very quiet today Andrea, I wonder if something is bothering you'. In an interpersonal group, the focus will be on the other group members and their role in initiating or perpetuating the situation, and the facilitator will say something like: 'Brian and Chris seem very talkative today, and perhaps that is preventing some of the other members from talking'. Finally, in a transpersonal group the focus will be on the group as an individual entity, and the facilitator will address her remarks to the group as a whole, saying something such as: 'I see that the group is allowing Della to remain silent today. What do you think might be the reason for this?'

REFLECTIVE WRITING

Think of a difficult individual that you have previously encountered in a group, either as a facilitator or a group member. Write a paragraph in response to each of the following questions:

What effect did the difficult group member have on you; what feelings did you have; how did you respond?

How did the difficult group member affect other group members and the task of the group?

Did the individual get some kind of pay off for their difficult behaviour? Can you identify what it was?

☐ Ending the group

Except for open life-span groups, all groups have a fixed life and a predetermined end-point. As Douglas (1976) observed, 'the termination of a group is part of its developmental sequence', and should therefore be anticipated and prepared for in advance. For some groups, the termination will coincide with the completion of the task for which it was established, and in these cases, the ending signals a job well done. In the case of supervision groups, however, the task must continue after the group has ended, and the termination is often seen in a more negative light, as the loss of a valuable support mechanism, almost as a bereavement. At the level of the whole group, Garland *et al.* (1965) noted a number of typical group reactions to termination that bear a striking resemblance to the grieving process, including denial that the facilitator ever mentioned that the group was going to finish, regression to an earlier stage of development or into chaos, and rose-tinted reminiscence about the early days of the group. Similarly, at an individual level, the end of the group often triggers thought about other bereavements that group members have suffered in the past, including some that might not have been fully resolved at the time. The end of the group is a potentially traumatic time, and it is therefore important for it to be well-planned and presented in a positive light, 'as a symbol of growth rather than loss' (Solomon 1968, cited in Douglas, 1976: 168).

Nichols and Jenkinson (1991) suggested three tasks for the final session of a group:

- For the group members to reflect on the aims and outcomes of the group by discovering what each has achieved since the group started, and hence to remind themselves just how far they had come.
- To reflect on the experience of being in the group by remembering how it had been along the way.
- To notice and share how they are now feeling at the end of the life of the group, to say their goodbyes, and to move on.

Nichols and Jenkinson went on to suggest a method of addressing these tasks that was both simple and effective:

To assist in this task the leader was directive at this point and invited members to sit quietly for a while and try to recapture the way they had felt when first

---

 FURTHER READING

There are, as far as we are aware, no books written specifically about group supervision in nursing and healthcare. However, Hawkins and Shohet devote two chapters of their text to group, team and peer-group supervision, and Bond and Holland have a very useful skills-based chapter that includes sections for both group supervisors and supervisees. In addition, a number of the more general groupwork texts, such as those by Brown and Douglas, have a strong social work orientation that is readily transferable to nursing and healthcare. Furthermore, Wright's book has a nursing focus, although his book is concerned with therapeutic groupwork rather than with supervision groups.

Bond, M. and Holland, S. (1998) *Skills of Clinical Supervision for Nurses*, Buckingham: Open University Press.

Brown, A. (1989) *Groupwork*, 2nd edn, Aldershot: Gower.

Douglas, T. (1976) *Groupwork Practice*, London: Tavistock.

Hawkins, P. and Shohet, R. (1989) Supervision in the Helping Professions, Milton Keynes: Open University Press.

Wright, H. (1989) *Groupwork: Perspectives and Practice*, Harrow: Scutari Press.

coming to the group. When they felt ready, they were to talk to one other member and listen carefully to what the other had to say, and then recount their own experience. Finally, if they wished, they could share anything they wanted to with the whole group. (Nichols and Jenkinson, 1991: 129)

Ultimately, though, the facilitator must put his faith in the group to say goodbye as they see fit. As Nichols and Jenkinson (1991) conclude, some groups do this in a flood of emotion, and others simply repair to the pub with very little fuss.

REFLECTIVE WRITING

Now turn back to the aims which you identified at the start of the chapter. To what extent have they been met? Write a paragraph outlining the scientific and experiential knowledge you have acquired through reading this chapter and doing the exercises. Write a second paragraph identifying any aims which you feel were only partially met or not met at all. As in previous chapters, divide your page into three columns. Head the first column 'What I need to learn', and make a list of any outstanding issues which you would like to learn more about. For example, you might wish to find out more about how to deal with difficult group members. Head the second column 'How I will learn it', and write down the ways in which your learning needs could be addressed; for example, through further reading, through attending study days, or through talking to other people. Head the third column 'How I will know that I have learnt it', and try to identify how you will know when you have met your needs.

Chapter 6

Reflection-in-action

■ Introduction

Most of our discussion up until now has focused on Donald Schön's notion of reflection-*on*-action, that is, thinking about practice after and away from the scene of that practice. However, Schön also explored the concept of reflection-*in*-action, which he saw as having far more significance for professional practice, and which we see as the distinguishing feature of the advanced practitioner. In very simple terms, reflection-in-action entails thinking about practice whilst doing it, and stands in contrast to reflection-on-action, in which the thought takes place after and away from the scene of the practice.

Although mindful practice of this kind might appear to be the norm, Schön noted that it is rarely recognised. Thus 'because professionalism is still mainly identified with technical expertise, reflection-in-action is not generally accepted – even by those who do it – as a legitimate form of professional knowing' (Schön, 1983). This is particularly true in nursing and the other healthcare professions, where Dartington (1994) observed that 'contemporary nursing has been dogged by a negative expectation that nurses should not think' and that 'it is an effort of will to make space for reflection in a working life dominated by necessity, tradition and obedience'. Similarly, Bond and Holland (1998) have pointed out that, although nurses are continuously making decisions and solving problems in their day-to-day practice, it is usually done at an unconscious level, and busy practitioners 'often express or display . . . difficulty in switching from paying attention to external events going on around to paying attention to thoughts and feelings going on within'. Particularly in nursing, the highest level of practice is usually associated with Benner's notion of the expert nurse who functions on an unconscious or intuitive level, and for whom conscious and mindful practice usually results in a deterioration in performance (see Chapter 1).

In attempting to move beyond this view of unconscious or intuitive practice, we have a number of aims for this chapter:

1   to help you to understand the complex and sometimes difficult concept of reflection-in-action as outlined by Donald Schön;
2   to discuss ways in which reflection-in-action could be applied to healthcare practice;
3   to enable you to reflect on the ways in which you might already employ reflection-in-action in your own practice; and
4   to suggest some strategies for developing your skills as a 'reflexive practitioner' through the use of reflection-in-action.

REFLECTIVE WRITING

Think carefully about our aims for Chapter 6. Now think about your own practice and how these aims might contribute towards developing it.

Based on our aims above, write down some of your own, both in terms of what you hope to know and what you hope to be able to do after reading Chapter 6. We will return to your aims at the end of the chapter.

■ Reflection-in-action and the advanced practitioner

Reflection-in-action is more than simply thinking whilst doing. As Schön pointed out:

> both ordinary people and professional practitioners often think about what they are doing, sometimes even while doing it. Stimulated by surprise, *they turn thought back on action and on the knowing which is implicit in action.* They may ask themselves, for example, 'What features do I notice when I recognise this thing? What are the criteria by which I make this judgement? What procedures am I enacting when I perform this skill? How am I framing the problem that I am trying to solve?' (Schön, 1983: 50, our emphasis)

From this description, we can see that reflection-in-action involves two separate and distinct components. Firstly, there is the turning of thought back on action, so that unlike Benner's intuitive expert, the advanced practitioner is thinking about what she is doing as she does it. But Schön also described the turning of thought back on the 'knowing which is implicit in action'. In other words, the advanced practitioner is not only conscious of what she is doing, but also of how she is doing it, of the practical knowledge that underpins her practice. Each of these components of reflection-in-action will be explored in detail, and we will conclude by suggesting some ways in which the skills of reflection-in-action can be employed and developed in healthcare practice.

Our task is made more difficult by the wealth of different terms that Schön often used to distinguish subtly different concepts, and in places we will introduce our own terminology where we feel that Schön's terms might result in confusion. However, reflection-in-action remains an elusive and difficult concept to grasp, although in our experience, practitioners who are already working at this level quickly recognise its main features.

□ Knowing-in-action

We shall start with the first of Schön's components of reflection-in-action, that of 'turning thought back on action'. Like many of his colleagues in the discipline of professional education, Schön was interested in the practical knowledge that accompanies skilled behaviour. For Schön, this practical 'know how' was part of the behaviour and could not be separated from it. As he pointed out, 'there is nothing strange about the idea that a kind of knowing is inherent in intelligent action' (Schön, 1983).

 FURTHER READING

Schön's notion of 'knowing-in-action' is similar to what we referred to in Chapter 1 as experiential practical knowledge. Other writers, mainly from the discipline of education, have described a similar concept, and it is clearly integral to a full understanding of how practitioners think and understand the practice setting. If you wish to explore this notion of 'a kind of knowing. . . inherent in intelligent action' (to use Schön's phrase), you might like to look at some of these texts. Usher and Bryant provide a broad overview of the issue in their chapter entitled 'Reconceptualizing Theory and Practice', while Carr and Kemmis discuss the notion of theory embedded in practice in Chapter 4 of their book, and Eraut does likewise in Chapter 3 of his. Gadamer's text offers a very readable introduction to practice theory in healthcare generally (and medicine in particular), and Rolfe, in the first two chapters of his book, argues for a greater recognition of experiential nursing theory.

Carr, W. and Kemmis, S. (1986) *Becoming Critical*, London: Falmer Press.
Eraut, M. (1994) *Developing Professional Knowledge and Competence*, London: Falmer Press.
Gadamer, H.-G. (1996) *The Enigma of Health*, Cambridge: Polity Press.
Rolfe, G. (1998) *Expanding Nursing Knowledge: Understanding and Researching Your Own Practice*, Oxford: Butterworth Heinemann.
Usher, R. and Bryant, I. (1989) *Adult Education as Theory, Practice and Research*, London: Routledge.

This synthesis of thinking and doing, which Schön called 'knowing-in-action', was seen as a form of practical experimentation 'which serves to generate both a new understanding of the phenomena and a change in the situation', such that 'when someone reflects-in-action, he becomes a researcher in the practice context' (Schön, 1983). Thus, if the nurse who reflects on action is a *reflective* practitioner, then the one who reflects in action is a *reflexive* practitioner. Although Schön referred to this advanced level of reflexive practice as on-the-spot experimenting, he was at pains to point out that he was not likening advanced practice to the controlled scientific experiment. Rather, he identified three ways in which reflection-in-action can be seen as a form of practical experimentation or action research.

Firstly, experimentation can be a simple pre-scientific method of discovery through doing: as Schön put it, 'to act in order to see what the action leads to'. This is a basic form of trial and error that Schön described as *exploratory* experimentation, which is 'the probing, playful activity by which we get a feel for things. It succeeds when it leads to the discovery of something there' (Schön, 1983). Secondly, experimentation can be seen as an action that is carried out in order to produce an *intended* change: 'any deliberate action undertaken with an end in mind is, in this sense, an experiment' (*ibid.*). Schön referred to this kind of experimentation as *move-testing*. Finally, experimentation can take the form of *hypothesis testing*, which is closest to the traditional scientific form of hypothetico-deductivism. In this mode of experimentation, the practitioner begins with a theory about what is happening in the clinical situation, formulates an hypothesis from that theory, and tests her hypothesis by acting on the situation. As Schön pointed out, 'If, for a given hypothesis, its predicted consequences fit what is observed, and the predictions derived from alternative hypotheses conflict with observation, then we can say that the first hypothesis has been *confirmed* and the others, *disconfirmed*' (*ibid.*, his emphasis).

For Schön, reflection-in-action encompasses all three modes of experimentation, such that 'When the practitioner reflects-in-action his experimenting is at once exploratory, move testing and hypothesis testing' (*ibid.*). In healthcare practice, where actions and judgements have to be made on the spot in a very short space of time, it is sometimes difficult to imagine how the practitioner has time to carry out even one of these modes of experimentation, let alone all three. We shall therefore begin with an example from outside of healthcare, in which the practitioner has the luxury of time to think, and in which her on-the-spot experimenting is done in a conscious manner.

☐   The reflective mechanic

Imagine, then, a car mechanic who is faced with a car that will not start. She might begin with the trial and error of *exploratory* experimenting, in which she simply tinkers with various wires and components. At this point, she has no clear ideas about why the car will not start, and is merely speculatively probing with no real expectation that it will resolve the problem. She might be lucky and find that the problem was caused by a loose wire that she has inadvertently moved back into place, but otherwise she will have to progress to the next stage of *move-testing*. In this case, the moves are deliberate and are intended to produce a particular outcome. The mechanic might test out the possibility that the spark plugs are damp by replacing them with a fresh set, or that the fuel pipe is blocked by looking to see whether any petrol is reaching the carburettor.

This approach works very well for simple problems, but most situations that mechanics and healthcare practitioners have to deal with are far more complex. The mechanic might narrow down the problem to the fact that there is no spark at the plugs. Now, there are many reasons why this might occur: a flat battery, damaged leads or faulty plugs, to name but three. And, of course, there are many reasons for each of these three causes. A flat battery might be caused by physical damage to the battery itself, by dirty connections, or by a broken alternator. As we can see, a simple move testing approach to resolving the problem might take some time, and if the problem is caused by two or more faults, then a linear approach in which potential causes are tested one by one might never uncover the problem.

This, then, brings us to Schön's third form of experimenting, that of *hypothesis-testing*. The aim here is not merely to try out simple moves such as replacing the spark plugs, but to formulate theories from the given symptoms. Our mechanic might have observed that there is no spark at the plug, but that her move testing strategy of replacing the battery only temporarily rectified the problem. She might theorise from this that the alternator is broken, which in turn is shorting out the battery and causing it to discharge. This theory would generate the hypothesis that the problem would be resolved by replacing the battery *and* the alternator at the same time. The hypothesis could then be tested by doing just that, and if the car now starts, then the hypothesis is confirmed (or, at least, strongly supported) and the mechanic has both generated knowledge about the car and fixed it by the same action. Clearly, such an hypothesis-testing approach requires a deep understanding of the situation that encompasses both scientific and experiential knowledge.

 DISCUSSION POINT

Recall a clinical situation in which you have had to make an on-the-spot judgement or assessment. With a colleague, discuss how you came to your clinical decision. Did you follow any of Schön's three forms of experimenting? If not, can you identify any sort of rational process, or were you acting 'intuitively'?

☐   The reflective healthcare practitioner

It might be argued that this model is all very well for car mechanics who are able to stop and think at every stage of fixing the car, but that there simply is not enough time in the midst of practice for the healthcare practitioner to employ this kind of reasoning to her on-the-spot clinical decisions. However, we have seen that Schön believed that the thought and the action components of reflection-in-action are not easily separated, but are two parts of the same process, what he described as 'a continual interweaving of thinking and doing'. The thinking component is a form of *practical* thinking, of thinking through doing, whilst the doing component is a *thoughtful* doing. Thus, the practitioner:

does not separate thinking from doing, ratiocinating his way to a decision that he must later convert to action. Because his experimenting is a kind of action, implementation is built into his inquiry. (Schön, 1983: 68)

Furthermore, for Schön, this process usually occurs so rapidly that it is performed unconsciously; what the baseball players whom he studied referred to as 'finding the groove', and what the jazz musicians spoke of as 'getting a feel for the music'. This might be the reason why some practitioners refer to their clinical decisions as intuitive. However, he also argued that practitioners are sometimes able to construct a 'virtual world' in which the pace of action can be slowed down in the practitioner's head so that *conscious* reflection is possible. Thus:

> Even when the action-present is brief, performers can sometimes train themselves to think about their action. In the split-second exchanges of a game of tennis, a skilled player learns to give himself a moment to plan the next shot. His game is the better for this momentary hesitation, so long as he gauges the time available for reflection correctly and integrates his reflection into the smooth flow of action. (Schön, 1983: 279)

The first aspect of reflection-in-action, then, is the conscious and mindful attention to the task at hand. The healthcare practitioner is sometimes able to stop and think in the midst of action and to describe and articulate the situation as she sees it; unlike Benner's example of the 'intuitive' psychiatric nurse, she is able to give a report of *why* the patient is psychotic rather than 'just knowing it'.

This conscious articulation of the situation is important, particularly when the practitioner is called upon to justify her actions or to teach them to others. However, as we have seen, there is a second aspect to reflection-in-action in addition to simply being mindful. As Schön noted, not only is the advanced practitioner aware of her thoughts as she practices, but '[s]he also reflects from time to time on [her] own performance, asking, in effect, Just what is it I spontaneously do in this situation?' (Schön, 1987). Bond and Holland (1998) described this as 'Level 4' reflection, in which the practitioner is not only aware of her own thought processes, but is also aware of her awareness of those thoughts. They borrowed Casement's (1985) term 'internal supervisor', since the practitioner is, in effect, acting as her own supervisor as she practices. We shall use the term 'meta-reflection' for this process of reflecting on our own reflections. Reflection-in-action therefore involves doing, thinking about doing, and thinking about thinking about doing (Figure 6.1).

Benner might be correct in her observation that experts often rely on their intuition and are able to practice without conscious thought, but, as we argued in Chapter 1, the advanced practitioner has moved beyond the limitations of such intuitive practice. The main difference between Benner's intuitive expert and the advanced practitioner, then, is that the latter is aware of her *modus operandi*, her methods of practice. Furthermore, she is not only reflecting on the details of the situation she is dealing with, but is also meta-reflecting on the process of how she is dealing with the situation.

Healthcare intervention	➡	'Intuitive' doing
Reflection on the intervention	➡	Thinking about doing
Meta-reflection on the reflection	➡	Thinking about thinking about doing

Figure 6.1   Three levels of reflection-in-action

 REFLECTIVE WRITING

Return to your reflective writing about your on-the-spot clinical judgement. At which of the three levels described in Figure 6.1 were you working? Write a paragraph to explore your reflection-in-action in this case.

■ Towards a model of reflexive practice

We can see, then, that reflection-in-action is far more than simply thinking about practice whilst doing it. Firstly, it involves a form of on-the-spot experimenting which brings together thinking and doing in a single act, and which Schön sometimes referred to as 'knowing in action'. Secondly, it also involves a meta-reflection on the process of knowing in action as it is taking place (Figure 6.2).

However, we saw earlier that Schön also divided the process of knowing in action or on-the-spot experimenting into three types, namely exploratory, move-testing and hypothesis-testing. In order to explore these further, we have associated each type of experimentation with a particular mode of thinking, doing and knowing (Table 6.1).

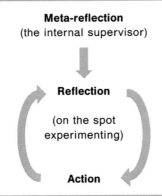

Figure 6.2   A basic model of reflection-in-action

Table 6.1   A model of knowing in action

	Thinking	Doing	Knowing
Exploratory experimentation	Engaging with the problem	Pre-theoretical probing (trial and error)	General knowledge and theory
Move-testing experimentation	Understanding the problem	Knowledge-based action	
Hypothesis-testing experimentation	Theorising/ hypothesising about the problem	Theory-based action	Specific knowledge and 'theory of the unique case'

This, of course, is an enormously over-simplified model of a very complex process, which we have constructed merely to facilitate thinking about reflection-in-action. In other words, the aim of the model is to stimulate your 'internal supervisor' rather than to provide a definitive description of how it functions.

☐   The reflexive practitioner

We will now use Benner's expert psychiatric nurse as an example of how a health-care practitioner might reflect-in-action. You will recall that Benner's nurse always knew when a patient was psychotic, even though she could not always say how she knew. Benner's explanation was that the nurse was engaged in some form of unconscious and arational pattern-matching that could not be explained in words. However, it is also possible to account for her expertise in terms of Schön's model of reflection-in-action. When she first meets the patient, the nurse has very little specific knowledge about him, and must rely on her broad knowledge of psychiatric patients in general. In her attempt to engage with the problem, her reflections are exploratory and her actions are based largely on trial and error, and correspond roughly to the car mechanic's initial tinkering (see Table 6.1 above). At this point she will have a number of possible diagnoses and treatment plans in her head, with little to guide her decisions about which might be the correct one.

As she gets to know the patient (which, for a skilled psychiatric nurse, might happen very quickly), she switches into move-testing mode (see Table 6.1). Her questions to herself now become more focused: 'Is this person depressed?'; 'What is the cause of his depression?'; 'Are his fears real or delusory?' She might ask questions of the patient to test her growing understanding of the problem: 'How long have you felt this way?'; 'Do you feel worse at night or in the morning?'; 'Does anything help to relieve your depression?' Her actions are no longer based solely on trial and error, but arise from her growing knowledge and understanding of the patient and his condition, as well as from established theories about psychosis and depression. She continues to reflect on the problem, but her thoughts now have more shape and direction.

As the nurse continues to build upon her understanding of the patient, she begins to develop her own personal theory about the presenting problem, what Schön called her 'theory of the unique case'. Perhaps his depression was caused by a loss; perhaps it is the depressive phase of a bipolar affective disorder; perhaps it is part of a toxic confusional state. At this point, her interventions will be centred around testing hypotheses based on these theories. If, for example, she theorises that the depression is symptomatic of a toxic state, then she will ask questions about fluid intake and might suggest blood tests to confirm or disprove her hypothesis. Her actions are therefore determined by her thoughts and theories, and those theories are in turn confirmed or modified by the results of her actions. This reflexivity of thinking and doing is precisely what Schön meant when he wrote about the on-the-spot experimenting that is so characteristic of reflection-in-action.

But, as we have seen, this on-the-spot experimenting or knowing in action is only part of the story of reflection-in-action, which also includes a meta-reflection on the process. Thus, not only is the advanced practitioner reflecting on the *content* of the practice situation ('if this patient is suffering from an acute toxic state, there is likely to be a spontaneous remission over the next 48 hours'), but she is also reflecting on the *process* of her reflective thoughts ('I am setting up an hypothesis which will confirm or disconfirm my theory'). The advanced practitioner is therefore aware both of the thoughts and reflections that underpin her clinical judgements and decisions, and also of the ways by which she arrives at those thoughts and reflections. This meta-reflection is important if the advanced practitioner is to explain and teach her skills to colleagues rather than merely to demonstrate them.

REFLECTIVE WRITING

Write a brief description of a clinical decision that you made intuitively. Attempt to reconstruct what you were thinking as you formulated your decision. To what extent were you aware of those thoughts at the time? Now write a paragraph in which you meta-reflect on those thoughts by asking yourself Schön's question: 'Just what is it I spontaneously do in this situation?'

As we emphasised earlier, this model is a gross oversimplification of the way in which the advanced practitioner arrives at her clinical judgements. In particular, it is unlikely that she will work sequentially through the three stages to arrive at a neat solution. She might, for example, begin with a hypothesis and only revert to the trial and error stage of exploratory reflection-in-action if her hypothesis is disproved. However, the important point that we wish to make is not about the exact nature of the process, but rather that such a process is possible. Contrary to

Benner's view, we are claiming that healthcare practitioners can not only reflect and meta-reflect on their practice while they are practising, but more importantly that this reflection-in-action can help both them and their colleagues to be better practitioners.

■ The reflexive practicum

Having explored Schön's notion of reflection-in-action, we will now turn our attention to his concept of the practicum as the means of developing the reflective skills of the advanced practitioner. Schön defined a practicum as:

> a virtual world, relatively free of the pressures, distractions, and risks of the real one, to which, nevertheless, it refers. It stands in an intermediate space between the practice world, the 'lay' world of ordinary life, and the esoteric world of the academy. (Schön, 1987: 37)

Sometimes the practicum is located in a classroom, sometimes it is located in a laboratory, and sometimes it is part of the real-life practice setting. However, a practicum is more than simply a physical space, since 'it embodies particular ways of seeing, thinking and doing that tend, over time, as far as the student is concerned, to assert themselves with increasing authority' (Schön, 1987). A practicum therefore also includes a theory of professional practice. In fact, Schön identified three types of practicum, related to different kinds of professional knowledge. Firstly, there is the technical practicum which aims to train the student in the 'correct' ways of solving problems for that particular profession by teaching her the facts, rules and procedures that members of the profession generally apply. In the second kind of practicum, the student is taught not only the facts and rules, but also the practical strategies that the professionals use to apply those rules. This kind of practicum operates at a deeper level, but it still teaches the student that there is a right response to every situation.

In healthcare education, we can see these two kinds of practicum in the classroom and the skills laboratory. Firstly, the student is taught the facts, and secondly she is taught how to apply them. However, it is only when the student is in the actual practice setting with actual practitioners and patients that the third kind of practicum is encountered. This 'reflective practicum' acknowledges 'neither that existing professional knowledge fits every case nor that every problem has a right answer', and focuses on 'the reflection-in-action by which, on occasion, students must develop new rules and methods of their own' (Schön, 1987). These three types of practicum are summarised in Table 6.2.

Reflective practicums are largely outside the control of the academy, and 'depend for their effectiveness on a reciprocally reflective dialogue of coach and student' (Schön, 1987). The role of the coach is rather different from that of the supervisor that we discussed in Chapter 3, since the supervisor tends to facilitate reflection-*on*-action outside of the practice setting, whereas the coach will be

Table 6.2   Schön's three types of practicum

	Usual location	*Focus*	*Coach*
Technical practicum	Classroom	Teaching the facts	Teacher
Applied practicum	Laboratory	Applying the facts	Teacher or practitioner
Reflective practicum	Practice setting	Dealing with unusual situations	Practitioner

working alongside the student in the clinical arena. In healthcare, we often refer to the coach as a mentor, whose role has been described as 'sharing their experience, thus teaching the best way of doing things, enhancing their proteges' skills and furthering their intellectual ability' (Butterworth and Faugier, 1992). However, Butterworth and Faugier continue by noting that 'such a demanding role obviously requires a competence over and above that of simply being able to function as a trained nurse'. In particular, many of the practitioners who will be fulfilling the role of mentor will not be skilled in initiating the kind of reflective dialogue demanded by Schön. Like Benner's psychiatric nurse, their ability to articulate the inner processes of their clinical decision-making will often be severely limited. If we are to facilitate the first generation of practitioners to reflect-in-action, then we cannot rely on the hit-and-miss environment of the 'raw' clinical area for our practicum.

 FURTHER READING

You might wish at this point to read a little more widely on the role of the mentor. This role is discussed by Butterworth and Faugier in chapter 1 of their book, where they contrast it with clinical supervision; it is given extensive treatment in chapter 3 of Morton-Cooper and Palmer; and is briefly discussed in chapter 1 of Bond and Holland. You might also wish to consider the extent to which these roles differ from Schön's description of the reflexive coach.

Bond, M. and Holland, S. (1998) *Skills of Clinical Supervision for Nurses*, Buckingham: Open University Press.
Butterworth, T. and Faugier, J. (1997) *Clinical Supervision and Mentorship in Nursing*, Cheltenham: Stanley Thornes.
Morton-Cooper, A. and Palmer, A. (1993) *Mentoring and Preceptorship*, Oxford: Blackwell Science.

The clinical area is not the ideal location for a reflective practicum, not only for practical reasons, but also for emotional ones. As Schön observed:

> For the student, having to plunge into doing – without knowing, in essential ways, what one needs to learn – provokes feelings of loss. Except in rare cases, students experience a loss of control, competence, and confidence; and with these losses come feelings of vulnerability and enforced dependency. It is easy, under these circumstances, to become defensive. (Schön, 1987: 166)

Similarly, the coach or mentor

> must accept the fact that he cannot tell his students about [practice] in any way they can at first understand, and then he must cope with their reactions to the predicament in which he has helped to place them. (*Ibid.*)

In the healthcare professions, not only must the student and mentor deal with feelings of inadequacy at not being able to master the tasks at hand, but also with feelings of anxiety. Unlike Schön's examples of the architect and the musician, the healthcare practitioner is working with vulnerable people, often in life or death situations, and therefore does not have the luxury of 'doing without knowing' or learning from her mistakes. What is required, then, is a *reflexive* practicum, a 'virtual messy world' in which the student can experiment with alternative approaches to problems for which the accepted solutions do not work, and in which the action can be slowed down or stopped altogether in order to allow her to explore her own reflection-in-action.

☐ Live supervision as a practicum

We wish to suggest one such approach to constructing a reflexive practicum that originated in the practice of family therapy. This approach is called live supervision, and, as its name suggests, it involves supervision *during the therapeutic session* from one or more colleagues. Live supervision was devised by Braulio Montalvo (1973) as a training technique for novice family thereapists, and was later extended to team work with peers (Brown, 1984), where it is sometimes referred to as live consultancy. Clearly, however, it has potential benefits in situations other than family therapy.

The main advantage of having access to clinical supervision during a session rather than afterwards is that it can address both the ongoing and developing therapeutic situation and also the process by which the practitioner is responding to that situation (her meta-reflection). Furthermore, it is far more reflexive than traditional supervision, since suggestions can be immediately implemented without having to wait until the next therapeutic session. Live supervision therefore provides training in the advanced skill of reflection-in-action for practioners at all levels from student to expert, and integrates the traditional roles of clinical supervisor and mentor.

Unlike much healthcare practice, live supervision involves a team, typically with two to four members. (Reimers and Treacher, 1995). One team member (whom we will refer to as the therapist) will be actively involved with the patient, whilst the other team members (the supervisors) will observe and occasionally intervene. There are a number of possible interventions that the supervisors could make. They might offer their own *hypotheses* about the ongoing therapeutic process, their *interpretation* of the interactions between the therapist and the patient, or simply provide *feedback* and *directions* to the therapist. As well as these more or less direct interventions, they might also offer *time out* from a difficult session for the therapist to collect her own thoughts. A discussion of the full range of possible interventions is provided by Kingston and Smith (1983).

The reflexive practicum for live supervision straddles the worlds of practice and education, and although it is most appropriately situated in a clinical setting, that setting requires some modification. The simplest arrangement is for the team of supervisors to be present in the room in which the therapist is practising (Kingston and Smith, 1983). However, this is not always an ideal situation, and it is often preferable for the supervisors to be physically separated and to view the session through a one-way mirror or on a video screen. This arrangement provides a number of options for live supervision. The most usual intervention involves the supervisors calling the therapist out of the room to offer one or more of the above forms of intervention. On other occasions, the therapist might recognise that she is stuck and leave the room to consult with her supervisors, whilst in exceptional cases, the supervisors might enter the room and directly intervene in the therapeutic process.

As you might expect from such an unusual approach to supervision, there are a number of difficulties. Firstly, there is the problem of extending an approach that was devised specifically for the practice of family therapy to the wider arena of healthcare practice, and it is important to recognise that there are certain settings in which it is not appropriate to employ live supervision. Secondly, live supervision runs counter to the expectations of patients, who are generally not used to having their treatment observed, nor to having their therapist called away at intervals during their treatment. And thirdly, it is undeniably resource-intensive, particularly in terms of staff. However, there are also a number of very valuable benefits to be had from live supervision. We have already seen how the supervisors can help the therapist in formulating hypotheses and generally making sense of the therapeutic situation, and can offer time out for the therapist to reflect and regain her thoughts. In addition, live supervision can offer added support and safety to both the therapist and patient, and can help to prevent burnout (Burnham, 1986). It is an ideal training tool for students and junior practitioners, and can increase flexibility and innovation in more senior staff by bringing fresh pairs of eyes and new perspectives to their practice.

We will now explore some of the ways in which live supervision can be utilised in practice. We shall begin with a case example from family therapy, and then discuss how it can be applied to a wide range of more common forms of healthcare practice. This is an actual case that one of us encountered when working in a family thereapy team, which we shall discuss with reference to the model of knowing in action presented in Table 6.1.

Case example: the bereaved father

Mr and Mrs X, both of who were thirty years old, had been referred for Mr X's unresolved grief following the death of their six-month-old son two years previously. The child was Mr X's first, although his wife had two daughters from a previous marriage. In the initial interview, the team learned that the baby died in his sleep during the night, and was discovered by the husband the following morning, who attempted to resuscitate him without success. Mr X claimed to feel particularly to blame since his wife had been out the previous evening and he had put the child to bed. When asked how he was now, he replied that he felt 'numb'. At this stage, the therapist hypothesised that, as well as feeling guilty and responsible for the death, Mr X might be feeling angry with his wife for being out and with the other children for being alive whilst his biological child was dead, and that these feelings of anger had been repressed, leading to him becoming stuck in the grieving process. We can see that, in this case, the therapist moved immediately to the hypothesis-testing mode of experimentation with a fully-formulated hypothesis.

The supervisory team of two trained family therapists and a student, who were observing through a one-way mirror, were less certain of this straightforward interpretation. However, they had no clear hypothesis of their own at this stage, and therefore reverted to the exploratory mode of experimentation. They did this by calling the therapist out and giving her the instruction to ask Mr X to talk about his feelings in the week following the death. She returned to the room and did so, and at this point Mr X became very angry and listed a catalogue of issues which he felt had been dealt with very badly by the hospital. These included a post-mortem being carried out against his will, seeing his son in the hospital chapel with the incisions from the post-mortem on full display, and being persuaded by the chaplain not to pursue his wish for the child to be buried in his garden.

This pre-theoretical probing produced some new information that allowed the therapist to see that Mr X's anger was not being repressed, but was simmering just below the surface. The therapist therefore refined the hypothesis to one of displaced anger, and left the room to consult with the supervisory team. Her question at this point was 'how is this man dealing with his anger?', and the supervisors suggested some move-testing experimentation to explore how Mr X was working through his feelings. He was initially very reluctant to discuss this issue, but it eventually emerged that he had coped with his distress by drinking 12–15 pints of beer every night and keeping a drunken vigil at the grave side in the early hours of the morning. His job was at risk because he was not sleeping, and his marriage was in crisis.

At this point, the supervision team further refined their hypothesis: Mr X was experiencing anger at a range of people (including himself) whom he could not confront either because they were inaccessible (the hospital staff) or because it seemed inappropriate (his wife and children). Seen in this light, his drinking was an unconscious attempt to punish himself and his family, and at this point the therapist left the room for a third time to discuss ways of testing this hypothesis and of helping the man to acknowledge and begin to address the problem.

The team decided to confront the problem head-on by employing the 'empty-chair' technique. Firstly, the wife was asked to imagine her husband in an empty chair that was facing her, and to tell him how she really felt about his drinking. This technique enabled her to say things to him that she could not say to his face, and she spoke for some time about her sadness at losing not only her child, but also her husband. Then it was her husband's turn. He was initially very resistive, but slowly began to tell his wife, through the empty chair, how he blamed her for not being there to put their son to bed, and how he was angry that she appeared to have come to terms with the death; indeed, to have almost forgotten about their son. The session ended with tears and some contemplative silences. This empty-chair work therefore not only confirmed the team's hypothesis, but also began to address the problem.

The process of this session is mapped out in Figure 6.3. It might appear to be a rather cold and dispassionate description of what was clearly a distressing encounter for all concerned. However, we have deliberately left out the emotional and social content of the session such as the comforting and empathising, so that the cognitive aspect might be seen more clearly.

It is important to note that this was not a miracle cure, but was simply the first stage in a long process of coming to terms with the death. However, it was a significant achievement for a single one-hour session, and such progress would not have been made had the technique of live supervision not been employed. Not only were the insights and hypotheses of the team essential for formulating the problem, but the possibility for the therapist to take time out towards the end to think about how to move the session forward probably meant that the progress which the team made in an hour was equivalent to about three sessions of traditional therapy. In addition, the live supervision had enabled the therapist to develop her ability to reflect in action, and had provided the student with a valuable insight into the clinical reasoning of a skilled practitioner.

☐   Establishing a reflexive practicum

Although the reflexive practicum of live supervision was developed by family therapists, it can be applied far more widely to almost any setting in which non-routine practice is (or should be) taking place. There are, of course, a number of issues that must be taken into account, but most can be resolved quite easily. First, there must be a facility for observation. In some settings, 'high-tech' equipment such as video cameras or one-way mirrors could be installed, whereas in other settings it might be more appropriate simply to have the supervision team sitting quietly and unobtrusively in a corner. Indeed, Kingston and Smith (1983)

142

Supervision	Practice

Practice

Information gathered about the
history of the event and
presenting features

reflection

Initial hypothesis:
Repressed anger leading to
repression of all feelings
(feeling numb)

rejected by team in favour of

Exploratory experimentation
(pre-theoretical probing)

intervention

Talk about feelings following
death

reflection

Tentative hypothesis:
Expressed anger directed at
hospital

resulting in

Move-testing experimentation
(knowledge-based action)

intervention

Talk with Mr X about how he is
working through his feelings

reflection

Hypothesis:
Anger displaced onto 'safe'
target through drinking.
Drinking is an unconscious
attempt to punish self and family

resulting in

Hypothesis-testing
experimentation
(theory-based action)

intervention

Empty-chair technique

reflection

Hypothesis confirmed

Figure 6.3   A map of a session

pointed out that one advantage of having the supervisors present in the room is that it introduces another powerful form of strategic intervention in which the supervisors are 'apparently speaking to the therapist but intending that the communication is received by the [patient]'.

Second, the team must decide in advance who will be acting as therapist and who will be offering supervision. We have already pointed out that it is appropriate for staff at all levels from student to advanced practitioner to take on any of the roles. For example, a team might consist of an advanced practitioner acting as therapist, with other practitioners and students as supervisors. This arrangement provides the advanced practitioner with important feedback on her performance and gives the more junior staff an opportunity to observe and discuss high-level practice. Alternatively, the student might be acting as therapist, in which case she is able to receive expert guidance and evaluation from advanced practitioners.

Third, it is vital that the patient is aware of this rather unusual method of working and gives her full and informed consent. It might be useful to point out to the patient that live supervision is a training tool which will maximise safety and best practice, and that it is the therapist who is being observed rather than the patient. However, it can still be a daunting prospect for the patient, particularly when the practice intervention is painful or intimate. It is sometimes better in such cases for the supervisors to be present in the treatment room rather than to monitor the situation with a video camera, since the patient can never be certain of just who is watching the video monitor, or indeed whether a recording is being made. In any case, it is important that the patient is introduced to the whole team before the therapeutic intervention, is reassured about confidentiality, and is given the opportunity to ask questions about such an unusual working arrangement.

Finally, we noted earlier that live supervision is most appropriate in non-routine situations where the therapist is called upon to make clinical judgements about problems that are not found in the text books. There might be some small advantage to giving live supervision to a nurse while she is making a bed, but it will be far outweighed by the cost implications.

 DISCUSSION POINT

Think about your own practice setting and discuss with a colleague from a similar setting how you might establish a live supervision practicum. In particular, think about who you might include in the team, how you would monitor practice, and some of the obstacles that you would need to overcome

☐   The reflexive practicum in action

We shall now briefly discuss a number of healthcare settings in which the reflexive practicum of live supervision might be appropriate. As we have already noted, live supervision is of most value in situations where non-routine decisions and clinical judgements have to be made in a well-controlled setting, particularly where the action can be slowed down or stopped altogether as and when required. One obvious situation in which live supervision could be of great benefit is the admission or assessment interview, particularly if it is seen as an opportunity to understand the patient and make a diagnosis of care rather than merely as a form-filling exercise. The simplest and least threatening arrangement of the assessment interview as a reflexive practicum is for a single supervisor to be present in the room whilst the assessment is conducted. The supervisor is then able to make hypotheses and judgements about care options and can intervene directly or call the assessor out of the session to offer feedback and suggestions. Furthermore, the arrangement works equally well with the more experienced practitioner as either therapist or supervisor, and provides a mutual learning experience for both practitioners.

A similar but more specialised setting is the practice nurse's surgery, since almost every new clinical encounter will involve some degree of assessment. As above, the most appropriate setting is for the supervisor to be present in the room and to intervene as required. This arrangement is an ideal training environment for the novice practice nurse, since it enables her both to observe a more experienced colleague in action and to practice under the watchful eye of an expert supervisor.

There are also a number of situations that are more conducive to a team of supervisors situated outside of the immediate practice area. An obvious example would be in group work, where a multidisciplinary supervision team might view a social skills group run by (say) an occupational therapist through a one-way mirror. This setting would be very similar to the family therapy example described above, in which the team would call out the therapist at regular intervals to offer hypotheses and feedback, and provides an ideal environment for trainee group facilitators to observe and participate in group work. It could also, of course, be used as a way of conducting group supervision as described in Chapter 4.

Finally, and more radically, it might be possible to install a video camera in a minor-injuries cubicle in an Accident and Emergency department of a hospital. It would, of course, be necessary to obtain consent from all patients who were treated in this 'live' cubicle, but it would provide an extremely effective multidisciplinary training facility which would enable junior staff from all professions to learn from their more senior colleagues.

These are just four of many different ways in which live supervision could be incorporated into everyday practice. As we have seen, it is an expensive and often challenging approach to practice, but it offers an unusual and very effective method for practitioners from all disciplines and at all levels to develop the ability

FURTHER READING

If you are planning to incorporate live supervision into your practice, we recommend that you read about how it has been employed in family therapy. Many of the key works such as Montalvo and Kingston and Smith were published in specialist journals that might be difficult to obtain, and so you might find it easier to read some of the many summaries that have appeared in textbooks. A good place to start is with John Carpenter's chapter 'Working Together: Supervision, Consultancy and Coworking' in Treacher and Carpenter. Philip Barker's book includes a useful chapter entitled 'Teaching and Learning Family Therapy', which explores a number of training methods including live supervision with and without a one-way mirror in their chapter entitled 'Research and Practice, Practice and Research'. To the best of our knowledge, there are no nursing or general healthcare texts that explore the use of live supervision.

Barker, P. (1986) *Basic Family Therapy*, London: Collins.

Kingston, P. and Smith, D. (1983) 'Preparation for Live Consultation and Live Supervision when Working Without a One-Way Screen', *Journal of Family Therapy*, **5**, 219–33.

Montalvo, B. (1973) 'Aspects of Live Supervision', *Family Process*, **12**, 343–59.

Reimers, S. and Treacher, A. (1995) *Introducing User-friendly Family Therapy*, London: Routledge.

Treacher, A. and Carpenter, J. (1984) *Using Family Therapy*, Oxford: Basil Blackwell.

 REFLECTIVE WRITING

Now turn back to the aims which you identified at the start of the chapter. To what extent have they been met? Write a paragraph outlining the learning about reflection-in-action you have acquired through reading this chapter and doing the exercises. Write a second paragraph identifying any aims which you feel were only partially met or not met at all. As in previous chapters, divide your page into three columns. Head the first column 'What I need to learn', and make a list of any outstanding issues which you would like to learn more about. For example, you might wish to find out more about live supervision. Head the second column 'How I will learn it', and write down the ways in which your learning needs could be addressed, for example, through further reading, through attending study days, or through talking to other people. Head the third column 'How I will know that I have learnt it', and try to identify how you will know when you have met your needs.

to reflect in action which Donald Schön and other writers see as essential for advanced practice. Furthermore, it offers an opportunity for students, novice practitioners and experts to explore the underlying thought processes of practice (what Schön called 'knowing in action') that often go unnoticed in the pressures of their everyday work.

Chapter 7

Research and the
reflective practitioner

■ Introduction

We have suggested in this book that as practitioners become more experienced, they begin to develop a knowledge-base derived from reflecting on their interactions with patients. Because this type of knowledge is not formally recognised by the traditional scientific model, and because reflection-on-action is not usually thought of as a research method, the reflective practitioner can sometimes feel discouraged and disempowered from contributing to the knowledge base of the profession. In addition, traditional models of research have tended to separate research and practice into discreet domains, thus widening the already substantial divide between theorists and practitioners, a divide which has been reinforced by academics who distinguish between the kind of thought that informs science (knowing that) and that which informs practice (knowing how). This in turn fosters a division in the ways of knowing rather than promoting integration, which merely reinforces the assumption that educators, researchers and practitioners occupy separate professional spheres. The emerging picture is therefore of a discipline consisting of academically-oriented researchers and service-oriented practitioners who never meet and rarely communicate.

The blame for the split between research and practice has traditionally been attributed to practitioners for failing to engage with research (see, for example, Hunt, 1981). Whilst it is certainly true that the level of participation by practitioners in generating and applying research findings is low, the responsibility for this does not lie totally with the practitioners themselves. Rather, a growing number of writers are beginning to recognise that the reluctance of practitoners to apply what can appear to be irrelevant research findings to their practice is due at least in part to the ever-widening gulf between researchers and practitioners and between research and practice. In order to reduce this gap, it is necessary to move beyond the traditional technical rationality paradigm of nursing research towards a model in which research and critical reflection are seen as fundamental aspects of everyday practice.

This chapter considers the challenges that practitioners face when trying to incorporate research into their everyday practice. Building upon the notion of a practicum (see Chapter 6), we propose an integral approach to practice that draws upon the concept of the practitioner-researcher (Jarvis, 2000) and reflection as research. We will further explore practice as a legitimate source of knowledge in its own right and examine the reflective processes that can be undertaken by skilled practitioners and field researchers as methods of generating knowledge. Through reflective research, the practitioner-researcher is encouraged to approach her practice with reflexivity; to make her private knowledge public whilst simultaneously maintaining a stance of professional accountability and responsibility.

We suggest that with the evolution of the practitioner-researcher, the practice arena becomes a place where evidence based practice no longer means the application of scientific research findings, but instead, is a site for the generation of the evidence base *from* practice. This chapter therefore aims:

1   to help you to understand the methodological issues which relate to and perpetuate the research–practice gap;
2   to help you to reflect upon the barriers to improving clinical effectiveness through research;
3   to enable you to understand methods of research which can become part of your everyday practice through the process of critical reflection; and
4   to explore the concept of the practitioner-researcher.

It is not possible in such a short space to enable you to develop the skills necessary to function as a competent practitioner-researcher. However, we hope that after reading this chapter you will begin to look beyond the rather narrow confines of traditional health care research methodologies towards a model that more fully integrates the practitioner and the researcher, and indeed, practice and research.

 REFLECTIVE WRITING

Think carefully about our aims for Chapter 7. Now think about your own practice and how these aims might contribute towards developing it.

Based on our aims above, write down some of your own, both in terms of what you hope to know and what you hope to do after reading Chapter 7. We will return to your aims at the end of the chapter.

■ Research or re-search?

Research has been described and defined by numerous authors from a broad range of disciplines, and there is an enormous number of definitions to be found in the wealth of available literature. Definitions originating from within the discipline of nursing include that of the International Council for Nursing (1996):

Research is a systematic approach and a rigorous method with the purpose of generating new knowledge. (p. 3)

Burns and Grove (1987) provided a similar definition, adding that the primary goal of nursing research is to:

> develop a scientific knowledge base for nursing practice. (p. 4)

The Department of Health (1993), for their part, stated that:

> Research is rigorous and systematic enquiry designed to lead to generalisable contributions to knowledge. (p. 6)

Whilst there is a common theme of generating knowledge running throughout these and other such definitions, the concept of research remains elusive and abstract. In addition, knowledge can be generated in a number of other ways, and as we saw in Chapter 1, what constitutes knowledge is open to debate. One way of operationalising these somewhat abstract definitions of research is to move beneath the generic purpose to the individual motivation of the researcher. Braud (1994) argued for three main motivations for research:

- to learn about the world and other people in order to predict and control;
- to understand the world in the service of curiosity and wonder; and
- to appreciate the world and delight in its myriad of entities.

Braud's first motivation for research is instrumental and has a utilitarian value. Knowledge is seen as power and the researcher enlists large and random samples in order to arrive at general principles. This motivation is in complete contrast to the second and third, which are clearly related. The second motivation for research is based on the assumption that the world is a puzzle, and that we have a need to understand how the pieces of that puzzle fit together. The third motivation is based on our need for variety, discovery and surprise, and requires from us the capacity to tolerate uncertainty. Whereas the scientific paradigm is driven almost exclusively by the first of Braud's motivations to predict and control, practitioners also have a need to understand and appreciate the world of practice.

According to Braud, the motivation for the research influences the subsequent choice of research question and methodology: research that stems from the first motivation is more likely to employ a quantitative methodology, whereas research that has its purpose in the second two motivations is more likely to employ methods originating from the qualitative paradigm. In addition, Braud's qualities of curiosity, wonder and delight are compatible with more aesthetic expressions such as narrative, poetry, literature and art, all of which are cognate disciplines in their own right. The nurse researcher who embraces the aesthetic dimension alongside other dimensions can be described as an integral inquirer, one who uses a pluralistic epistemology, polling all aspects of the self including bodily reactions, emotions, feelings, intuitions, cognitions and aesthetic sensibilities (Braud, 1994).

DISCUSSION POINT

What has been your experience of research both in your clinical setting and in a broader social context? For example, think about the times you have been stopped in the street and asked to help fill in a questionnaire. How did you feel about it?

Discuss with a colleague how your practice has been influenced by research. What might be the purpose of conducting research into your own practice? How would you go about choosing the appropriate research method?

Think back to a piece of research you have read or have been involved in. What was the purpose of the research? Were the motivations of the researcher made explicit?

■ Methodological considerations

Qualitative and quantitative approaches to research have often been viewed as deriving from opposing and conflicting philosophies of science, each with their own specific methodologies, and the debate about the potential merits and short-comings of each approach is as much rehearsed in nursing as in all social sciences (Webb, 1996; Duffy, 1985). Mishler (1979) distinguished the salient points of the two philosophies as follows:

- *Qualitative research*
  - intertwines observer and phenomena;
  - has many different but equal truths;
  - seeks to understand the meaning of phenomena;
  - has a holistic approach to analysis;
  - has increased validity.

- *Quantitative research*
  - relies on an outside observer being separate from the phenomena;
  - seeks one truth to explain a phenomenon;
  - examines causal relationships;
  - strips the context of assumptions;
  - has increased reliability.

Quantitative or positivist research aims to test hypotheses by using 'objective' measures and predicting and controlling phenomena (cf Braud's first motiva-tion). Hypotheses are generated by logical inference from previous research, library searches and intuitive grasp (Morse and Field, 1996), and this deductive style of research therefore commences with sets of concepts which are then made operational. Morse and Field state that:

> Quantitative research looks for relationships between variables so that causality may be explained and accurate prediction becomes possible. The aim is to examine the experimental variables, while controlling the intervening variables that arise from the context. (1996: 9)

The context is therefore stripped of its meaning.

In contrast, qualitative or interpretative (sometimes referred to as anti-positivist) research focuses on the process of understanding human experience (cf. Braud's second motivation) rather than seeking to control or predict it (Webb, 1996; Polit and Hungler, 1993), and is concerned with the meaning in the context. Quantitative and qualitative methodologies both evoke criticisms of their epistemological bases, and each has its methodological limitations. Whilst it is not possible to do justice to both sides of the quantitative–qualitative debate here, some issues are pertinent to this chapter and will be attended to in brief.

Firstly, there is the issue of the legitimisation and trustworthiness of the findings. In quantitative research, a well-defined set of criteria is applied to the methodology to evaluate the worthiness of the study and its results, utilising concepts such as reliability, validity and generalisability (Burns and Grove, 1987). Validity refers to the extent to which the research instrument measures what it set out to measure, thus ensuring authenticity of the content. Reliability, on the other hand, pertains to whether or not the research instruments would continually produce the same result when applied in identical situations on different occasions, and is thus a measure of consistency. However, these concepts are seen as irrelevant in the legitimisation of qualitative research, and researchers talk instead of credibility, dependability and transferability (Denzin and Lincoln, 1994). In order to demonstrate rigour, the researcher has to make her research practices visible and auditable (Alvesson and Skoldberg, 2000; Sandelowski, 1993), and this can be achieved in a number of ways, one of which involves leaving a decision trial by making the research practices visible through reflection-on-action and reflection-in-action (reflexivity).

Secondly, there is the objectivity–subjectivity debate. Quantitative research methods are often criticised for reducing individuals to objects made up of separate parts rather than a dynamic whole. However, this objective approach is viewed positively by the scientific world as producing more valid and reliable data, since the researcher also treats herself as an object within the research process by, as far as possible, excluding her own beliefs, attitudes and feelings from of the research findings. Porter (1993) likened this approach to the philosophical position of naïve realism (see Chapter 1) and the positivist adherence to the language of neutral observation. In contrast, qualitative methodology tends to focus far more on the subjects of the research within their context, moving between the parts by way of perceiving the whole picture. It is therefore a much more subjective approach which acknowledges the experiences both of the participants and of the researcher.

Thirdly, there is the issue of whether qualitative research actually fulfils its promise of subjectivity. The qualitative approach has been adopted by a number of nurses almost without question, with many taking a critical stance towards the positivist paradigm which has hitherto dominated the profession. Examples include nursing theorists Margaret Newman (1994) and Rosemary Parse (1985),

---

 FURTHER READING

The library shelves are straining under the weight of available texts on research and research methods, and making an appropriate choice can require a research study in itself. There are, however, some generic texts which lay down the foundations of the main research approaches, and as such provide a good starting point.

Burns, N. and Grove, S.K. (1987) *The Practice of Nursing Research*, Philadelphia: W.B. Saunders.
Morse, J. and Field, P.A. (1996) *Nursing Research: The Application of Qualitative Approaches*, 2nd edn, London: Chapman & Hall.
Polit, D.F. and Hungler, B.P. (1991) *Nursing Research: Principles and Methods*, 4th edn, Philadelphia: Lippincott.

There are many research texts which describe the varying methods of collecting and analysing research data, although not all fully explicate the philosophical underpinnings of the methods and the way in which this influences the role of the researcher in the research process. You may wish to read a little more widely into the role of the researcher and the process of hermeneutics:

Benner, P. (ed.) (1994) *Interpretive Phenomenology*, California: Sage.
Murray, M. and Chamberlain, K. (eds) (1999) *Qualitative Health Psychology*, London: Sage.
Rolfe, G. (1998) *Expanding Nursing Knowledge: Understanding and Researching Your Own Practice*. Oxford: Butterworth Heinemann.

Many practitioners find the terms 'research' and 'audit' confusing. For a useful explanation of the differences between them, read:

Closs, J. and Cheater, F.C. (1996) 'Audit or Research – What is the Difference?' *Journal of Clinical Nursing*, **5** (4 Jul), 249–57.

who write of a human science approach to research that is useful when working with subject matter not amenable to the experimental and investigative methods of the natural sciences. This human science approach has been built over a period of time, with writers such as Leonard (1994) and Newman (1994) arguing that personhood cannot be approached scientifically. However, whilst there is little doubt that some qualitative methods (for example some branches of phenomenology) allow for the subjectivity of the researcher, Porter (1993) argued that many qualitative approaches are flawed insofar as they still assume the possibility of objective knowledge, which is mirrored in the language they employ. In contrast, reflexivity is posited as a method that fully embraces and exploits the subjectivity of the researcher. It therefore moves beyond the more traditional research methods which retain the possibility of objectivity, and offers an alternative theoretical base for nursing research that is grounded in practice.

Whilst an active engagement in the debate about the epistemological and methodological credibility of nursing research is commendable, there is always a danger of the debate becoming self-limiting, since the researcher is apt to find herself polarised into an either/or position rather than seeing an alternative beyond the two opposing approaches. In the heat of the debate, a power struggle often ensues, with each researcher seeing her own paradigm as the 'right' one for the job, and becoming blind to the real issues such as whether her chosen methodology will result in an improvement to practice. It is to this problem of the theory–practice gap (Rolfe, 1996a; 1996b; McCaughterty, 1991) that we shall now turn.

■ Research into practice

□ The theory–practice gap

The development of a theoretical base and the acknowledgement of differing sources of knowledge has highlighted the need for nursing to have a scientific basis (Freshwater and Broughton, 2000; Salvage, 1998; Akinsanya, 1985). This is hardly a new proposition (see for example, Chater, 1975), although the move towards research-based practice has been accelerated by recent developments in nursing and the caring professions. Dramatic changes in the provision of health care and the trend towards care pathways and integrated care delivery systems have focused practitioners' attention on clinical effectiveness, often measured against prescribed clinical guidelines, on a medical model of evidence-based practice, and on patient outcomes as determined by national policies and agendas.

Despite this move towards a more research-based profession, nursing care and treatment remains largely unaffected by research findings (Coombs, 1999; Walsh *et al.*, 1995), and it often seems as if the research process ends when the data analysis has been completed and the paper submitted for publication. However, this ignores the whole issue of the translation of research into practical action, and this regular failure of research findings to be applied to practice is usually blamed on the practitioners (Fox, 1999).

This so-called theory–practice gap in nursing has an established history and a well-rehearsed debate of its own. Clarke (1986), for example, highlighted three main problems around the relationship between theory and practice:

- the separation of theory from practice;
- reality versus the ideal; and
- adherence to a scientific paradigm versus adherence to an arts paradigm.

It has been argued that in order to address the theory–practice gap:

> There has to be recognition of the interdependent and dynamic relationship between theoretical and practical knowledge. One is not superior to the other, and both are essential to improving patient care. (Nolan *et al.*, 1998: 275)

Many authors have expressed their concern about the apparent lack of impact that nursing research has made on practice (Le May *et al.*, 1998; Bircumshaw, 1990). As early as 1986, Sheehan asserted that applying research findings to practice is perhaps the biggest challenge facing nursing research, whilst Walsh and Ford (1989) identified the problem of myth and ritual in nursing practice, arguing that nurses behaved in certain ways regardless of the findings of research simply because they had always behaved in those ways. Greenwood (1984) rationalised that nurses did not use research because of a lack of knowledge and a lack of belief regarding the findings, adding that often nurses do not find the research findings relevant to their practice. She concluded that:

> Nursing is a practical activity, it is aimed at bringing about change in the physical, emotional and social status of persons – the problems that confront nurses are essentially practical problems concerning what to do. (Greenwood, 1984: 78)

Greenwood added that researchers have tended to approach nursing as if it was a theoretical activity, and Miller (1989) concluded that theory and research which is grounded in practice has far greater potential for improving the effectiveness and the knowledge base of nursing practice and reducing the theory–practice gap. These comments were echoed almost 10 years later in the findings of a study to explore the research culture of nursing (Le May *et al.*, 1998).

Further barriers to the implementation of nursing research include organisational issues (time and finances), cultural issues (embedded negative attitudes), lack of preparation, lack of education, and methodological issues (not just competing paradigms but also the restrictions imposed by the current NHS Research and Development strategy).

Practitioners often 'do' research as part of an academic course, and this can provide some theoretical grounding in the methods of searching and appraising the research literature. However, once back in practice, the knowledge and experience gained is not always followed through or reevaluated in the context of a dynamic clinical environment (Freshwater and Broughton, 2000).

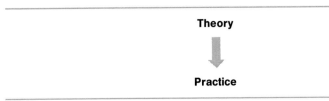

Figure 7.1 A technical rationality model

A further reason for the lack of impact on practice is that nursing research is mainly carried out by academics and nursing theorists who are removed from the area of practice (Rolfe, 1996a). As Rafferty and Traynor (1999) comment, there is a belief that researchers and practitioners occupy separate spheres with rival versions of reality. This view, which is sometimes referred to as technical rationality, holds that evidence travels in one direction (from researcher to practitioner), and that the practitioner is passive in this process, that is to say, that evidence is applied uncritically and without reflection (Figure 7.1).

☐   Case study research

One approach to research which attempts to address some of the above problems is single-case study methodology. A single-case study can be defined as:

> A strategy for doing research which involves an empirical investigation of a particular contemporary phenomenon within its real life context. (Robson, 1993: 146)

Case studies are a helpful way to focus attention on specific issues that cannot be sufficiently explicated within a larger-scale research project. The data generated from case studies allow for a far more in-depth examination of the phenomena, and can call attention to the ordinary as well as the extraordinary. Case studies are of particular relevance to the theory–practice gap in nursing, as they offer a technique to generate research as part of everyday practice, with the purpose of investigating a phenomenon within its real life context (Yin, 1994). Furthermore, it is possible for the practitioner to study and make changes to an aspect of her own practice through reflection-on-action and other reflexive methods in what Rolfe (1998) refered to as 'reflective case study' research.

On of the most common criticisms directed at case study methodology is its lack of generalisation to a wider population. However, this has been countered by Rolfe (1998), who contends that reflection-on-action as a research method is concerned primarily with the uniqueness of the nurse–patient relationship, and therefore makes no claim for generalisability (Koch, 1998; Rolfe, 1996b). Indeed, there is a certain uniqueness about *every* practice performance:

Since the emergencies of practice in the caring profession frequently preclude repetition, it is hard to conceptualise practice situations as being anything other than unique. (Jarvis, 2000: 32)

Robson (1993), in response to the aforementioned criticisms, identified two methods by which (non-statistical) generalisations can be made from the findings of case studies. The first of these is 'direct demonstration', and the second is 'making a case'. Robson describes these methods as theoretical generalisations on the basis that the researcher is generalising to a theory rather than to a population. In addition, Schön (1987) advocated the use of case studies and practicum experience to develop skilful reflective thinking, and Kuhn *et al.* (1988) suggested that the use of reflective strategies in concrete cases may promote their generalisation. An example of this is clinical supervision, which, when viewed as a conversation with a purpose, is the reflective equivalent of case study research facilitated through skilful interviews.

Case example: reflective case study research

A nurse working on a cancer-care ward wished to explore how she and her colleagues broke bad news to patients' relatives. She decided to conduct a single-case study using a variety of methods, including:

- participant observation, where she collected data about how her colleagues dealt with breaking bad news by observing them in action;
- interviews with her colleagues to determine their attitudes and feelings about breaking bad news;
- a reflective interview during her own clinical supervision to collect data about her own attitudes, feelings and actions; and
- document analysis to discover what was written in the notes about cases where bad news was broken to relatives.

From these data, a comprehensive picture was built up which enabled the nurse and her colleagues critically to examine their own practice. As we have already discussed, the findings were not meant to be generalised to other wards or situations, but might nevertheless be useful in formulating a more general theory.

☐ Research as critical intent and reflection

Case study research to some extent spans both the qualitative (Stake, 1995) and the quantitative (Yin, 1994) paradigms. However, one of the reasons why it is rarely employed in healthcare settings might be that in a discipline dominated by the medical paradigm, practitioners continue to perpetuate the research–

DISCUSSION POINT

Working with a colleague, spend a few minutes reflecting back on your own experience of case studies. You might find that you have several different understandings of the term case study; if so, compare some of these to the notion of case study research. How might case study research be applied to your current practice setting?

FURTHER READING

If you are interested in finding out more about case study research, you might wish to look at the following:

Robson, C. (1993) *Real World Research*, Oxford: Blackwell Science.
Rolfe, G. (1998) 'Reflective Case Study Research', in G. Rolfe, *Expanding Nursing Knowledge*, Oxford: Butterworth Heinemann.
Sharp, K. (1998) 'The Case for Case Studies in Nursing Research: The Problem of Generalisation', *Journal of Advanced Nursing*, **27**, 785–9.
Stake, R.E. (1995) *The Art of Case Study Research*, London: Sage.
Yin, R.K. (1994) *Case Study Research*, 2nd edn, London: Sage.

practice gap by their (often unconscious) adherence to the technical rationality model of science. Thus, in response to the criticisms of both the qualitative and quantitative paradigms, a third approach to social research has emerged, calling itself critical science (Fay, 1987). Critical science aims at critique, and its mode of inquiry is derived from the epistemological base of emancipatory cognitive interest (Mezirow, 1981). One of the aims of critical science is to expose power imbalances by revealing to people the nature of the crisis within their lives, and this requires that the individuals concerned have an interest in self-knowledge and self-reflection. By adopting an active stance towards developing critical self-awareness, the individual can take action to emancipate self, and feeling empowered by this new awareness, can develop practice (Fay, 1987; Mezirow, 1981). You might recall that we briefly discussed critical science in Chapter 2 when we examined Kim's model of critical reflection.

As a critical theorist and a central figure in the hermeneutic tradition, Habermas (1978) categorised human knowledge into the technical (empirical), the practical (interpretative) and the emancipatory (critical knowledge), and Mezirow (1981) further framed these categories in terms of social existence by relating them to work, interaction and power. Fay (1987) conceptualised critical social science in much the same way, describing it as scientific, practical and critical. Habermas (1978) argued that one of the purposes that knowledge serves is to maintain the influence of powerful people and regimes, keeping other people down (cf. the postmodern view on knowledge and power which is briefly discussed in Chapter 1). Critical theory offers freedom from subordination through systematic reflection and critique, and change is therefore the main interest of critical reflection. As Taylor (1998) remarked, this 'may mean freedom from people's previous perceptions of themselves and their circumstances, and freedom to change to something that is better for them'.

 DISCUSSION POINT

Think back to the different types of knowledge we outlined in Chapter 1. Now review these ways of knowing in light of the work of Habermas, Mezirow and Fay. Discuss with a colleague how knowledge has been used in relation to work, interaction and power in your own experience. You might reflect on situations in which someone else has information that you require, or on the power of 'secrets'. What is it like when you know something about another person that they don't know? Examples of this occur in clinical practice in the breaking of bad news, the reporting of diagnosis/prognosis, and in health education.

The act of bringing critical intent to bear on a problem is an act of reflection (Habermas, 1978) which may lead to perspective transformation (Mezirow, 1981). Mezirow (1981) suggested that insights gained from critical intent are only emancipatory insofar as they transform consciousness, such that the individual is not only more aware of her own biography (history) but also feels more of an authority on how the story will continue to be written. However, a transformation of consciousness does not necessarily lead to a change in action, which in turn does not necessarily equate with improvement to practice. As Rolfe (1996a) commented, '... although this approach is guaranteed to bring about *change* by impacting directly on the clinical situation, it does not necessarily bring about *improvement*'. Thus, when using critical science as an underpinning philosophy for research, the practitioner-researcher 'is the main judge of the quality of an intervention, and her evaluation is made not on some external, objective criteria, but on her own professional judgement' (Rolfe, 1996a). This judgement is always made in relation to the intended outcome and subsequent deliberate action. Thus, whilst the (advanced) practitioner refers to her own professional judgement she does not do this in isolation, and the context of the intended change is seen as inextricably linked to the change itself.

Systematic investigation of nursing practice is a relatively new phenomenon in the nursing profession, and it is even more novel to suggest that the investigation might be carried out by the practitioner herself, particularly using a critical science approach which relies so heavily on her own subjective professional judgements. However, the development of such agendas as clinical governance and evidence-based practice means that organisations must make a commitment to address the barriers to research utilisation in creative and innovative ways, including practitioner-based approaches.

Practitioner-based research is particularly associated with clinical governance in that it:

- develops and maintains multidisciplinary partnerships;
- provides a forum for reporting on how the quality of services is developing;
- promotes ownership of national agendas and policies;
- develops responsiveness to dynamic clinical practice;
- promotes examination of beliefs and values that underpin decision-making;
- explores reasons for deviating from national guidelines and standards;
- addresses the issue of public accountability and professional standards; and
- promotes continuing professional development through the utilisation of a practicum.

Research which reflects the values of critical science and which provides a framework for the practitioner to explore and improve her own practice is often referred to as action research.

■ Action research

Action research involves the practitioner directly in the research process, and has been growing in popularity in nursing over the past decade as a way of bridging the theory–practice gap. Lewin (1946) viewed action research as a democratic approach, not because it explicitly introduced democracy into the research process, but because it embodied democratic principles. Thus, Hughes (1997) described it as a tool for changing society and generating knowledge, which at its best is emancipating and empowering. For example, educational action research has been used to help teachers cope with the challenges of change, and to carry through innovation in a reflective and collaborative manner (Altrichter *et al.*, 1993). Similarly, Winters (1989) identified action research as an activity which is integral to professional work, thus avoiding the split between theoretical and practical understanding. Action research can therefore act as a bridge between research, theory and practice.

There are many varieties of action research, and three main types have been identified within the literature: technical and positivist; collaborative and interpretative; critical and emancipatory (McTaggart, 1992; Zuber-Skerritt, 1991). Zuber-Skerritt (1991) explicated these three levels of action research further:

1   Technical action research aims at effectiveness and efficiency in performance and changes in social practices. Participants are often co-opted and rely on an outside expert/researcher.

2   Practical action research involves transformations of the consciousness of participants as well as change in social practices. The expert/researcher acts as a process consultant, engaging in dialogue to encourage both the cooperation of the participants and self-reflection.

3   Emancipatory action research includes the participants' emancipation from tradition, self-deception and coercion. The expert/researcher is a process moderator, collaborating and sharing equal responsibility with the participants. In having more involvement with the participants, emancipatory action research offers the potential to generate and test action theories, thereby developing and empowering practitioners.

In discussing the three types of action research, Zuber-Skerritt (1991) does not make it clear what he means by the term 'expert', and this can lead to some confusion, not least because action research is more often deemed to be not only participative, but also collaborative. It would seem, however, that Zuber-Skerritt uses the term to refer to the role of the researcher rather than as someone who is an expert practitioner in Benner's (and our) sense.

Cohen and Manion (1989) suggest that action research is situational, that is, concerned with diagnosing a problem in a specific context and attempting to solve it in that context. As action research is usually collaborative, the researchers and the participants work together, the research practice is self-evaluative, and modifications are continuously made within the ongoing situation. Action research, therefore, is essentially developmental, longitudinal and multidimensional, requiring reflection at different levels. The evaluation itself consists of two stages: firstly a diagnostic stage in which the problems are analysed and hypotheses are developed; and secondly a therapeutic stage when the hypotheses are tested by a consciously directed change experiment.

The self-evaluative aspect of action research is also an essential component both of nursing (Greenwood, 1984) and of reflective practice (Johns, 1998). You might be wondering whether or not research carried out by the practitioner and involving self-evaluation can ever be reported in an unbiased or undistorted way, but as Rolfe (1996a) pointed out, the kind of theory that is generated from this type of research is intended to be neither generalisable nor objective and is, in fact, unashamedly biased. However, as Alvesson and Skoldberg (2000) highlighted, 'To grant a role for the knowledge of practice does not mean the abandonment of a critical stance in favour of undisciplined subjectivism'.

In fact, it might be more meaningful to talk about interest (in both its meanings) rather than bias. As Stenhouse (1981) pointed out, the practitioner-researcher should both *take* an interest in what she is researching (it should be an issue about which she is curious, as opposed to the disinterested 'objective' stance of the scientific researcher), and also *have* an interest in the outcome (it should be an issue that matters to her, for example an improvement in patient care). The practitioner-researcher does not merely wish to bring about change, she wants improvement, and that entails making a subjective value-judgement, what Reason (1988) termed 'critical subjectivity'. As Schön (1983) pointed out, the practitioner-researcher 'has an interest in transforming the situation from what it is to something he likes better'.

Viewing action research as biased or distorted misses its purpose of facilitating self-reflection in the practitioner, who will hopefully discover previously unrecognised shortcomings and in turn endeavour to make improvements to her practice. Hence, all interpretations of meaning from action will always be contextual.

 REFLECTIVE WRITING

Think back to a time when you attempted to implement a change in practice. Examples might include changing a patient's regime of care, a change of routine in the practice area, implementing a new system such as computerised care plans or care pathways, changing documentation or setting up mentorship/preceptorship.

Write a reflective account of the change, considering the following questions:

- How did you start?
- What was your plan of action?
- Did you implement the change alone or did you enlist the help of other people?
- What were the difficulties you encountered?
- What modifications (if any) did you make along the way?
- Was the change successful?
- How did you evaluate it?
- What did you learn from the process?

☐ Action research as reflexive praxis

We can see, then, that action research generates theory and action that is of more relevance to practitioners than the theory and subsequent changes to practice offered by the traditional model of technical rationality. However, it is also a method by which we can come to understand our practice, that is, a way of generating theory from and about practice. Action research therefore closes the feedback loop of technical rationality (Figure 7.1 above) by allowing practice to influence theory as well as being influenced by it (Figure 7.2).

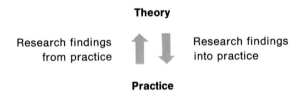

Figure 7.2 A reflexive model

Research that simultaneously describes and constitutes or modifies a social set-ting has been termed reflexive research (Alvesson and Skoldberg, 2000). In this approach, the objective/subjective dichotomy is seen as unproductive (Porter, 1993), and, as Kemmis (1993) pointed out, it is impossible to analyse reflexive action research from a value-free, neutral stance. Rather than attempting to eliminate the effects of the researcher (that is, of herself), the reflexive researcher tries to understand and utilise them.

Reflexivity is clearly an important concept, not only in critical science, where it is employed to ensure that the object of critical intent is far as possible critically appraised, but also in conducting action research and reflective practice. Rolfe (1998) explored the reflexive process in nursing through the work of Benner (1984) and Schön (1987), arguing that the reflexive practitioner is able to modify her practice on the spot by responding to her hypothesis testing (see Chapter 6). This cycle of continuous conscious reflection-in-action has also been explored both in education and research processes, for example in Kolb's (1984) experien-tial learning cycle and Pfeiffer and Jones' (1980) learning cycle both of which follow a similar pattern.

Action research has also been described as a cycle or a spiral of steps (Lewin, 1946) of planning, acting, observing and reflecting. The four stages in the action research cycle comprise a careful and systematic approach to developing changes and innovations in the social world. The initial steps in the cycle are to design and execute a plan of action, followed by a period of reflection. Changes and modifi-cations are made to the plan and the cycle is then repeated. It is important to note, however, that reflection also occurs continuously throughout the cycle. Generally, it is claimed that in action research, any phase of data gathering and interpretation can only be a tentative step forward and not a final answer (Elliot, 1991). Indeed, from a feminist standpoint, reflexivity assumes that all work is incomplete and requires a response from others who are positioned differently (Marcus, 1994). This serves to highlight the importance of the cyclical format and the reflexive approach to the research problem.

An important aspect of reflexive action research is that it addresses the reality of practice in both teaching and nursing, thereby bringing theory and prac-tice closer together, and also aims to help participants to understand and act on their particular situations. Wheeler and Chinn (1984) refer to this as praxis research, which they define as 'thoughtful reflection and action that occur in synchrony, in the direction of the transforming world'. Praxis is action informed by practical theory, which in turn may inform and transform that theory, and the practitioner-researcher who employs the methodology of reflexive action research or praxis research therefore integrates knowledge, thought and theory with professional skills, action and practice in a spiral of reflexive cycles.

Action research has no particular techniques or methods of its own; it is not technique that distinguishes action research from other research methodologies, but the process of reflection and a commitment to the improvement of practice. Hence, it is not the method that makes action research different from other more

Table 7.1 Approaches to research (adapted from Askew and Carnell, 1998)

	Action research	Qualitative research	Quantitative research
Purpose	To bring about informed change	To illuminate meaning and understanding	To increase knowledge and find universal laws and generalisations
Framing	Concerned with the whole picture	Concerned with understanding phenomena	Focus on behaviour not context
Rationale for planning	Research planned to investigate practice	Research planned to investigate phenomena	Research planned to test hypotheses
Techniques	Draws on qualitative and quantitative	Ethnography, case study	Uses measuring techniques
Rigour	Based on logical coherence, interpretations in the reflections	Through discussion of bias and constraints	Statistical analysis and meta techniques for establishing validity and reliability
Objective–subjective dichotomy	Enables practitioners to clarify values on which research is built	Recognition of the subjective nature of research	Sets out to be objective and value-free
Evaluation	By reflective questions	Evaluated by questions related to meaning and understanding	Evaluated by questions referring to reliability and duplication

traditional approaches to research, but its underlying principles. Hart and Bond (1995) devised a useful action research typology in order to make this point, asserting that action research is able to retain a distinct identity whilst simultaneously spanning the entire spectrum of research approaches. Askew and Carnell (1998) also demonstrated that action research is a distinct entity when they outlined the fundamental differences in principles underpinning qualitative, quantitative and action research, some of which are shown in Table 7.1.

Action research is validated by evaluating the impact of actions in a continuous process of data-collection, reflection and analysis, interpretation, action and evaluation (Altrichter, Posch and Somekh, 1993). Hence, the rigour of action research:

> derives from the logical, empirical, and political coherence of interpretations in the reconstructive moments of the self reflective spiral (observing and reflecting) and the logical, empirical, and political coherence of justifications of proposed action in its construction or prospective moments (planning and acting).
> (Kemmis, 1993: 185)

Action research deals with local problems, and therefore the findings cannot always be generalised to other situations. However, this is only a problem when viewed from the perspective of traditional science, which assumes that findings must be generalisable in order to impact on practice. Indeed, the Department of Health (1993a) specifically defined research as 'rigorous and systematic enquiry ... designed to lead to generalisable contributions to knowledge'. However, action research is essentially a qualitative endeavour, and as such, it has a different relationship to practice (Rolfe, 1996a). Thus, whereas the social and political context in which the research is carried out might have some resonance with other organisations, the outcomes will always be different, as the learning is unique to each situation and each learner and therefore cannot be replicated exactly. Every practice situation is therefore a separate and unique case (Jarvis, 2000).

Case example: reflexive action research

A ward manager wished to improve the admission procedure on her ward by following Lewin's action research circle:

Plan	She first ascertained the need for change and explored various options by interviewing staff and patients, by visiting other wards, and by conducting a search of the literature.
Act	She then designed and introduced a new procedure based on the above data.
Observe	Following a trial period, she conducted interviews and participant observations to assess the impact of the new procedure.

Reflect	She next conducted focus groups with staff and patients to discover whether they felt that the new procedure had led to improvement in the way that admissions were carried out.
Plan	She then planned further modifications to the procedure in a second action research cycle.

DISCUSSION POINT

Look back to the earlier reflective writing exercise on implementing a change in practice. With a colleague, discuss how you might approach this innovation using a reflexive action research framework. What does the action research framework add to your understanding of implementing a change in practice?

FURTHER READING

There are a number of texts written specifically about action research. Lewin produced the first major theories of action research, and whilst his earlier work can be difficult to locate, many of the more recent texts make reference to Lewin's initial work and his influence on the development of subsequent theories. Altrichter *et al.* write specifically about action research for educators, although the book provides a useful introduction to the practicalities of the research process itself, with much of the text being easily transferable to the healthcare setting.

Altrichter, H., Posch, P. and Somekh, B. (1993) *Teachers Investigate their Work: An Introduction to the Methods of Action Research.* London: Routledge.

Hart, E. and Bond, M. (1995) *Action Research for Health and Social Care. A Guide to Practice.* Buckingham: Open University Press.

Hughes, I. (1997) *Action Research Electronic Reader.* Internet site http://www.beh.cchs.usyd.edu.au

Lewin, K. (1946) 'Action Research and Minority Problems', *Journal of Social Issues*, **2** (4), 34–46.

Rolfe, G. (1998) 'Reflexive Action Research', in G. Rolfe, *Expanding Nursing Knowledge*, Oxford: Butterworth Heinemann.

Zuber-Skerritt, O. (1991) *Action Research for Change and Development*, Aldershot: Avebury.

We can see that this action research study produced a local solution to a local problem, and is not necessarily generalisable to other settings. This study also provides a good example of subjective evaluation, since it is the staff and patients who make the final judgement in the reflective stage as to whether or not they feel that the admission procedure has improved.

■ Towards a science of practice

In the pursuit of a science of practice (as opposed to a science *for* practice, which is the aim of technical rationality), it is essential that we 'avoid methodology being perceived as peripheral to research practice as a result of it being "intellectualised"' (Alvesson and Skoldberg, 2000). The task of making methodological issues more accessible and central to the work of the practitioner-researcher is certainly a challenge for all those concerned with healthcare practice, and one in which critical reflection plays a significant role by utilising human science methodology to check on the validity of practice knowledge. The prime motivation of research for the science of practice is therefore to inform and develop practice through reflexivity. Reflexive research has two basic characteristics, namely careful interpretation and reflection, characteristics which are not alien to the practice of the advanced practitioner (Alvesson and Skoldberg, 2000).

A science of practice based in reflexive research methods is not devoid of theory or knowledge, but is rather pregnant with theory. As we have tried to show throughout this book, knowledge and theory can be created by all of us from our own practice, and

> the test of knowledge is not whether it corresponds exactly to reality, as it is impossible to ascertain whether there is such a direct correspondence. Instead, the test for knowledge is whether it serves to guide human action to attain goals. (Hoshimond and Polkinghorne, 1992: 58)

Evidence of having achieved our intended outcomes can be assessed through reflexive strategies, but only:

- if the appropriate frameworks are used;
- with the development of suitable estimations of rigour;
- if the environment is conducive, for example that of a practicum; and
- if collaborative inquiry, dialogic reflection and conscientization are valued by practitioners in pursuit of clinical effectiveness.

In conclusion, then, where action research is an integral part of the practitioner's daily work, she can feel empowered to make changes in her practice (Somekh, 1995). The idea of the practitioner-researcher learning about the process of researching through carrying out research is congruent with both the action learning and the action research cycles. Further, it fulfils the notion of lifelong learning espoused by the UKCC (1996) and is fundamental to the process of reflective practice. Research as reflexivity views the practitioner as a professional learner, whom Askew and Carnell described as:

> engaged in the process of action learning and action research, reflecting on experiences, developing understanding, gaining insights into practice, making important professional judgements and bringing about actions for change. (1998:152)

This embodies the concept of what we have previously defined as the advanced practitioner.

Research, then, is also concerned with systematically and rigorously controlled learning, and its practitioners are often well placed to learn systematically about their own practice (Jarvis, 1996). From this viewpoint, the practitioner is not seen as a technician delivering a programme of care, but as an open and professional learner/educator in action, a concept that will be explored further in the following chapter. In fact, this is often reflected in the reality of clinical practice, and as such, the patient is always teaching the carer.

Using the self as a research instrument does invoke some criticism, not least when the researcher declares that the research is also a tool for personal and professional development, and the researcher must be able to demonstrate a reflexive awareness of the factors influencing the various stages of her research practices. However, as we have attempted to show throughout this book, 'interpretation free, theory-neutral facts do not, in principle exist' (Alvesson and Skoldberg, 2000), and it is impossible for the researcher not to bring something of herself to the research process.

REFLECTIVE WRITING

Now turn back to the aims that you identified at the start of the chapter. To what extent have they been met? Write a paragraph outlining the learning about research and the reflective practitioner you have acquired through reading this chapter and doing the exercises. Write a paragraph identifying any aims you feel were only partially met or not met at all.

As in previous chapters, divide your page into three columns. Head the first column 'What I need to learn', and make a list of any outstanding issues you would like to learn more about. For example you might wish to learn more about practitioner based research. Head the second column 'How will I learn it', and write down the ways in which your learning needs could be addressed. Head the third column 'How will I know that I have learnt it', and try to identify how you will know when you have met your needs.

Chapter 8

Education and the reflective practitioner

■ Introduction

We started this book by exploring the relationship between knowledge and practice, and proposed a model that conceptualised practice development in terms of knowledge rather than skills acquisition. We further suggested that scientific knowledge is only one of many possible foundations for nursing practice, and that the expert or advanced practitioner employs a combination of experiential and scientific 'knowing-how' and 'knowing-that' when she makes on the spot clinical judgements. Subsequent chapters explored a variety of ways for developing experiential knowledge through reflection-on-action and reflection-in-action, and proposed the idea of the advanced practitioner as an active and reflexive experimenter in practice.

One of the consequences of this model is that if the advanced practitioner is developing knowledge through reflection on and in action, then she is both a researcher and, as we suggested at the end of the previous chapter, an active learner. In this final chapter we shall explore in more detail some of the implications of active learning and suggest ways in which you might maximise your learning from practice. The aims of this chapter are therefore:

1 to discover and explore your own style(s) of learning;
2 to begin to map out your own learning needs and write learning contracts to address them;
3 to consider critically a number of models of open learning; and
4 to help you to continue the process of lifelong learning.

 REFLECTIVE WRITING

Think carefully about our aims for Chapter 8. Now think about your own practice and how these aims might contribute towards developing it.

Based on our aims above, write down some of your own, both in terms of what you hope to know and what you hope to do after reading Chapter 8. We will return to your aims at the end of the chapter.

■ Learning and practice

We have claimed above that there is a close correspondence between how we learn and how we practice. The educationalist David Kolb (1984) suggested that different people are predisposed towards different styles of learning, and that these could be represented along the two axes of 'Concrete Experience versus Abstract Conceptualisation' (CE–AC) and 'Active Experimentation versus Reflective Observation' (AE–RO). Thus, by plotting your position on each of these axes it is possible to determine which of four learning styles suits you best (Figure 8.1). For example, if you are towards the 'concrete experience' end of one axis and towards the 'reflective observation' end of the other axis, then you will have a 'divergent' learning style.

Divergent learners are imaginative and capable of viewing situations from a variety of perspectives. As Kolb *et al.* (1995) pointed out, 'the divergent learning style … emphasises concrete evidence and reflective observation'. They are 'feelers' rather than 'doers', and are good at brainstorming new ideas. In contrast, convergent learners are good at abstract conceptualisation and active experimentation. They prefer technical problems to interpersonal issues, and are adept at scientific or hypothetical-deductive reasoning. Assimilative learners also tend towards abstract conceptualisation, but they are observers rather than doers. As Kolb *et al.* (1995) pointed out, 'the greatest strength of this orientation lies in inductive reasoning, in the ability to create theoretical models and in assimilating disparate observations into an integrated explanation'. Finally, accommodative learners have the opposite strengths to assimilative learners, and are interested in concrete experience and active experimentation. Kolb *et al.* (1995) note that 'The greatest strength of this orientation lies in doing things, in carrying out plans and tasks, and in getting involved in new experiences'. Furthermore:

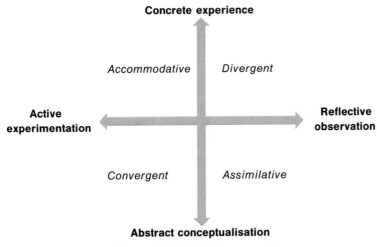

Figure 8.1   Kolb's learning styles

In situations where the theory or plans do not fit the facts, those with an accommodative style will most likely discard the plan or theory. People with an accommodative orientation tend to solve problems in an intuitive trial and error manner, relying on other people for information rather than on their own analytic ability. (Kolb *et al.*, 1995: 54)

Kolb related each of the four styles to particular kinds of work. For example, the convergent style is typical of many engineers and technical specialists, the divergent style is characteristic of caring and welfare activities and the arts, the assimilative style relates to the pure sciences, and the accommodative style relates to technical or practical fields such as business. This is, of course, something of an overgeneralisation, and we might expect all four 'types' to be found in any particular profession. Thus, nursing and the caring professions might have higher numbers of divergent learners, but they will also include practitioners from each of the other three orientations.

You might notice from Kolb's descriptions of his four types that the divergent learner who 'emphasises concrete experience and reflective observation' is similar to our reflective practitioner who reflects *on* action, and that Kolb's accommodative learner who 'tend[s] to solve problems in an intuitive trial and error manner' shares many characteristics with our reflexive practitioner who reflects *in* action. Furthermore, Kolb's assimilative learner is clearly a theoretician and model builder, whereas his convergent learner who relies on 'abstract conceptualisation and active experimentation' would appear best-suited to scientific research.

Since we are suggesting a knowledge acquisition model of practice development, we should not be surprised at this close correlation between learning styles and modes of theorising and practising. In fact, we need only slightly alter Kolb's two axes for his model of learning styles to be transformed into a model of practice development styles. Thus, his Concrete Experience versus Abstract Conceptualisation (CE–AC) axis becomes Experiential Knowledge versus Scientific Knowledge, and his Active Experimentation versus Reflective Observation (AE–RO) axis becomes Reflection-In-Action versus Reflection-On-Action (Figure 8.2).

We can see that this model suggests four ways of developing practice: by reflecting in action; by reflecting on action; by carrying out controlled scientific research; and by developing models and theories. Furthermore, each of these ways of developing practice is associated with one of the four types of practitioner knowledge discussed in Chapter 1 (see Figure 1.3). We have argued that reflection on and in action are associated with expert and advanced practice, and it is therefore likely that practitioners who prefer these approaches will tend to remain in clinical practice, whereas those who prefer the latter two approaches of researching and theorising will tend to move into academic or research posts, or else will be attracted to more technical healthcare roles in which there are clear-cut procedures and answers. We have also argued in this book that

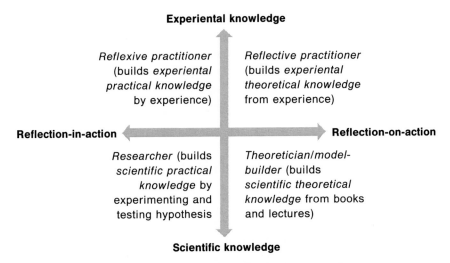

Experiental knowledge

Reflexive practitioner
(builds *experiental*
practical knowledge
by experience)

Reflective practitioner
(builds *experiental*
theoretical knowledge
from experience)

Reflection-in-action

Reflection-on-action

Researcher (builds
scientific practical
knowledge by
experimenting and
testing hypothesis

Theoretician/model-
builder (builds
scientific theoretical
knowledge from books
and lectures)

Scientific knowledge

Figure 8.2   A model of practice development styles

the profession of nursing in particular, and healthcare in general, has been dominated by these latter technical approaches at the expense of the former reflective approaches.

☐   Experiential learning

We have seen, then, that there is a close relationship between the way in which we practice and the way in which we learn. Reflective and reflexive practitioners build experiential theoretical knowledge and experiential practical knowledge by reflecting on and in their own practice, and might therefore be described as experiential learners. Thus, whereas the traditional learner learns *about* practice, usually from those who profess to know more about it than she does, the experiential learner predominantly learns *from* and *in* practice. Bines (1992) has referred to the former model of learning as 'technocratic education', which is characterised by 'the development and transmission of a systematic knowledge base . . . [and] the interpretation and application of the knowledge base to practice'. Technocratic education therefore requires a core curriculum of knowledge that is designed and delivered by an educationalist with expertise in both theory and practice, and that is relevant and appropriate to all students on a particular course. This model of technocratic education is passive in that the student has no role to play in the choice or delivery of the material; she has merely to absorb the content of what is being taught, and is not even expected to decide how the theory should be applied to practice.

In contrast, experiential or active learning is located within a 'post-technocratic' model (Bines, 1992) which assumes that the most appropriate knowledge for practice is located not in books or even in universities, but in the practice itself.

If this is the case, then as Schön (1987) pointed out, 'what aspiring practitioners most need to learn, professional schools seem least able to teach'. Carl Rogers (1957) went even further to suggest that 'anything that can be taught to another is relatively inconsequential and has little or no significance on behaviour', whilst Boud *et al.* (1985) added that:

> Only learners themselves can learn and only they can reflect on their own experiences. Teachers can intervene in various ways to assist, but they only have access to individuals' thoughts and feelings through what individuals choose to reveal about themselves. At this basic level the learner is in total control. (1985:11)

Clearly, then, the educationalist has a very different role to play in the post-technocratic model than in traditional passive learning. Indeed, as Rogers claimed and Boud *et al.* implied above, the role of the *teacher* is largely redundant.

This does not mean that the educationalist has no place in the education of the reflective practitioner, simply that her role is not to teach in the traditional sense of delivering knowledge and theory. Rather, she is concerned with facilitating the practitioner to construct, gain access to, and critically explore her own experiential knowledge from her own practice. Just as the practitioner is an expert in the practice and process of healthcare, so the educationalist should be an expert in the practice and process of education. What the educationalist possesses that the healthcare practitioner does not, is experiential knowledge about the process of learning; it is not her 'know-that' that is important in post-technocratic education, but her 'know-how'.

Post-technocratic education is therefore concerned far more with process than with content. This distinction is particularly important in the education of more

---

 FURTHER READING

You might like to think about your own preferred way of learning. For example, do you consider yourself to be an active or a passive learner? More specifically, which of Kolb's four learning styles is closest to your own? To find out more about Kolb's model of learning, see:

Kolb, D.A. (1984) *Experiential Learning: Experience as the Source of Learning and Development*, Englewood Cliffs, New Jersey: Prentice Hall.

A simplified version of his Learning Style Inventory can be found in:

Kolb, D.A., Osland, J.S. and Rubin, I.M. (1995) *Organizational Behavior: an Experiential Approach*, Englewood Cliffs, New Jersey: Prentice Hall: 46–7.

experienced or advanced practitioners, since it removes the necessity for the educator to know more about healthcare practice than the practitioner herself. The role of the educator is not to teach the practitioner how to practice, but to help her to learn from her own reflections on her own practice. Of course, the practitioner might also need access to scientific knowledge, but it is not the job of the educator to tell her what she needs to know, but rather to help her to seek out, gain access to, and evaluate the relevant published material. Seen in this way, the healthcare practitioner and the practitioner of education form a partnership of equals, each with their own expertise in their own realm of practice.

In this book, we have offered a number of approaches to active experiential learning, including writing-to-learn (Chapter 3), individual and group supervision (Chapters 4 and 5) and reflection-in-action (Chapter 6). We now wish to distil these approaches into a process model of learning for the post-technocratic reflective and reflexive practitioner in order to help you to become a lifelong learner.

■ A process model of experiential learning

Education has often been described as a journey, and it might be instructive to compare the metaphorical educational journey with a real journey from one place to another. For example, we might think about what happens when we stop someone in the street and ask her for help in getting to our destination. There are basically three ways that a passer-by might offer help if I am lost: firstly, she might personally take me to where I want to go; secondly, she might give me directions (for example, take the first road on the left, turn right at the traffic lights, etc.); and thirdly, she might draw a map for me.

Similarly, there are three main ways to get from A to B in education. Firstly, the educator can personally take the student. This is usually known as the apprenticeship model, or what Bines (1992) referred to as pre-technocratic education, and involves the student working alongside a more experienced educator/ practitioner or clinical teacher. The apprenticeship model is the basis of most traditional courses in professional education, but is now usually thought of as being too *ad hoc* and unaccademic for most professions. It can be successful, but depends largely on the educational skills and qualities of the practitioner. Furthermore, it lacks a formal structure and relies primarily on the gradual and largely unconscious absorption of skills by the student. Rather like being driven along a route that she does not know, the student tends not to pay too much attention to where she is going, and probably could not retrace the route by herself.

Secondly, the educationalist could give directions to the student in the form of a syllabus backed up with lectures and set reading, with an examination or other form of assessment to check whether the route has been followed. This is Bines' model of technocratic education, and is the foundation of most modern courses in professional education such as *Project 2000* for pre-registration nurses, and many taught post-qualifying courses. The implicit or (sometimes) explicit aim of such courses is not to learn what the student finds interesting or relevant, but what is set out in the syllabus. This sends a clear message to the student that the educator knows best what she needs to learn, and usually how best she might learn it. The aim when writing assignments is therefore to attempt to guess the 'right' answers, that is, the answers dictated by the syllabus.

The technocratic model clearly favours Kolb's convergent and assimilative learners, and the proliferation of courses of this type might partly explain the dominance of scientific knowledge over experiential knowledge in most of the healthcare professions. Furthermore, whilst this model might be appropriate for neophyte practitioners (although Rolfe, 1993, argues otherwise), it is clearly arrogant of the educator to assume that she knows best what the advanced practitioner needs to learn, and indeed, how she might best learn it.

Thirdly, the educator can give the student a map. This is a fairly new approach to learning, what Bines referred to as 'post-technocratic' education and what others have referred to as 'open learning', and it gives the student a degree of control over how to get from A to B. She still has to get there (there are still learning outcomes to be achieved), but she has some degree of choice about which route she wishes to take, and sometimes about the precise location of point B. As we shall see, this post-technocratic model is most appropriate for reflective and reflexive practitioners.

 FURTHER READING

If you would like to read more about open learning, you might like to start with the work of Carl Rogers (who referred to it as student-centred learning) and Malcolm Knowles (who referred to it as andragogy), who are usually acknowledged as the modern-day founders of this approach. Abercrombie has (to a limited extent) applied the model to medical education in the form of 'free group discussion', and A.S. Neill has taken it to its logical conclusion in his school 'Summerhill'. If you are interested in the philosophical roots of open learning, you might wish to read John Dewey's short book *Experience and Education*, or Jean Jacques Rousseau's seminal and more poetic book *Emile*.

Abercrombie, M.L.J. (1979) *Aims and Techniques of Group Teaching*, Guildford: SRHE.
Dewey, J. (1963) *Experience and Education*, New York: Collier Books.
Knowles, M. (1984) *The Adult Learner: A Neglected Species* (3rd edn), Houston: Gulf.
Neill, A.S. (1968) *Summerhill*, Harmondsworth: Penguin.
Nias, J. (ed.) (1993) *The Human Nature of Learning: Selections from the Work of M.L.J. Abercrombie*, Buckingham: Open University Press.
Rogers, C. (1983) *Freedom to Learn for the 80s*, Columbus: Merrill.
Rousseau, J.J. (1911) *Emile, or Education*, London: Dent.

DISCUSSION POINT

Think about a previous course you have been on. Try to identify which of the three educational models described above was mainly employed. With a colleague, discuss the things you liked and disliked about that approach. How did it suit your style of learning?

☐ A map of professional practice

At the start of his book *Educating the Reflective Practitioner,* Donald Schön observed that:

> In the varied topography of professional practice, there is a high, hard ground overlooking a swamp. On the high ground, manageable problems lend themselves to solution through the application of research-based theory and technique. In the swampy lowland, messy, confusing problems defy technical solution. The irony of this situation is that the problems of the high ground tend to be relatively unimportant to individuals or society at large, however great their technical interest may be, while in the swamp lie the problems of greatest human concern. The practitioner must choose. Shall he remain on the high ground where he can solve relatively unimportant problems according to prevailing standards of rigor, or shall he descend to the swamp of important problems and nonrigorous inquiry? (Schön, 1987: 3)

We maintain that only post-technocratic reflective and reflexive practitioners are able to (and would wish to) explore Schön's 'messy confusing problems [that] defy technical solution', and that this can only be achieved through an open learning model of education. Few educationalists are qualified or experienced to take the student through the swamp from A to B themselves, and providing a list of directions is hardly appropriate for practitioners at this level, even supposing that the educator had enough experiential knowledge to compile one. It clearly makes far more sense to give her a map (Figure 8.3).

The first thing to note about a map is that you are able to get more information out than was originally put into it, inasmuch as it allows you to go to places that were never intended by the map maker. This particular map (partially) represents the practice of nursing, and we can see from it that there are some fairly well-trodden paths that lead from novice practice to various destinations such as community psychiatric nursing and stoma-care nursing. However, we cannot go too far beyond these points without running into the swampy lowlands of

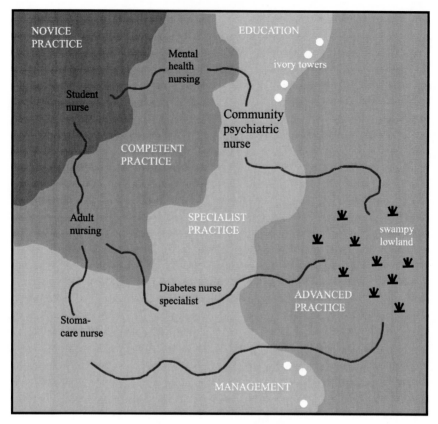

Figure 8.3 A map of nursing practice

advanced practice, where there are no paths and very few landmarks. Unfortunately, a large number of more experienced practitioners are out there, often on their own, and they probably feel that sometimes they are slowly sinking into the swamp.

Being offered a map might be useful for less-advanced practitioners who are in areas of practice that are well-charted, and it might also be useful for showing the advanced practitioner where she has been, and for helping her to get back onto firm ground. However, advanced practitioners are in largely uncharted territory, and the educationalist is usually unable to provide them with a map that can help them to move forward. Indeed, many advanced practitioners are not even certain where they are moving to. There are some ivory towers along the coast from which educationalists can look out over the swampy lowlands and shout directions but, essentially, the advanced practitioner is out there on her own. In the absence of a reliable map, the aim of the post-technocratic educator is to help the advanced practitioner to make her own, and this, in a nutshell, is the purpose of open learning.

■ Applying the process model of learning

□ Mapping out your learning needs

What would a map of your practice look like? It would certainly contain far more detail than the one shown in Figure 8.3. If you think of that map as a map of a country, showing the main 'cities' such as community psychiatric nursing, diabetes nurse specialism and stoma-care nursing, then your own map might be a street plan of just one of those cities. Your map might show the qualifications recognised in your particular specialism, it might mark out routes in terms of experiences to be gained, or it might be a plan of the different posts you need to work in on your road to the ideal job. It might show the 'main roads' that most practitioners use to move forwards in their learning and in their careers, as well as the dirt tracks that are slower and less well-travelled. However you decide to design your map, there are four issues that you will need to think about.

Firstly, you will need to determine just where on the map you currently are. What is your present location in terms of qualifications, experience or job title? Secondly, you will need to decide where you wish to go. Your destination might be the high, hard ground of specialist practice, of management, or of education, or it might be out in the swampy lowlands developing your experiential knowledge and becoming a more reflective or reflexive practitioner. Thirdly, you will need to decide how you are going to get there. Do you wish to travel along the quickest or the most scenic route? What is your favoured mode of transport; that is, when, where and how do you learn best? Finally, you will need some way of identifying when you have arrived. If your chosen destination is a particular job or qualification, there will be some familiar landmarks to signal your arrival. If, on the other hand, you have chosen to develop your experiential or scientific knowledge-base, then it might not be quite so obvious that you have arrived.

If we put these four issues together – identifying the current state of your knowledge and theory; deciding what it is that you want and need from education; planning how these wants and needs are going to be met; and identifying how you will know that your wants and needs have been met – we have the framework for a simple learning contract (Table 8.1).

Table 8.1   A framework for a simple learning contract

Learning contract

- What do I already know?
- What do I want to learn?
- How do I want to learn it?
- How will I know, and be able to demonstrate, that I have learnt it?

Learning contracts are the basis for lifelong learning, and represent both short- and long-term plans of what the practitioner hopes to achieve. Learning contracts might be made between the practitioner and an educationalist as part of a formal course, or else they might be made by the practitioner with herself. You have probably noticed that each chapter of this book ends by asking you to assess what you have learnt from reading it (What do I already know?), to identify what other knowledge you still need (What do I want to learn?), how you might go about obtaining it (How do I want to learn it?), and how you will know that you have achieved it (How will I know, and be able to demonstrate, that I have learnt it?). If you have carried out these exercises, you have therefore written a series of learning contracts to give structure and direction to your individual lifelong learning about reflective practice.

 REFLECTIVE WRITING

Draw a map of your current practice in whatever style you choose. Try to be imaginative and include as much detail as you can. Now identify where you are on your map, and think about your next destination. What is your most immediate educational need in moving towards your goal?

Using the above format, try to write a learning contract to meet part of that need. For example, you might identify the need to learn more about evidence-based practice, and choose to write a learning contract to help you to conduct a systematic literature review.

☐   Developing a learning community

Learning by yourself can be a very lonely business, and just as clinical supervision can be carried out either individually or in groups, so too can learning, particularly if the focus is on learning from your own experience, that is, on reflection-on-action. We have already looked in detail at setting up a supervision group in Chapter 5, and many of the same issues apply to establishing a community of learners, such as group size, composition, venue, ground rules and so on. The one major difference is that whereas we recommended that supervision groups should usually be facilitated, this is rarely the case for learning communities, which is why we prefer to refer to them as communities rather than as groups. Nevertheless, learning communities are subject to the same developmental stages and dynamic forces as any group, and in the absence of a facilitator, particular care and consideration should be given to these issues. You might find it helpful at this point to look again at the sections of Chapter 5 that deal with establishing and running a group. Furthermore, the three models of intra-, inter- and transpersonal group dynamics which we applied to supervision groups also apply to learning communities, and we shall now consider each in turn.

Firstly, we shall briefly examine the intrapersonal model in which learners meet together in order to pursue their own individual needs through their own individual learning contracts. As we discussed in Chapter 5, the intrapersonal model of group behaviour views each individual as striving to meet her own agenda, and the role of the other members is to help her to achieve her personal learning objectives. The other members of the learning community therefore offer support and suggestions and act as an external check and validation to ensure that her learning outcomes are being met. The main (and not insignificant) advantage of this model is that it helps to alleviate the loneliness of the long-distance learner. The disadvantage, however, is that each learner will spend the majority of the group time facilitating others rather than having her own learning needs met.

Secondly, we shall turn our attention to the interpersonal model, in which the community works together on a shared learning project rather than individual members pursuing their own individual agendas. For example, the community might decide to focus on learning more about research methods, and would produce a shared learning contract in which different roles and tasks were given to different individuals. This model has a number of advantages over both individual learning and the intrapersonal model described above. Not only does it allow each individual to benefit from the work of her colleagues in a way rarely encountered (and often discouraged) in more formal learning environments, but it plays to the strengths of each of those individuals. When Kolb identified his four learning orientations, he pointed out that none was superior to any other, and that 'the key to effective learning is being competent in each mode when it is appropriate' (Kolb *et al.* 1995). A group that contains individuals from all four orientations therefore has a distinct advantage over an individual with strengths in only one or two. For example, the convergent learners in the group might conduct a literature search of the topic area, the assimilators might organise the findings into a coherent and logical format, the accommodators might offer alternative and more creative perspectives, and the divergers might relate the emerging findings to the real world. The disadvantage of this approach to learning is that the learning aims and outcomes are decided upon by the community as a whole, and the individual learner might find herself engaged in a project for which she has little personal interest.

Thirdly, we shall look at the transpersonal model, in which the focus is on the process of learning rather than the content. This model can operate either with a group project or with a number of individual projects. For example, the input of the learning community to an individual learning project would be to explore *how* the individual would go about learning rather than *what* she might learn. When examining her learning contract, the group would be focusing less on the first and second questions of 'what do I already know?' and 'what do I want to learn?', and more on the third and fourth questions of 'how do I want to learn it?' and 'how will I know that I have learnt it?'. To return to the map analogy, the learning community will be more concerned with the route and with the mode of transport than with the final destination.

This task becomes more complex with a group learning project, because the community will be reflexively exploring its own underlying processes rather than those of a (temporarily) external individual. In the absence of a detached and impartial facilitator, the learning community has the difficult dual role of monitoring both the content and the (often unconscious) process of learning.

Most learning communities find that they slip in and out of all three of the above models to suit the task at hand. The community might well have one or more group projects as well as a number of individual ones, and might focus sometimes on process and at other times on content. At their best, learning communities provide support and assistance to the individual whilst not stifling their individual aims and objectives.

☐ An open learning course for reflective and reflexive practitioners

We have already explored the use of learning contracts as a way of identifying and planning your individual and group learning needs. However, learning contracts can also be negotiated with an educationalist as part of an open learning course. The term 'open learning' is often misused, partly because it is sometimes confused with the term 'distance learning'. The former is a philosophy of education, whereas the latter is a way of delivering what can be (and often is) a very traditional 'closed' course. The purpose of open learning courses is not to tell you what or how you should be learning, but to give you access to some experienced educational map-makers who can offer help and advice on planning your own route through a series of learning contracts. In fact, we might regard an open learning course as a particular kind of facilitated learning community. We shall now briefly examine some of the key features of an open learning course for reflective (experienced) and reflexive (advanced) practitioners.

☐ *What do I already know?*

To continue our map analogy, the first question to be addressed in the learning contract is the equivalent of establishing point A (where am I now?) on the map. Unlike in the examples of being taken or of being given directions, it is essential when reading a map to know where you are at the moment, that is, the current state of your knowledge and practice. Furthermore, this is likely to be something that is different for each student, and all that most post-registration students have in common is that they each bring a unique and individual body of theoretical and practical knowledge with them to a course. Traditional courses assume or require that all the students are at the same point on starting, whereas open learning courses work with the student in order to help her to identify her own starting point.

☐ *What do I want to learn?*

The second question in the learning contract is concerned with deciding on the location of point B. Unlike on most traditional courses, where your learning destination is established in advance by the syllabus, open learning usually requires you to decide where it is on the map that you wish to go. By writing a learning contract, the student is therefore to some extent writing her own course syllabus.

One of the difficulties with taking such an open approach to course design is that the student is often spoilt for choice: she has so many learning needs, so many potential destinations, that it is difficult for her to make decisions about which is the most pressing. In attempting to resolve this problem, we should always bear in mind the first tenet of experiential learning; that the most meaningful learning arises from practice. It is only when undertaking a new project that the practitioner runs up against the limitations of her own knowledge and understanding, just as it is only when we move out of our own familiar locality that we have to stop and consult our map.

Ideally, then, open learning courses for reflective practitioners should be project-based, since it is only through planning and implementing new practice-based projects that the practitioner can begin to identify the learning she needs in order to support and carry out that project. And since most practitioners are very busy people, courses should be based largely around *real* projects that they have recently completed, are currently involved in, or are about to commence.

☐ *How do I want to learn it?*

The third question asks you to decide on your mode of transport. To some extent, different kinds of knowledge are best acquired by particular methods of learning. Some knowledge (for example, scientific theoretical knowledge) is most easily and appropriately learnt in a classroom from an expert in that particular kind of knowledge or else from reading a book. Other kinds of knowledge (for example, experiential practical knowledge) can only be learnt from other practitioners or from yourself through discussion and reflection-on-action, and it should be borne in mind that learning *about* practice often means learning *from* practice, and for the reflective practitioner, that usually means learning from her own practice.

However, although different kinds of knowledge lend themselves to different forms of learning, most students also have their favoured style. Some learn best in a classroom, some from private study, some from reflective writing and some from group discussions and seminars. In open learning courses, then, the student should have a large degree of freedom in deciding exactly how she will get from A to B; that is, on *how* she wishes to learn as well as *what* she wishes to learn.

☐ *How will I know, and be able to demonstrate, that I have learnt it?*

Finally, the fourth question is concerned with verifying that you actually are at point B where you think you are. The simple answer to this question is that you write an assignment that is marked by a tutor. In traditional courses, where the destination is set in advance by the syllabus, the assessment often drives the course, and the first question that most new students ask is 'what do I need to do in order to pass this course?' In open learning courses, the assessment depends on the location of point B and the mode of transport employed in order to get there, and will often be decided by the student herself.

The more complex answer to the question concerns the nature of the assignment, particularly when the course is centred on a practice-based project. We have already asserted that open learning involves collaboration between an experienced practitioner and an experienced educationalist, each with her own specific experiential and scientific knowledge. However, if the educationalist is an expert in education rather than in health care practice, then there are very real concerns surrounding her ability to assess the practice-based work of the practitioner. Indeed, it might be argued that the person best placed to assess practice-based projects is the practitioner herself.

This notion of critical self-appraisal fits perfectly with the philosophy of open and/or lifelong learning, which should be concerned not only with self-education, but also with self-evaluation. The role of the educationalist should therefore be to provide the knowledge and theory to enable the reflective practitioner to critically evaluate her own practice-based projects, and to support and facilitate her through the process. Of course, there is still a requirement on most academic courses for the assignment to be marked and accredited by an educationalist, but her role is to assess the practitioner's evaluation of her own project rather

Table 8.2 Some questions to ask about open learning courses for experienced and advanced practitioners

---

- Is the course structured through learning contracts negotiated between the practitioner and an educationalist?

- Is it organised around real practice-based projects in the practitioner's own workplace?

- Does it offer access to a wide range of taught and self-directed units of education of relevance to each individual practitioner?

- Does it facilitate and encourage the practitioner to explore her experiential knowledge base through reflection-on-action?

- Does it facilitate the practitioner to critically evaluate her own project work?

- Does it facilitate the sharing of knowledge and experience between practitioners, both within and outside of the practitioner's own specialism, through seminars, discussions and group work?

- Is it structured to fit the busy schedule of the practitioner rather than that of the educationalist?

- Does it promote a relationship between practitioner and educationalist as a partnership of equals, each with skills, knowledge and expertise in their own discipline?

---

than directly to evaluate the project herself. This approach separates assessment (which is the job of the educationalist) from evaluation (which is the job of the reflective practitioner), so that what is required from an assignment is not necessarily a successful project, but a skilled evaluation, even of an unsuccessful project.

We can see, then, that open learning courses are likely to look very different from more traditional taught courses, and some of the questions you might wish to ask when choosing such a course are suggested in Table 8.2.

DISCUSSION POINT

Try to imagine what an open learning course of this type would be like, and how it might be structured. With a colleague, discuss some of the pros and cons of such a course.

It is unlikely that any course will meet all of the criteria suggested in Table 8.2, and perhaps not all will be appropriate to your own needs. However, it is important that you have your own shopping list when looking at prospective courses.

REFLECTIVE WRITING

Now think about what issues are important to you in an open learning course. Write down your own list of questions that you would wish to ask the tutor of a course that you might apply for.

■ Conclusion: becoming a lifelong learner

In this final chapter, we have attempted to make links between different modes of practice and different approaches to learning. Clearly, since the development of our practice is a lifelong endeavour, then so too is our learning. For reflective and reflexive practitioners, the two activities cannot be separated: the very act of reflecting on and in practice generates experiential knowledge, and so to practice is also to learn (and, indeed, to research).

In many ways, then, this entire book has been concerned with learning: through critical reflection, through reflective writing, through individual and group supervision, through reflection-in-action and through practitioner-research. However, in most of these activities the learning is *ad hoc* and often secondary to some other goal such as developing practice or doing research. In this chapter we have focused on learning as an end in itself, and discussed some of the ways that the reflective and reflexive practitioner can structure her learning experiences either alone, with colleagues, or through a formal taught course.

The most important learning, however, is what we might call meta-learning, that is, learning about how you learn. This meta-learning is the basis of life-long learning. If we help a practitioner to learn about (say) depressive illness and to work with people suffering from depressive illness, then we have equipped her to carry out a task for a limited time-span until her knowledge and skills become outdated. But if we help a practitioner to learn how to learn, then we have equipped her for life.

Let us return once more to our map analogy. If we take a traveller to where she wants to go, or if we give her directions, we will help her to reach her next destination but no further. If we give her a map, she will be able to navigate without further help until she comes to the edge of that map or until the map becomes out of date. If, on the other hand, we show her how to make her own maps, then she can continue with her travels for as long and as far as she wishes. Our hope is that, having read this book, you have begun to sketch out your first maps and will continue to work on refining them throughout your life as a practitioner. To reiterate the quotation cited at the very start of this book, 'to read means to borrow; to create out of one's reading is paying off one's debts' (Lichtenberg, 1969).

REFLECTIVE WRITING

Now turn back to the aims which you identified at the start of the chapter. To what extent have they been met? Write a paragraph outlining the scientific and experiential knowledge you have acquired through reading this chapter and doing the exercises. Write a second paragraph identifying any aims which you feel were only partially met or not met at all. Now divide your page into three columns. Head the first column 'What I need to learn', and make a list of any outstanding issues which you would like to learn more about. Head the second column 'How I will learn it', and write down the ways in which your learning needs could be addressed, for example, through further reading, through attending study days, or through talking to other people. Head the third column 'How I will know that I have learnt it', and try to identify how you will know when you have met your needs.

You have just written the last learning contract of this book, but not, we hope, the last of your career.

References

Abercrombie, M.L.J. (1979) *Aims and Techniques of Group Teaching*, Guildford: SRHE.

Adair, J. (1968) *Training for Leadership*, London: Macdonald.

Agazarian, Y. and Peters, R. (1981) *The Visible and Invisible Group*, London: Routledge & Kegan Paul.

Akinsanya, J. (1985) 'Learning about life', *Senior Nurse*, **2** (5), 24–5.

Allen, D.G., Bowers, B. and Diekelmann, N. (1989) 'Writing to Learn: A Reconceptualization of Thinking and Writing in the Nursing Curriculum', *Journal of Nursing Education*, **28** (1), 6–11.

Altrichter, H., Posch, P. and Somekh, B. (1993) *Teachers Investigate their Work: An Introduction to the Methods of Action Research*, London: Routledge.

Alvesson, M. and Skoldberg, K. (2000) *Reflexive Methodology*, London: Sage.

Andrews, M. (1996) 'Using Reflection to Develop Clinical Expertise', *British Journal of Nursing*, **5** (8), 508–13.

Argyris, C. and Schön, D.A. (1974) *Theory in Practice: Increasing Professional Effectiveness*, San Francisco: Jossey Bass.

Askew, S. and Carnell, E. (1998) *Transformatory Learning: Individual and Global Change*, London: Cassell.

Atkins, S. and Murphy, K. (1994) 'Reflective Practice', *Nursing Standard*, **8** (39), 49–54.

Bacon, F. (1994) *Essays* (ed. Michael J. Hawkins), London: Dent.

Bandura, A. (1969) *Principles of Behaviour Modification*, London: Holt, Reinhart & Winston.

Barker, P. (1986) *Basic Family Therapy*, London: Collins.

Beck, A.T. (1976) *Cognitive Therapy and the Emotional Disorders*, New York: International Universities Press.

Benner, P. (1984) *From Novice to Expert*, California: Addison-Wesley.

Benner, P. (ed.) (1994) *Interpretive Phenomenology*, California: Sage.

Benner, P. and Tanner, C. (1987) 'Clinical Judgement: How Expert Nurses Use Intuition', *American Journal of Nursing*, **87** (1), 23–31.

Benner, P., Tanner, C. and Chesla, C. (1996) *Expertise in Nursing Practice: Caring, Clinical Judgment, and Ethics*, New York: Springer.

Benner, P., Hooper-Kyriakidis, P. and Stannard, D. (1999) *Clinical Wisdom and Interventions in Critical Care: A Thinking-in-Action Approach*, Philadelphia: W.B. Saunders.

Bertcher, H.J. and Maple, F.F. (1977) *Creating Groups*, London: Sage.

Bhaskar, R. (1989) *Reclaiming Reality*, London: Verso.

Billig, M. (1994) 'Sod Baudrillard! Or Ideology Critique in Disney World', in H.W. Simons and M. Billig (eds), *After Postmodernism: Reconstructing Ideology Critique*, London: Sage.

Bines, H. (1992) 'Issues in Course Design', in H. Bines & D. Watson (eds), *Developing Professional Education*, Buckingham: Open University Press.

Binnie, A. and Titchen, A. (1995) 'The Art of Clinical Supervision', *British Journal of Nursing*, **4**, 327–34.

Bion, W.R. (1959) *Experiences in Groups*, London: Tavistock.

Bircumshaw, D. (1990) 'The Utilisation of Research Findings in Clinical Nursing Practice', *Journal of Advanced Nursing*, **15**, 1272–80.

Bishop, V. (1998a) 'Clinical Supervision: What Is It?', in V. Bishop (ed.), *Clinical Supervision in Practice*, London: Macmillan – now Palgrave: 1–21.

Bishop, V. (1998b) 'Clinical Supervision: What Is Going On? Results of a Questionnaire', *NT Research*, **3** (2), 141–50.

Bond, M. and Holland, S. (1998) *Skills of Clinical Supervision for Nurses*, Buckingham: Open University Press.

Bond, T. (1986) *Games for Social and Life Skills*, London: Hutchinson.

Borton, T. (1970) *Reach, Touch and Teach*, London: McGraw-Hill.

Boud, D., Keogh, R. and Walker, D. (1985) *Reflection: Turning Experience into Learning*, London: Kogan Page.

Boychuk Duchscher, J.E. (1999) 'Catching the Wave: Understanding the Concept of Critical Thinking', *Journal of Advanced Nursing*, **29** (3), 577–83.

Boyd, E. and Fales, A. (1983) 'Reflective Learning: The Key to Learning from Experience', *Journal of Humanistic Psychology*, **23** (2), 99–117.

Boydell, T. (1976) 'Experiential Learning', *Manchester Monograph No. 5*, University of Manchester, Department of Continuing Education.

Brandes, D. (1984) *Gamesters' Handbook Two*, London: Hutchinson.

Brandes, D. and Phillips, H. (1979) *Gamesters' Handbook*, London: Hutchinson.

Brandes, P.L. and Ginnis, P. (1985) *A Guide to Student Centred Learning*, Oxford: Basil Blackwell.

Braud, W. (1994) 'Integral Inquiry', in W. Braud and R. Anderson (eds), *Transpersonal Research Methods for the Social Sciences*, ch. 3, London: Sage.

Briant, S. and Freshwater, D. (1998) 'Exploring Mutuality in the Nurse–Patient Relationship', *British Journal of Nursing*, **7** (4), 204–11.

Brookfield, S.D. (1987) *Developing Critical Thinkers: Challenging Adults to Explore Alternative Ways of Thinking and Acting*, San Francisco: Jossey Bass.

Brookfield, S. D. (1995) *Becoming a Critically Reflective Teacher*, San Francisco: Jossey-Bass.

Brown, A. (1984) *Consultation for Social Workers*, London: Heinemann Educational.

Brown, A. (1989) *Groupwork* (2nd edn), Aldershot: Gower.

Bullock, A. Stallybrass, O. Trombley, S. and Eadie, B. (eds) (1988) *The Fontana Dictionary of Modern Thought*, London: HarperCollins.

Burnham, J.B. (1986) *Family Therapy*, London: Tavistock Publications.

Burns, N. and Grove, S.K. (1987) *The Practice of Nursing Research*, Philadelphia: W.B. Saunders.

Burrows, D. (1995) 'The Nurse Teacher's Role in the Promotion of Reflective Practice', *Nurse Education Today*, **15**, 346–50.

Butterworth, T. and Faugier, J. (eds) (1997) *Clinical Supervision and Mentorship in Nursing*, Cheltenham: Stanley Thornes.

Butterworth, T., White, E., Carson, J., Jeacock. J. and Clements, A. (1998) 'Developing and Evaluating Clinical Supervision in the United Kingdom', *EDTNA/ERCA Journal*, **24** (1), 2–8.

Carper, B. (1978) 'Fundamental Patterns of Knowing in Nursing', *Advances in Nursing Science*, **1** (1), 13–23.

Carper, B. (1992) 'Philosophical Inquiry in Nursing: An Application', in J.F. Kikuchi and H. Simmons (eds), *Philosophic Inquiry in Nursing*, Newbury Park: Sage.

Carr, W. and Kemmis, S. (1986) *Becoming Critical*, London: Falmer Press.

Casement, P. (1985) *On Learning from the Patient*, London: Routledge.

Casement, P. (1985) *On Learning from the Patient*, London: Tavistock.

Cavanagh, S.J., Hogan, K. and Ramgopal, T. (1995) 'The Assessment of Student Nurse Learning Styles using the Kolb Learning Styles Inventory', *Nurse Education Today*, **15**, 177–83.

Chater, S. (1975) *Understanding Research in Nursing*, Geneva: World Health Organisation (WHO).

Clarke, M. (1986) 'Action and Reflection: Practice and Theory in Nursing', *Journal of Advanced Nursing*, **11**, 3–11.

Closs, J. and Cheater, F.C. (1996) 'Audit or Research – What is the Difference?' *Journal of Clinical Nursing*, **5** (4 Jul), 249–57.

Cohen, L. and Manion, L. (1989) *Research Methods in Education*, London: Routledge.

Coombs, M. (1999) 'Building Bridges between Nursing Research and Practice', in V. Bishop and I. Scott (eds), *Working towards a Research Degree, Insights from the Nursing Perspective*, ch. 7, London: EMAP Healthcare Ltd.

Dartington, A. (1994) 'Where Angels Fear to Tread: Idealism, Despondency and Inhibition of Thought in Hospital Nursing', in A. Obholzer and V.Z. Roberts (eds), *The Unconscious at Work*, London: Routledge.

Davison, A. and Gordon, P. (1978) *Games and Simulations in Action*, London: The Woburn Press.

Dawson, P. (1998) 'The Self ', in S. Edwards (ed.), *Philosophical Issues in Nursing*, London: Macmillan, ch. 9.

Denzin, N.K. and Lincoln, Y.S. (eds) (1994) *Handbook of Qualitative Research*, London: Sage.

Department of Health (1993a) *Report of the Taskforce on the Strategy for Research in Nursing, Midwifery and Health Visiting*, London: HMSO.

Department of Health (1993b) *A Vision for the Future: The Nursing, Midwifery and Health Visiting Contribution to Health and Health Care*, London: HMSO.

Department of Health (1994) *The Allitt Inquiry (The Clothier Report)*, London: HMSO.

Dewey, J. (1916) *Democracy and Education*, New York: The Free Press.

Dewey, J. (1938) *Experience and Education*, New York: Macmillan – now Palgrave.

Dewey, J. (1963) *Experience and Education*, New York: Collier Books.

Douglas, T. (1976) *Groupwork Practice*, London: Tavistock.

Dreyfus, H.L. (1992) *What Computers Still Can't Do*, Cambridge, Mass.: MIT Press.

Dreyfus, H.L. and Dreyfus, S.E. (1986) *Mind Over Machine*, Oxford: Basil Blackwell.

Dreyfus, H.L. and Dreyfus, S.E. (1996) 'The Relationship of Theory and Practice in the Acquisition of Skill', in P. Benner, C.A. Tanner and C.A. Chesla (eds), *Expertise in Nursing Practice*, New York: Springer.

Duffy, M.E. (1985) 'Designing Nursing Research: The Qualitative–Quantitative Debate', *Journal of Advanced Nursing*, **10**, 225–32.

Elliott, J. (1991) *Action Research for Educational Change*, Buckingham: Open University Press.

Elliott, J. and Ebbutt, D. (1985) *Issues in Teaching for Understanding*, Harlow: Longmans.

Ennis, R.H. (1985) 'A Logical Basis for Measuring Critical Thinking Skills', *Educational Leadership*, **43** (2), 44–8.

Eraut, M. (1994) *Developing Professional Knowledge and Competence*, London: Falmer Press.

Ersser, S. J. (1998) 'The Presentation of the Nurse: A Neglected Dimension of Therapeutic Nurse-Patient Interaction?', in R. McMahon and A. Pearson (eds), *Nursing as Therapy*, Cheltenham: Stanley Thornes, ch. 3.

Facione, P.A. (1990) *The Delphi Report. Critical Thinking: A Statement of Expert Consensus for Purposes of Educational Assessment and Instruction. Executive Summary*. Millbrae California: The California Academic Press.

Facione, P.A., Facione, N.C. and Sanchez, C.A. (1994) 'Critical Thinking Disposition as a Measure of Competent Clinical Judgement: The Development of the California Critical Thinking Disposition Inventory', *Journal of Nursing Education*, **33**, 345–50.

Farrington, A. (1995) 'Models of Clinical Supervision', *British Journal of Nursing*, **4** (15), 876–8.

Faugier, J. (1992) 'The Supervisory Relationship', in T. Butterworth and J. Faugier (eds), *Clinical Supervision and Mentorship in Nursing*, London: Chapman Hall: 18–36.

Faugier, J. and Butterworth, T. (1994) *Clinical Supervision: A Position Paper*, Manchester: University of Manchester.

Fay, B. (1987) *Critical Social Science*, Cambridge: Polity Press.

Fiedler, F.E. (1967) *A Theory of Leadership Effectiveness*, New York: McGraw-Hill.

Fisher, M. (1996) 'Using Reflective Practice in Clinical Supervision', *Professional Nurse*, **11** (7), 443–44.

Fitzgerald, M. (1994) 'Theories of Reflection for Learning', in A. Palmer, S. Burns and C. Bulman (eds), *Reflective Practice in Nursing*, Oxford: Blackwell Scientific.

Fitzgerald, M. (2000) 'Clinical Supervision and Reflective Practice', in C. Bulman and S. Burns (eds), *Reflective Practice in Nursing* (2nd edn, ch. 5), Oxford: Blackwell Scientific.

Flanagan, J. (1954) 'The Critical Incident Technique', *Psychological Bulletin*, **51** (4), 327–58.

Foucault, M. (1980) *Power/Knowledge; Selected Interviews and Other Writings 1972–77*, Brighton: Harvester Press.

Fowler, M. (1996) 'The Organisation of Clinical Supervision within the Nursing Profession: A Review of the Literature', *Journal of Advanced Nursing*, **23**, 471–8.

Fowler, J. and Chevannes, M. (1998) 'Evaluating the Efficacy of Reflective Practice within the Context of Clinical Supervision', *Journal of Advanced Nursing*, **27**, 379–82.

Fox, N.J. (1999) *Beyond Health. Postmodernism and Embodiment*, London: Free Association Books.

Freire, P. (1972) *Pedagogy of the Oppressed*, Harmondsworth: Penguin.

Freshwater, D. and Broughton, R. (2000) 'Research and Evidence Based Practice', in V. Bishop and I. Scott (eds), *Challenges in Clinical Practice: Professional Developments in Nursing*, ch. 3, London: Macmillan – now Palgrave.

Gadamer, H.-G. (1996) *The Enigma of Health*, Cambridge: Polity Press.

Garland, J.A., Jones, H.E. and Kolodny, R.L. (1965) 'A Model for Stages of Development in Social Work Groups', in S. Berstein (ed.), *Explorations in Groupwork*, Boston: Boston University Press.

Gibbs, G. (1988) *Learning by Doing: A guide to Teaching and Learning Methods*, Oxford: Further Education Unit, Oxford Polytechnic.

Greenwood, J. (1984) 'Nursing Research: A Position Paper', *Journal of Advanced Nursing*, **9**, 77–82.

Habermas, J. (1974) *Theory and Practice*, London: Heinemann.

Habermas, J. (1978) *Knowledge and Human Interest*, London: Heinemann.

Habermas, J. (1984) *The Theory of Communicative Action*, Vol. 1, Boston: Beacon.

Hart, E. and Bond, M. (1995) *Action Research for Health and Social Care. A Guide to Practice*, Buckingham: Open University Press.

Hawkins, P. and Shohet, R. (1989) *Supervision in the Helping Professions*, Buckingham: Open University Press.

Heath, H. & Freshwater, D. (2000) 'Clinical Supervision as an Emancipatory Process: Avoiding Inappropriate Intent', *Journal of Advanced Nursing*, **32** (5), 1298–306.

Heron, J. (1981) *Assessment*, Guildford: Human Potential Resource Group, University of Surrey.

Holloway, E. (1995) *Clinical Supervision. A Systems Approach*, London: Sage.

Holly, M. (1984) *Keeping a Personal Professional Journal*, Victoria: Deakin University Press.

Holm, D. and Stephenson, S. (1994) 'Reflection – A Student's Perspective', in A. Palmer, S. Burns and C. Bulman (eds), *Reflective Practice in Nursing*, Oxford: Blackwell Scientific: 53–62.

Hoshimand, L.T. and Polkinghorne, D.E. (1992) 'Redefining the Science–Practice Relationship and Professional Training', *American Psychologist*, **47** (1), 55–66.

Hughes, I. (1997) *Action Research Electronic Reader*, internet site *http://www.beh.cchs.usyd.edu.au*

Hunt, J. (1981) 'Indicators for Nursing Practice: The Use of Research Findings', *Journal of Advanced Nursing*, **6** (3), 189–94.

International Council of Nurses (1996) *Better Health through Nursing Research*, Geneva: ICN.

Jacobs, M. (1991) *Psychodynamic Counselling in Action*, London: Sage.

Jacobs, M. (ed.) (1996) *In Search of Supervision*, Buckingham: Open University Press.

Jarvis, P. (1996) *The Practitioner-Researcher: Developing Theory from Practice*, San Francisco: Jossey-Bass.

Jarvis, P. (2000) 'The Practitioner-Researcher in Nursing', *Nurse Education Today*, **20**, 30–5.

Jasper, M. (1995) 'The Potential of the Professional Portfolio for Nursing', *Journal of Clinical Nursing*, **4**, 249–55.

Jasper, M. (1998) 'Using Portfolios to Advance Practice', in G. Rolfe and P. Fulbrook (eds), *Advancing Nursing Practice*, Oxford: Butterworth Heinemann, chapter 15.

Jasper, M.A. (1999) 'Assessing and Improving Student Outcomes through Reflective Writing', in C. Rust (ed.), *Improving Student Learning – Improving Student Learning Outcomes*, ch. 1, Oxford: Oxford Centre for Staff Development.

Johns, C. (1993) 'Professional Supervision', *Journal of Nursing Management*, **1**, 9–18.

Johns, C. (1998) 'Opening the Doors of Perception', in C. Johns and D. Freshwater (eds), *Transforming Nursing through Reflective Practice*, Oxford: Blackwell Science: 1–20.

Johns, C. (2000) *Becoming a Reflective Practitioner*, Oxford: Blackwell Science.

Johns, C. and McCormack, B. (1998) 'Unfolding the Conditions where the Transformative Potential of Guided Reflection (Clinical Supervision) might Flourish or Flounder', in C. Johns and D. Freshwater (eds), *Transforming Nursing through Reflective Practice*, ch. 6, Oxford: Blackwell Science.

Kadushin, A. (1992) *Supervision in Social Work*, New York: Columbia University Press.

Kemmis, S. (1993) 'Action Research', in M. Hammersley (ed.), *Educational Research: Current Issues*. Milton Keynes: Open University Press.

Kim, H.S. (1999) 'Critical Reflective Inquiry for Knowledge Development in Nursing Practice', *Journal of Advanced Nursing*, **29** (5), 1205–12.

Kingston, P. and Smith, D. (1983) 'Preparation for Live Consultation and Live Supervision when Working Without a One-Way Screen', *Journal of Family Therapy*, **5**, 219–33.

Kintgen Andrews, J. (1991) 'Critical Thinking and Nursing Education: Perplexities and Insights', *Journal of Nursing Education*, **30**, 152–7.

Knowles, M. (1984) *The Adult Learner: A Neglected Species* (3rd edn), Houston: Gulf.

Koch, T. (1998) 'Story-Telling: Is It Really Research?', *Journal of Advanced Nursing*, **28** (6), 1182–90.

Kohner, N. (1994) *Clinical Supervision in Practice*, London: Kings Fund Centre.

Kolb, D.A. (1984) *Experiential Learning: Experience as the Source of Learning and Development*, New Jersey: Prentice-Hall.

Kolb, D.A., Osland, J.S. and Rubin, I.M. (1995) *Organizational Behavior* (6th edn), Englewood Cliffs, New Jersey: Prentice-Hall.

Kolb, D.A., Osland, J.S. and Rubin, I.M. (1995) *Organizational Behavior: an Experiential Approach*, Englewood Cliffs, New Jersey: Prentice Hall: 46–7.

Kuhn, D., Amsel, E. and O'Loughlin, M. (1988) *The Development of Scientific Thinking Skills*, California: Academic Press.

LeMay, A., Mulhall, A. and Alexander, C. (1998) 'Bridging the Research–Practice Gap: Exploring the Research Cultures of Practitioners and Managers', *Journal of Advanced Nursing*, **28** (2), 428–37.

Leonard, V.W. (1994) 'A Heideggarian Phenomenological Perspective on the Concept of the Person', in P. Benner (ed.), *Interpretative Phenomenology, Embodiment, Caring and Ethics in Health and Illness*, London: Sage.

Levine, B. (1979) *Group Psychotherapy, Practice and Development*, New York: Prentice-Hall.

Lewin, K. (1946) 'Action Research and Minority Problems', *Journal of Social Issues*, **2** (4), 34–46.

Lichtenberg, G.C. (1969) *Aphorisms*, London: Jonathan Cape

Lippitt, R. and White, R.K. (1953) 'Leader Behaviour and Member Reaction in Three Different Climates', in D. Cartwright and A. Zander (eds) (1968), *Group Dynamics* (3rd edn), New York: Harper & Row.

Lufe, J. (1969) *Of Human Interactions. The Johari Model*, Palo Alto: Mayfield.

Lyotard, J.-F. (1984) *The Postmodern Condition: A Report on Knowledge*, Manchester: Manchester University Press.

Lyotard, J.-F. (1988) *The Differend: Phrases in Dispute*, Minneapolis: University of Minnesota Press.

Mackintosh, C. (1998) 'Reflection: A Flawed Strategy for the Nursing Profession', *Nurse Education Today*, **18**, 553–7.

Marcus, E. (1994) 'Early Clinical Skills Training', *Academic Medicine*, **69** (5), 191–2.

McCaugherty, D. (1991) 'The Use of a Teaching Model to Promote Reflection and the Experiential Integration of Theory and Practice in First Year Student Nurses: An Action Research Study', *Journal of Advanced Nursing*, **16**, 534–43.

McGrowther, J. (1995) *Profiles, Portfolios and How to Build Them*, London: Scutari Press.

MacGuire, J. (1998) 'Tailoring Research for Therapeutic Nursing Practice', in R. McMahon and A. Pearson (eds), *Nursing as Therapy*, Cheltenham: Stanley Thornes, ch. 9.

McNiff, J. (1993) *Teaching as Learning: An Action Research Approach*, London: Routledge.

McTaggart, R. (1992) 'Action Research: Issues in Theory and Practice', Paper presented to Methodological Issues in Qualitative Health Research Conference, Deakin University.

Menzies-Lyth, I.E.P. (1970) *The Functioning of Social Systems as a Defence against Anxiety*, London: Free Association Books.

Menzies-Lyth, I.E.P. (1988) *Containing Anxiety in Institutions: Selected Essays*, London: Free Association Books.

Mezirow, J. (1981) 'A Critical Theory of Adult Learning and Education', *Adult Education*, **1**, 3–24.

Mezirow, J. (1981) 'A Critical Theory of Adult Learning and Education', *Adult Education*, **32**, 3–24.

Miller, A. (1989) 'Theory to Practice: Implementation in the Clinical Setting', in M. Jolley and P. Allan (eds), *Current Issues in Nursing*, London: Chapman & Hall.

Mishler, E. (1979) 'Meaning in Content: Is There Any Other Kind?', *Harvard Educational Review*, **49**, 1–19.

Montalvo, B. (1973) 'Aspects of Live Supervision', *Family Process*, **12**, 343–59.

Moon, J. (1999) *Learning Journals. A Handbook for Academics, Students and Professional Development*, London: Kogan Page.

Morse, J. and Field, P.A. (1996) *Nursing Research: The Application of Qualitative Approaches* (2nd edn), London: Chapman and Hall.

Morton-Cooper, A. and Palmer, A. (1993) *Mentoring and Preceptorship*, Oxford: Blackwell Science.

Morton-Cooper, A. and Palmer, A. (2000) *Mentoring , Preceptorship and Clinical Supervision: A Guide to Support Roles in Clinical practice*, (2nd edn), Oxford: Blackwell Scientific Publications.

Murray, M. and Chamberlain, K. (eds) (1999) *Qualitative Health Psychology*, London: Sage.

Neill, A.S. (1968) *Summerhill*, Harmondsworth: Penguin.

Newman, M. (1994) *Health as Expanding Consciousness* (2nd edn), New York: National League for Nursing Press.

Nias, J. (ed.) (1993) *The Human Nature of Learning: Selections from the Work of M.L.J. Abercrombie*, Buckingham: Open University Press.

Nichols, K. and Jenkinson, J. (1991) *Leading a Support Group*, London: Chapman & Hall.

Nolan, M., Lundh, U. and Tishelman, C. (1998) 'Nursing's Knowledge Base: Does it Have to be Unique?', *British Journal of Nursing*, **7** (5), 270–5.

Ottman, H. (1982) 'Cognitive Interests and Self-Reflection', in J.B. Thompson and D. Held (eds), *Habermas: Critical Debates*, London: Macmillan – now Palgrave.

Page, S. and Woskett, V. (1994) *Supervising the Counsellor*, London: Routledge.

Palmer, A. (2000) 'Freedom to Learn – Freedom to Be: Learning, Reflecting and Supporting in Practice', in D. Humphris and A. Masterson (eds), *Developing New Clinical Roles: A Guide for Health Professionals*, London: Harcourt Health Sciences.

Parse, R.R. (1985) *Nursing Science: Major Paradigms, Theories and Critiques*, Philadelphia: Saunders.

Pfeiffer, J. and Jones, J. (1980) *Structured Experience Kit – Users Guide*, California: University Associates, San Diego.

Polanyi, M. (1962) *Personal Knowledge: Towards a Post-Critical Philosophy*, London: Routledge & Kegan Paul.

Polit, D.F. and Hungler, B.P. (1991) *Nursing Research: Principles and Methods* (4th edn), Philadelphia: Lippincott.

Popper, K. (1979) *Objective Knowledge: An Evolutionary Approach* (revd edn), Oxford: Clarendon Press.

Porter, S. (1993) 'Nursing Research Conventions: Objectivity or Obfuscation?', *Journal of Advanced Nursing*, **18**, 137–43.

Proctor, B. (1986) 'Supervision: A Co-operative Exercise in Accountability', in M. Marken and M. Payne (eds), *Enabling and Ensuring*. Leicester: National Youth Bureau and Council for Education and Training in Youth and Community Work.

Progoff, I. (1975) *At a Journal Workshop: The Basic Text and Guide for Using the Journal*, New York: Dialogue House Library.

Rafferty, A.M. and Traynor, M. (1999) 'The Research–Practice Gap in Nursing: Lessons from the Research Policy Debate', *Nursing Times Research*, **4** (6), 458–65.

Reason, P. (1988) *Human Inquiry in Action*, London: Sage.

Redl, F. (1951) 'Art of Group Composition', in S. Schulze (ed.), *Creative Living in a Children's Institution*, New York: Free Association Press.

Reece Jones, P. (1995) 'Hindsight Bias in Reflective Practice: An Empirical Investigation', *Journal of Advanced Nursing*, **21**, 783–8.

Reimers, S. and Treacher, A. (1995) *Introducing User-friendly Family Therapy*, London: Routledge.

Richardson, G. and Maltby, H. (1995) 'Reflection on Practice: Enhancing Student Learning', *Journal of Advanced Nursing*, **22**, 235–42.

Robson, C. (1993) *Real World Research*, Oxford: Blackwell Science.

Rogers, C. (1957) 'Personal Thoughts on Teaching and Learning', *Merrill-Palmer Quarterly*, **3**, 241–3.

Rogers, C.R. (1969) *Freedom to Learn*, Ohio: Merrill.

Rogers, C. (1983) *Freedom to Learn for the 80s*, Columbus: Merrill.

Rogers, C.R. (1991) *Client Centred Therapy*, London: Constable.

Rolfe, G. (1988) *Expanding Nursing Knowledge: Understanding and Researching your own Practice*, Oxford: Butterworth Heinemann.

Rolfe, G. (1993) 'Towards a Theory of Student-Centred Nurse Education: Overcoming the Constraints of a Professional Curriculum', *Nurse Education Today*, **13**, 149–54.

Rolfe, G. (1996a) 'Going to Extremes: Action Research, Grounded Practice and the Theory–Practice Gap in Nursing', *Journal of Advanced Nursing*, **24**, 1315–20.

Rolfe, G. (1996b) *Closing the Theory–Practice Gap. A New Paradigm for Nursing*, Oxford: Butterworth Heinemann.

Rolfe, G. (1998) *Expanding Nursing Knowledge: Understanding and Researching Your Own Practice*, Oxford: Butterworth Heinemann.

Rolfe, G. (1998) 'Advanced Practice and the Reflective Nurse: Developing Knowledge out of Practice', in G. Rolfe and P. Fulbrook (eds), *Advanced Nursing Practice*, Oxford: Butterworth Heinemann.

Rolfe, G. (1998) 'Reflective Case Study Research', in G. Rolfe, *Expanding Nursing Knowledge*, Oxford: Butterworth Heinemann.

Rolfe, G. (1999) 'Insufficient Evidence: The Problems of Evidence-Based Nursing', *Nurse Education Today*, **19**, 433–42.

Rolfe, G. (2000) *Research, Truth and Authority: Postmodern Perspectives on Nursing*, Oxford: Macmillan – now Palgrave.

Rorty, R. (1989) *Contingency, Irony and Solidarity*, Cambridge: Cambridge University Press.

Rousseau, J.J. (1911) *Emile, or Education*, London: Dent.

Ryle, G. (1963) *The Concept of Mind*, Harmondsworth: Penguin.

Salvage, J. (1998) 'Evidence Based Practice: A Mixture of Motives?' *Nursing Times Research*, **3** (6), 406–18.

Sandelowski, M. (1993) 'Rigor or Rigor Mortis: the Problem of Rigor in Qualitative Research Revisited', *Advances in Nursing Science*, **16**, 21–8.

Schön, D. (1983) *The Reflective Practitioner*, London: Temple Smith.

Schön, D. (1987) *Educating the Reflective Practitioner*, San Francisco: Jossey-Bass.

Schutz, W.C. (1958) *FIRO: A Three Dimentional Theory of Interpersonal Behaviour*, New York: Holt, Rinehart & Winston.

Sharp, K. (1998) 'The Case for Case Studies in Nursing Research: The Problem of Generalisation', *Journal of Advanced Nursing*, **27**, 785–9.

Sharples, M. (1999) *How We Write,* London: Routledge.

Slevin, O. and Basford, L. (eds) (1995) *Theory and Practice of Nursing,* Edinburgh: Campion Press.

Somekh, B. (1995) 'The Contribution of Action Research to Development in Social Endeavours: A Position Paper on Action Research Methodology', *British Educational Research Journal,* **21,** 339–55.

Stake, R.E. (1995) *The Art of Case Study Research,* London: Sage.

Stenhouse, L. (1981) 'What Counts as Research?', *British Journal of Educational Studies,* **29** (2), 103–14.

Stenhouse, L. (1985) 'Reporting Research to Teachers: The Appeal to Professional Judgement', in J. Ruddock and D. Hopkins (eds), *Research as a Basis for Teaching,* Oxford: Heinemann.

Stoltenberg, C.D. and Delworth, V. (1987) *Supervising Counsellors and Therapists,* San Francisco: Jossey-Bass.

Taylor, B. (1998) 'Locating a Phenomenological Perspective of Reflective Nursing and Midwifery Practice by Contrasting Interpretative and Critical Reflection', in C. Johns and D. Freshwater (eds), *Transforming Nursing through Reflective Practice,* ch. 11, Oxford: Blackwell Science.

Thatcher, D. and Robinson, J. (1984) *Perspectives on Gaming and Simulation 8: Business, Health and Nursing Education,* Loughborough: SAGSET

Treacher, A. and Carpenter, J. (1984) *Using Family Therapy,* Oxford: Basil Blackwell.

Tuckman, B. (1965) 'Developmental Sequences in Small Groups', *Psychological Bulletin,* **63,** 384–99.

United Kingdom Central Council for Nursing, Midwifery and Health Visiting (1996) *Position Statement on Clinical Supervision for Nursing and Health Visiting,* London: UKCC.

Usher, R. and Bryant, I. (1989) *Adult Education as Theory, Practice and Research,* London: Routledge.

Van Ments, M. (1989) *The Effective Use of Role-play* (rev edn), London: Kogan Page.

Van Ments, M. and Hearnden, K. (1985), *Effective Use of Games and Simulation,* Loughborough: SAGSET.

Van Ooijen, E. (2000) *Clinical Supervision. A Practical Guide,* London: Churchill Livingstone.

Walsh, M. and Ford, P. (1989) *Nursing Rituals, Research and Rational Actions,* Oxford: Butterworth Heinemann.

Walsh, K., Ham, C. and Appelby, J. (1995) 'Given in Evidence', *Health Service Journal,* 29 June, 28–9.

Webb, C. (1996) 'Action Research', in D.F.S. Cormack (ed.), *The Research Process in Nursing,* ch. 18, Oxford: Blackwell Scientific.

Wheeler, C.E. and Chinn, P.L. (1984) *Peace and Power: A Handbook of Feminist Process,* Buffalo: Margaret Daughters.

Winnicott, D.W. (1971) *Therapeutic Consultations in Child Psychiatry,* London: Hogarth Press.

Winters, R. (1989) *Learning from Experience: Principle and Practice in Action Research,* London: Falmer.

Wright, H. (1989) *Groupwork: Perspectives and Practice,* Harrow: Scutari Press.

Wyllie, R. (1993) 'On the Road to Discovery: A Study of the Composing Strategies of Academic Writers using the Word Processor', MA thesis, University of Lancaster, cited in Sharples *ibid.*

Yalom, I.D. (1970) *The Theory and Practice of Group Psychotherapy,* New York: Basic Books.

Yegdich, T. (1999) 'Clinical Supervision and Managerial Supervision: Some Historical and Conceptual Considerations', *Journal of Advanced Nursing,* **30** (5), 1195–204.

Yin, R.K. (1994) *Case Study Research* (2nd edn), London: Sage.

Zuber-Skerritt, O. (1991) *Action Research for Change and Development,* Aldershot: Avebury.

Index